THE NEW PROFESSIONAL'S HANDBOOK

Your guide to information services management

THE NEW PROFESSIONAL'S HANDBOOK
Your guide to information services management

Sheila Corrall
University Librarian, University of Reading

Antony Brewerton
Subject Team Leader, Oxford Brookes University Library

LIBRARY ASSOCIATION PUBLISHING
LONDON

Published by
Library Association Publishing
7 Ridgmount Street
London WC1E 7AE

Library Association Publishing is wholly owned by The Library Association.

First published 1999

British Library Cataloguing in Publication Data

A catalogue record for this book is available from the British Library.

ISBN 1-85604-311-8

Typeset in 11/14pt Savoy and Franklin Gothic Condensed from authors' disks by Library Association Publishing.
Printed and made in Great Britain by MPG Books Ltd, Bodmin, Cornwall.

Contents

Acknowledgments

Our thanks are due to many colleagues at Reading University Library and in the wider professional community, who have shared ideas with us and helped to shape our thinking. We are particularly grateful to the Interlibrary Loans team at Reading for their speed and efficiency in supplying us with journal articles; and to the four trainee liaison librarians who provided valuable feedback on early drafts of this book: Christopher Cipkin, Neil Dalley, Jennifer Ross and Joanna Snelling. We are indebted to Ian Burn for his help with the diagrams and general technical assistance. We must also thank Nick Smith and John Matthews for allowing us to reproduce the Aston University LIS Guidelines for Customer Care Tours in Chapter 9.

gy should not be restricted to our organizations. We also need a strategic approach to our own professional and personal development.

These concerns account for the content, and to a large extent the approach, of what follows. As its title suggests, this book is aimed predominantly at new professionals, thrown in at the sharp end of information services management. The thematic arrangement means that each chapter can be used for self-directed learning or as the basis of a session with a mentor. Indeed, the material on which this book is based was originally used as part of our modular Library Association 'Route A' Chartership Training Programme at Reading University Library. But this is not its only purpose and we hope this handbook (with its mix of theory and practical applications) will act as a useful aid to LIS students and lecturers, staff development officers, those returning to the profession after a break and established professionals in search of a fresh perspective.

In some ways this may seem like a sizeable tome, but it is really only an introduction. We have tried to provide a global cross-sectoral view of information services, but have inevitably had to be selective in both our choice of topics covered and the depth of treatment. There is so much more we could have included (you should see the state of our cutting room floor!) and we have had to be disciplined in our approach. Increasingly, as managers, we have recourse to employ Kipling's six honest serving men, always starting with Why – if you cannot answer that, do not do it! This is how we have tried to tackle many of the areas covered.

The new professional's handbook is intended to be a starting-point and with that in mind we have provided references to key sources and also suggestions for further reading (with annotations) at the end of each chapter, to encourage you to explore topics of interest. We are aware that the current pace of change in our field makes professional updating a real challenge, so our aim here has been to offer a representative selection of material which will assist you by indicating where to look as well as what to read. We hope this book proves useful and helps to stimulate and focus the mind. It has certainly concentrated ours!

Sheila Corrall and Antony Brewerton

List of figures

Part 1   The service in context

1

The service environment

Introduction

Information and library services do not exist in isolation. They are part of a larger environment, but usually exist within a specific organizational context to serve a particular community. As an information professional, you need to understand your operational environment in order to perform effectively. In these times of rapid change you need to be alert to events and developments in the wider world and to assess their significance for service planning and delivery. This chapter introduces some concepts and techniques to assist with environmental monitoring. It also provides a selective overview of recent trends and developments in business generally and in information services, and shows how developments in the latter reflect more general trends in organizations and society.

Environmental appraisal

The environment is hard to define in precise terms. It comprises facts, events and issues that might have a large impact on an organization's performance, but over which it may have little influence – though in turn its actions may affect other organizations and individuals. It is easier to think of the environment as a complex set of *variables*, and to use a model or framework to focus appraisal and assessment.

We can break down our analysis in various ways, and a common first step is to separate out the **macro-environment**, sometimes referred to as the *societal* environment, representing the outside world in general or those conditions that have a broad – and therefore indirect – impact upon the organization. In contrast, factors and forces in the **micro-environment**, have a major and direct effect on the organization and its services. We can then subdivide this latter analysis into the *task* environment – the industry sector or business world in which the organization operates – and the *corporate* or *internal* environment, to include consideration of the organization itself (its structure, culture, resources, etc).

The conventional way of viewing the macro-environment is to consider issues and influences under four headings: Political, Economic, Social and Technological. This is generally referred to as a **PEST** or **STEP** analysis, depending on the order in which the headings are taken. The **SEPTEMBER** formula (see Figure 1.1) is a less common mnemonic, but potentially more useful as it can be expanded to cover a longer list of key variables that need to be taken into account in such an analysis. The full list then extends from the wider macro-environment into the narrower task/operational environment for the organization/service.

Society   Economics   Politics   Technology   Education
Marketplace   Business   Ethics   Regulations

Fig. 1.1 *The SEPTEMBER formula*

Here are some examples of the variables to consider under each heading:

- **Society** – includes socio-cultural issues and demographic trends, such as life-style changes, consumer activism, birth rates, population distribution, life expectancies

- **Economics** – issues such as national productivity, interest rates, currency fluctuations, employment patterns, energy costs, price controls, wage settlements, globalization
- **Politics** – including factors like government stability, public expenditure, industrial policy (eg privatization, deregulation), taxation (eg VAT) and special incentives
- **Technology** – hardware and software developments, relating to both business and consumer markets, including issues such as transferability, standards and security
- **Education** – all aspects of lifelong learning (at home, school or in the workplace) including issues such as literacy levels, skills shortages, vocational qualifications
- **Marketplace** – the nature and number of products, services, customers, partners, suppliers, competitors, and pertinent factors like growth, maturity and pricing
- **Business** – general trends and specific developments in relevant sectors, including the information and service industries, and the particular industrial/business sector served
- **Ethics** – organizational policies on corporate/social responsibility, codes of professional conduct, statements of service values, ethical dilemmas in the workplace
- **Regulations** – health and safety, employment, data protection and copyright legislation; trends in contracts and licensing arrangements (eg for information services/software).

REFLECTION

What forces or factors in the economy or society at large are likely to have a significant impact on your organization and service over the next three years? What are their implications?

The process of looking at – or looking for – information related to the environment is known as **environmental scanning**. In a primarily historical review of the topic, Chun Wei Choo and Ethel Auster offer the following definition: 'Environmental scanning is thus defined as the acquisition and use of information about events and trends in an organization's external environment, the knowledge of which would assist management in planning the organization's future course of action.'[1]

In a separate article reporting their survey of scanning activity in the Canadian publishing and telecommunications industries, Auster and Choo elaborate this description as follows:

> Scanning not only concerns seeking information to address a specific question (for example, 'How big is this market?'), but also includes doing a broad sweep of the horizon to look for signs of change and opportunities ('Where are the new markets?'). Scanning activities could range from gathering data deliberately such as by doing market research, to informal conversations with other executives, or reading the newspaper.'[2]

Note that the term 'scanning' is thus used not just to cover the viewing or seeking of information but to include also the subsequent processing of the information obtained, typically involving some form of analysis and assessment, and often then extending to forecasts and predictions. While the prime focus of such activity tends to be on the external or macro-environment, commentators also stress the need to search an organization's internal environment to identify important elements that might affect future performance.

REFLECTION

Are you aware of any plans or proposals within your own organization, or the sector more generally, that would require development or changes to your service operations and management?

Stakeholder interests

Organizations and services do not consist of impersonal entities. They consist of people – individuals and groups – and their day-to-day operation and longer-term development depends on how these people interact with each other, and with the outside world. A **stakeholder analysis** is a convenient way of identifying people whose opinions and activities affect the organization. John Bryson explains the purpose of such an analysis thus: 'A stakeholder analysis is the means for identifying who the organization's internal and external stakeholders are, how they evaluate the organization, how they influence the organization, what the organization needs from them, and how important they are.'[3]

A **stakeholder** can be defined as any individual or group with an involvement or interest in the organization, actual or potential - in the past, present or future. Bryson provides the following definition: 'A stakeholder is any person, group or organization that can place a claim on an organization's resources, attention or output, or is affected by its output.'[3]

Examples of an information service's stakeholders include not only its clients or customers (subdivided into various categories), but also top management in the host organization, information service staff, funding bodies and other regulators, suppliers, partners, competitors, trade unions, professional associations and 'the local community'. These groups can usefully be divided into *internal* and *external* stakeholders, and also into those *directly* and *indirectly* affected by the service. A point to note is that groups are not mutually exclusive, but often overlap, with some people featuring under several headings. There are also many different ways of categorizing individuals - for example, as spokespersons, or 'key opinion formers', which may cut across conventional classifications. In addition, groups can be successively divided into further subgroups almost indefinitely, but a balance must be struck to ensure that the resulting categories are sufficient to represent the main viewpoints without making the ensuing analysis too complicated and unmanageable.

ACTIVITY

Make a list of all the categories of individuals and groups you consider have some involvement or interest in your service. Aim to be as inclusive as possible. (You may find it helpful to compile the list over several days.)

After identifying who the stakeholders are, the analysis can be pursued at various levels. Common approaches include rating and ranking stakeholders on the basis of their interest and *influence*. The latter can cover the nature and extent of the group's influence on the service, as well as the service manager's capacity to influence the group.

ACTIVITY

For each of your stakeholder categories, think about the group's level of *interest* and assess this on a five-point scale (where a score of five signifies a high level of interest or dependence, and one indicates only marginal interest). Assess each group again, this time for their power to *influence* your service (where five suggests a powerful voice in policy and decision-making, and one represents very limited ability to influence decisions). Taking account of both scores, draw a diagram or **map** showing who your stakeholders are, placing your service at the centre and positioning stakeholders to reflect your perception of their relative importance to the management of the service.

A more penetrating analysis will look at what *criteria* the different stakeholder groups use to judge the organization or service, and then try to assess performance from these stakeholder perspectives. Evaluations can be based on a range of 'hard' and 'soft' inputs, from explicit statements through observed behaviour to informed guesswork. Peter Block identifies four generic categories of stakeholders in a matrix model, positioning them according to perceived levels of *agreement* about where the organization is heading, and trust concerning the way it operates in pursuit of that future.[4] He suggests different approaches for these groups, assigning them time and energy in the following order of priority:

- **Allies** (high agreement, high trust). Typical examples include customers who are successful users of products or services. Embrace them as members of the organization, and ask them for advice and support.
- **Opponents** (high trust, low agreement). Includes trusted but dissatisfied customers who test your thinking in a positive way. Regard them as great assets, and engage them in conversation and problem-solving.
- **Bedfellows** (high agreement, low trust). Accept some responsibility for having contributed to the difficulty in the relationship; resist the temptation to be manipulative, and try to agree how you can work together.
- **Adversaries** (low agreement, low trust). Stop trying to persuade them, but avoid doing anything to undermine or destroy them; reduce tension and threat, and either break off contact or help them feel understood.

REFLECTION
Who are your Allies, Opponents, Bedfellows and Adversaries?

Business trends and organizational developments

Without doubt **information technology** (IT) is the driving force and transforming factor for business and all kinds of organization as we approach
the 21st century. The impact of IT is not limited to the development of
products and services and their underlying systems and processes. IT is
already having a significant effect on organizational structures and cultures,
and will ultimately affect all aspects of our working and domestic lives, as
we move toward 'the informational age'. The scale of change envisaged is
persuasively described here by Manuel Castells (Professor of Sociology and
Planning at the University of California, Berkeley):

> For all the science fiction ideology and commercial hype surrounding the
> emergence of the so-called Information Superhighway, we can hardly under-
> estimate its significance. The potential integration of text, images, and sounds
> in the same system, interacting from multiple points, in chosen time (real or
> delayed) along a global network, in conditions of open and affordable access,
> does fundamentally change the character of communication . . . Because cul-
> ture is mediated and enacted through communication, cultures themselves,
> that is our historically produced systems of beliefs and codes, become
> fundamentally transformed, and will be more so over time, by the new tech-
> nological system. At the moment of this writing, such a new system is not yet
> fully in place, and its development will occur at uneven pace and with uneven
> geography in coming years. Yet it is a certainty that it will develop and
> embrace at least the dominant activities and the core segments of the popu-
> lation in the whole planet. Furthermore, it already exists in bits and pieces,
> in the new media system, in the rapidly changing telecommunications sys-
> tems, in the networks of interaction already formed around Internet, in the
> imagination of people, in the policies of governments, and on the drawing
> boards of corporate offices. The emergence of a new electronic com-
> munication system characterized by its global reach, its integration of all
> communication media, and its potential interactivity is changing and will
> change forever our culture.[5]

Reinforcing this theme, Melanie Norton and June Lester (professors of Information Science) explain how IT has been the enabler of concepts such as the *network organization*, the *horizontal revolution* and the *boundary-less firm*, providing the technological infrastructure to support all sorts of organizational trends and business developments over the past decade. Characteristic features, which are touched on in this piece, include flatter structures, devolved decision-making and self-managed teams; strategic alliances, joint ventures between companies, and outsourcing of non-core activities; customization of products and services, based on closer contact with consumers; and knowledge management, systematically capturing information of value to the organization and recognizing its 'intellectual capital'. Of course, just as IT has the power to open up organizations and make them more inclusive, it can also be divisive and create new hierarchies or elite groups, excluding those who lack the equipment and/or skills to participate in the exchange of information.

> Essentially, the evolution of computer technology, and especially networking systems, has impacted every aspect of the traditional organization. Electronic mail, electronic bulletin boards, shared files and other similar systems allow information transfer without the typical channels of hierarchy, breaking down rigid organizational structures by circumventing the hierarchy and allowing information to flow through the electronic structure rather than the traditional one. This openness is what allows organizations to expand the personnel involved in projects and to network outside of themselves. Boundaries become blurred, both within work groups and within the organization. Decision making becomes less centralized, more dispersed and, certainly at some levels, less institutional in nature. The composition of the organization changes. Over time even the 'walls' of the organization change to encompass the customers within the evolving information net. As some organizations have experienced, the voice – or rather e-mail – of the customer can indeed cause them to appear interior to the organization.[6]

These comments serve to flag up the fact that while it is convenient to think about environmental forces under different headings – such as those suggested in the SEPTEMBER model – the various factors tend to *overlap* and *interact*, and it is their cumulative effect and combined impact that we need to track. Often it is difficult to categorize these trends and developments satisfactorily, but we must remember that the purpose of using such a model is to stimulate and focus our thinking about these issues.

The following section continues our overview of business trends within this framework:

- **Social trends** affecting organizations include the changing balance and relative influence of men and women as employees and customers; a growth in part-time employment and home/teleworking; and continuing diversity of populations in terms of ethnic backgrounds.
- **Economic forces** include global competition, with new entrants in many markets; budget pressures, in both public and private sectors, resulting in short-term employment contracts; and industry restructuring, especially (multi-national) company mergers and acquisitions.
- **Political pressures** are requiring public sector organizations to become more accountable to stakeholders; to deliver value for money, improved quality and consumer choice; and to demonstrate cost-effectiveness in comparison with private sector operators.
- **Technological advances** have moved us from the PC era to the network age, featuring web browsers and groupware, making communications bandwidth the enabling/limiting factor – instead of memory size or microprocessor speed – and electronic data interchange (EDI), facilitating the seamless supply chain, with cost reductions and quicker turnaround.
- **Educational matters** have become a universal concern, with the promotion of concepts such as the *learning organization*, *lifelong learning* and the *learning society*; the desire to empower individuals; and the need to improve skill levels in line with business needs.
- **Markets** generally are characterized by intensified competition, arising from globalization; IT is enabling much more sophisticated approaches, including *relationship marketing*; and consumers are expecting improved quality, with faster service and customized products.
- **Business changes** include *lean organization* initiatives (eg downsizing, outsourcing and process re-engineering) with continuing interest in *quality management* and *strategic alliances*, and intensified management control (supported by performance-related pay).
- **Ethical themes** include concern about the effects of economic development on the environment and social well-being; pressure on

organizations to accept their responsibilities to their local communities; and realization of the importance of shared values in business.

- **Regulatory issues** for the networked environment include controls for the conduct of electronic commerce; problems over intellectual property rights; and tensions between freedom of information and personal privacy (and protection from offensive material).

All this adds up to a dynamic and competitive business environment, with rapidly changing technology, assertive and demanding customers, shifting organizational boundaries and a flexible and multiskilled workforce, operating under tight constraints and controls, but expected to accept more responsibility (including a commitment to self-development).

Information and library service developments
Economic and electronic imperatives

Budget pressures and technological advances have been the dominant influences on information service developments over the past decade, arguably having even more impact than in organizations generally, as most information services are critically dependent on IT, and the cost of books, periodicals and other information sources has continued to rise at a much faster rate than other areas of the economy. Information service managers in both public and private sectors have also been affected by political forces. In the UK, libraries in higher education and local government have received special attention as a result of major reviews during this period,[7-8] and the Irish Department of the Environment initiated a policy review for public libraries in 1998.

Many of the service and management trends evident in the wider business world have been reflected in the information sector, except that a characteristic feature of information and library services continues to be an assumption of the need to maintain all or most of their traditional operations in addition to taking on new activities. 'Doing more with less' is a familiar description of the current situation, and the quickening pace of change, combined with heightened interest in value for money and performance indicators, is testing managerial competence and ingenuity to an unprecedented degree. However, there is published evidence from around the world of radical solutions being considered in relation to all types of information and library services.

Service trends and developments

General trends evident in all sectors include the move from *holdings* to *access*, especially in academic libraries; the shift from *print* to *electronic* media, particularly networked resources; and the development of *self-service facilities* combined with desktop delivery and electronic enquiries, in a more distributed model of information provision. Major research and development programmes in the USA, the UK and the European Union are bringing the concepts of the electronic, digital and virtual library closer to realization, and the migration of library 'housekeeping' systems from proprietary hardware and software to industry-standard models is enabling better integration of information services with other organizational applications, notably utilizing Internet and web technologies.

The rôles and responsibilities of information services staff are changing as a result of the 'end-user revolution', with training and support for users assuming more importance, and 'upskilling' of paraprofessional and other support staff becoming a common means of dealing with the need to free up specialist staff time to develop and deliver new services. Management structures and styles are also changing in keeping with other developments, with client-oriented teams and project-based working replacing the traditional hierarchies typically found in academic libraries, bringing them more into line with practices in other sectors. Staff development and training are also being given more attention, with explicit acknowledgment that continuing professional development is essential to ensure the sustainable development of IT skills and the interpersonal and managerial competencies required to deliver quality services.

REFLECTION

Have you read or heard of any developments in information services elsewhere – in your own sector or others, locally or globally – that you think your service could or should introduce?

Further illustrations of information service developments reflecting more generic organizational trends include the following:

- **Boundary shifts.** Academic and special libraries have converged with other information-related functions in their organizations to form combined or integrated services, aimed at streamlining support for users (for example, convergence with academic computing/IT services and audiovisual/media services, with teaching and learning institutes; and mergers with records management and archives units).
- **Customization.** Academic and public libraries have developed special services for customer groups with particular needs, recognizing the diversity of the communities they now serve (for example, academic library services for part-time and distance-learning students, and for those with disabilities; public library homework help clubs, and open learning centres).
- **Joint ventures.** Information and library services in all sectors are forming partnerships of many kinds with other services and with suppliers to optimize resources and reduce costs (for example, consortium-based purchasing of materials, and contracting out or outsourcing of technical services, including cataloguing; entire information services have also been sub-contracted).

The challenge facing information service managers is evident in the obvious difficulty of trying simultaneously to exploit technology, improve quality and reduce costs – usually in the context of growing customer demand. Some have chosen an entrepreneurial path, typically by looking for *new income streams* from value-added services or fundraising, or alternatively *repositioning* the service within the organization by changing or expanding its rôle – notably special libraries/information centres seeing opportunities offered by the current widespread interest in *knowledge management*. Others have opted for – or had imposed upon them – *restructuring* and transformation via the less palatable process of downsizing (or 'rightsizing'). For all services, it is certain that the future will continue to bring change; successful managers today are already looking ahead and anticipating the information landscapes of tomorrow.

Sources of environmental information

There is a huge number of sources potentially available to help you find out what is happening in the wider community, and even more possibilities since the phenomenal growth of information available electronically via the Internet and the world wide web. Sources can be broadly categorized as documentary (impersonal) and human (personal) on the one hand, external/publicly available or internal/organizationally generated on the other. Commonly used sources include:

- **published documents** – for example, newspapers and periodicals, research reports, conference proceedings, statistical series, directories and yearbooks
- **professional meetings** – from major conferences to informal gatherings, especially events with exhibitions, demonstrations and cross-sectoral participation
- **organizational contacts** – colleagues at work, especially experts in their field, senior managers and people with formal planning or research rôles
- **personal observations** – for example through visits to other information services, and also to suppliers, customers, other service providers/retail outlets
- **electronic 'listservs'** – discussion lists offer scope for initiating and participating in debate, or just observing and learning from exchanges.

Your choice of sources will naturally depend on both the topic and timescale for your research, and your familiarity with the subject matter. Your needs will vary over time, but it makes sense to look ahead as far as possible. In addition, it is good practice to acquire the habit of regularly scanning a core list of newsletters, journals and electronic sources.

ACTIVITY

Draw up a short list of the themes or topics which you consider most important to track in relation to your present job, current projects and future career development. Identify potential sources of information and ideas about your chosen subjects, grouping these under appropriate headings (such as publications, organizations, people, etc). Include a few general cross-sectoral and interdisciplinary sources as well as specialist ones, preferably covering developments in more than one country.

An obvious starting-point is your professional association(s) and related special interest groups, which will enable you to obtain an overview through generalist journals, such as *Managing Information*, the *Library Association Record*, the *Bulletin of the American Society for Information Science* and *American Libraries* – as well as more specialist titles, like *Public Library Journal*, *Program: Electronic Library and Information Systems*, *Information Technology and Libraries*, and *College & Research Libraries*. The suggestions for further reading in this and other chapters will help you to identify other relevant titles from our growing body of professional literature.

Beyond the literature of information and library studies, you will need to consider publications specifically related to the sector or industry served by your information service (for example, health service, higher education, local government, pharmaceutical industry). It is important too to read outside your immediate speciality and to cover interdisciplinary subjects: daily newspapers are obviously useful here, but consider also a weekly current affairs periodical (such as *The Economist*) or a digest of news stories (eg *The Week*) and a popular general science magazine (eg *New Scientist*).

ACTIVITY

Formulate an action plan to enable you to monitor trends and developments on a regular basis. Think about how you will capture, record and apply the knowledge gained.

References

1   Choo, C W and Auster, E, Environmental scanning: acquisition and use of information by managers. In Williams, M E (ed) *Annual review of information science and technology*, Vol 28, Learned Information, 1993, 279.

2   Auster, E and Choo, C W, Environmental scanning by CEOs in two Canadian industries, *Journal of the American Society for Information Science*, **44** (4), 1993, 194-203.

3   Bryson, J M and Alston, F K, *Creating and implementing your strate-gic plan: a workbook for public and non-profit organizations*, Jossey-Bass, 1996, 43.

4   Block, P, *The empowered manager: positive political skills at work*, Jossey-Bass, 1987 (paperback edn 1990), 130-51.

5   Castells, M, *The rise of the network society*, Blackwell, 1996, 328-9.

6   Norton, M J and Lester, J, 'Digital accessibility: information value in changing hierarchies', *Bulletin of the American Society for Information Science*, 22 (6), 1996, 21-6.

7   Joint Funding Councils' Libraries Review Group, *Report*, The Councils, 1993 (Chairman: Professor Sir Brian Follett).

8   Department of National Heritage, *Reading the future: public libraries review*, Department of National Heritage, 1997.

Suggestions for further reading

Future directions, *New Library World*, 96 (1120), 1995, 6-48.
Special issue containing six articles reflecting on current trends and speculating about future developments from different perspectives. Covers academic, healthcare and school library services; two views of the public library; and comments from the (UK) Library Association Chief Executive on 'The librarian at the end of the galaxy'.

Library and Information Commission, *New library: the people's network*, Library and Information Commission, 1997 (available at http://www.ukoln.ac.uk/services/lic/newlibrary/).
Report (c150 pp) commissioned by the Department for Culture, Media and Sport, recommending actions to enable public libraries to respond effectively to the challenges of new technology, including the development of coordinating mechanisms, the technical infrastructure, network services/content, and a comprehensive staff training strategy.

Service developments

Nicholson, H, Uncomfortable bedfellows: enterprise and academic libraries, *Journal of Librarianship and Information Science*, 24 (1), 1992, 9-13.

Discusses motives, benefits and pitfalls of introducing income-generating activities in public-sector institutions. Includes guiding principles, comments on staffing and a matrix of examples of revenue-earning services categorized by type, size and risk.

Green, A, Open and flexible learning opportunities, *Public Library Journal*, **10** (5), 1995, 123-6.

Describes planning and promotion of a network of open learning centres in Staffordshire public libraries and prisons, including development of complementary advice/guidance services, PC and teleworking facilities, and collaborative involvement of other local agencies, with reference to relevant national and European initiatives.

Heery, M, Academic library services to non-traditional students, *Library Management*, **17** (5), 1996, 3-13.

Discusses diversification in the UK student population and service issues arising from the difficulties encountered by overseas students, part-timers, distance learners and students with disabilities. Describes initiatives taken by the University of the West of England and other academic libraries to improve provision for 'non-traditional' users.

Restructuring

Lovecy, I, *Convergence of libraries and computing services*, Library & Information Briefings 54, Library Information Technology Centre, 1994.

Ten-page overview of trend towards convergence in the UK, covering pressures and issues, managerial justification, practical arrangements and perceived problems. Refers to two dozen American and British publications and an informal UK e-mail survey.

Brin, B and Cochran, E, Access and ownership in the academic environment: one library's progress report, *Journal of Academic Librarianship*, **20** (4), 1994, 207-12.

Describes how the University of Arizona Library used a literature review, focus groups and user studies to inform policy and decisions on access and ownership. Discusses the task force's report and outcomes, including a new team-based organizational structure with extra systems staff, an access unit and a Staff Creativity Lab for software training.

Stanley, N M and Branche-Brown, L, Reorganizing acquisitions at the Pennsylvania State University Libraries: from work units to teams, *Library Acquisitions: Practice & Theory*, **19** (4), 1995, 417-25.

Describes radical restructuring and cultural change, removing three management layers with use of quality techniques and self-directed teams. Key features include a phased approach, ownership of the whole process and back-up support through cross-training.

Marcum, J W, Outsourcing in libraries: tactic, strategy, or 'meta-strategy'? *Library Administration & Management*, **12** (1), 1998, 15-25.

Explains the background and development of outsourcing in its various forms, with reference to general management literature and placing it within the context of other organizational trends. Discusses its application in libraries, drawing on recent practical accounts, and offers a rationale and advice for deciding which activities to outsource.

Repositioning

McClure, C R, Network literacy: a role for libraries? *Information Technology and Libraries*, **13** (2), 1994, 115-25.

Discusses educational and social policy issues arising from the evolving networked environment. Defines different types of literacy and links with information problem-solving skills. Argues need to reinvent schools and libraries, and assert public library rôle in ensuring access by training and educating people to use networked information.

Hunt, P J, Interpreters as well as gatherers; the librarian of tomorrow . . . today, *Special Libraries*, **86** (3), 1995, 195-204.

Considers copyright as a concept in relation to the digital revolution, information society and knowledge management. Discusses future rôles for libraries and librarians, presents views of other commentators, and concludes that the future offers exciting new opportunities to those who understand the context of information as well as its content.

Stoffle, C J, Renaud, R and Veldof, J R, Choosing our futures, *College & Research Libraries*, **57** (3), 1996, 213-25.

Argues that academic libraries must change fundamentally, irreversibly and quickly. Outlines reasons for change, and identifies outmoded assumptions and approaches; advocates strategic reallocation of

resources and development of effective two-way relationships with customers, with partners (on and off campus) and with all staff.

Line, M B, What do national libraries do in the age of the Internet?
Ariadne, **13**, 1998, 6-7 (available, with references, at **http://www.
ariadne.ac.uk/issue13/main/**).

Discusses the threats and opportunities presented to national libraries
by information technology and globalization, in relation to their traditional functions and unique rôles, and concludes that they will continue to exist, evidenced by several recent new buildings.

Knowledge management

Klobas, J E, Information services for new millennium organizations: librarians and knowledge management. In Raitt, D (ed) *Libraries for the new
millennium: implications for managers*, Library Association Publishing,
1997, 39-64.

Discusses opportunities and threats facing librarians as other professional groups develop knowledge management skills. Argues the need
for librarians to improve their analytical skills, business focus and understanding of information technology and systems, and suggests
'information science' may be a more helpful label than 'librarianship'
for rôles in the new era.

Stear, E B and Wecksell, J, Information Resource Center Management
(IRCM), *Bulletin of the American Society for Information Science*, **23**
(4), 1997, 15-17.

Traces IRC development from information repository through centre
for distributed interactive information to new rôle with enterprise
knowledge management systems, noting organizational and technological imperatives, and predicting high failure rates.

Broadbent, M, The phenomenon of knowledge management: what does it
mean to the information profession? *Information Outlook*, **2** (5), 1998,
23-36.

Explains the concept of knowledge management, drawing on examples
of good practice and published literature. Emphasizes the significance
of organizational learning and information politics, stressing the need
for an holistic and multidisciplinary approach, and considers the potential rôle of librarians and their capacity for knowledge work.

Corrall, S, Knowledge management: is it our business? *Ariadne*, **18**, 1998, 16–18 (available with references and further reading at **http://www. ariadne.ac.uk/issue18/knowledge-mgt/**).
Defines knowledge management and related concepts (such as intellectual capital) and explains the background and purpose of current developments. Outlines typical applications, key technologies and the skills required by staff involved, referring to examples in the corporate sector and speculating about applications in higher education.

2
Strategic management

Introduction

As an information professional, you will be expected to develop strategies or produce plans for your service, for a particular purpose or as part of regular organizational reviews of objectives and resources. Strategic planning has evolved from a rather abstract top-down model to a more open and inclusive process, involving many stakeholders in a dynamic and holistic approach to managing the business. This chapter explains some of the concepts and techniques of strategic management adopted by organizations in both public and private sectors. It also explores the use of strategic management techniques within information services, and provides models and examples of practical application.

Thinking strategically

Irrespective of whether you opt for or are obliged to have a formal strategic planning process, all information professionals need to acquire a *strategic mindset* – you need to develop the ability to think (and manage) 'strat-

egically'. It is common for people to be criticized for not 'thinking strategically', but comments of this sort are seldom supported by any explanation
or advice on addressing the alleged shortcoming! It is quite difficult to
define what we mean by **strategic thinking**, but here are some characteristics that may help to convey this in understandable terms:

- scanning widely
- seeing the 'big picture'
- selecting the right data
- exploring systematically
- linking process and output
- integrating data with theory
- discriminating between events
- having a conceptual framework
- dealing with many inputs at once
- being creative – moving beyond logic
- responding to an audience/environment
- transferring learning from one experience to another.

Failure to think strategically is often associated with *compartmentalization*.
For example, in planning specific aspects of information services, it is essential to take an overall or *holistic* view of the total information resourcing
process. Cutting journal subscriptions to reduce acquisitions expenditure
may have a knock-on effect on other budgets, notably interlibrary loan or
document delivery services. Even if these costs are not picked up directly
by the information service, someone needs to consider whether it is more
cost-effective for the organization as a whole to invest in an upfront subscription or pay for the supply of individual articles on demand.

There is no standard definition of **strategic management**, but the following description from Gerald Cole will serve as a starting point:

> Strategic management is a process, directed by top management, but engaged
> in throughout the management structure, which is aimed at determining the
> fundamental aims or goals of the organisation, including those concerned
> with satisfying customers' legitimate needs and wants, and ensuring the
> attainment of those fundamental aims and goals through the adoption of ade-
> quate decision-making mechanisms and the provision of adequate resources

in support of a planned direction for the organisation over a given period of time.[1]

The above quotation counters a common misconception of strategic management as something which is the exclusive preserve of top management. There must be leadership at the top, but widespread participation is essential for an organization to operate efficiently and effectively. Other words or phrases associated with strategic management include 'holistic', 'action-based', 'context-specific', 'future-oriented', 'individual and collective'. Many people are more familiar with the term *strategic planning*, but the broader concept of strategic management is increasingly preferred by academics and practitioners as better reflecting the fact that effective planning cannot be divorced from *strategy implementation*, which in turn must include continuous monitoring, evaluation and review, with adjustment of plans if necessary. Related topics, also covered in this chapter, include managing change and quality management.

Strategic planning

In the 1960s, long-range planning was a logical exercise based on the assumption that present trends would continue into the future and any change would be evolutionary or incremental. In the 1980s, strategic planning emerged as a way of coping with the turbulence which characterized the contemporary environment. Strategic planning is in effect a process of relating an organization and its products, services and people to the changing environment and the opportunities and threats in the marketplace. It is a process in which purposes, objectives and action programmes are developed, implemented, monitored, evaluated and reviewed. Again, there is no standard definition, but John Bryson's description captures the essential points: 'a disciplined effort to produce fundamental decisions and actions that shape and guide what an organization (or other entity) is, what it does, and why it does it.'[2]

Strategic planning is particularly concerned with anticipating and responding to environmental factors, taking responsibility for change, and providing unity and direction to an organization's activities. It differs from traditional long-range planning in its focus on identifying and resolving *issues*, its expectation of new trends and *discontinuities*, and its association with *multiple* futures and *qualitative* shifts in direction. Bryson character-izes the process in this way: '[it] requires broadscale information gathering, an exploration of alternatives, and an emphasis on the future implications of present decisions.'[2]

Strategic planning involves several conceptually distinct elements, but in practice it is not a linear process – rather one which is both iterative and interactive, as the information and ideas generated at each stage will often prompt rethinking and reworking of earlier statements. In turbulent times it must be a *continuous process*, requiring *communication with stakehold-ers*, and in its implementation and monitoring modes can be likened to a *combination of projects* within a *coherent framework* supporting a *com-mon purpose*. The key components of strategic planning and management can be elaborated thus:

- **environmental scanning** – researching and analysing the outside world, including your own industry/sector and its marketplace, as well as reviewing and auditing the internal situation, especially your organiza-tion's competitive position
- **strategic profiling** – discussing and agreeing fundamental issues, such as the purpose and functions of your organization, its guiding princi-ples, your view of the future and the direction in which you wish to go, represented by a series of succinct statements
- **strategy development** – formulating and selecting strategies, action pro-grammes and resource plans, after identifying and evaluating options and sensitivities, considering supporting strategies and contingency plans, and specifying performance measures
- **programme management** – implementing actions and monitoring progress, reviewing objectives and refining plans, elaborating tasks and incorporating targets into annual budgets and operational plans, bal-ancing strategic projects and day-to-day operations.

It is worth noting that the process will not necessarily result in a document labelled 'strategic plan'. Moreover, while planning exercises of this type might previously have taken place over a year or longer, managers today are often required to develop plans very quickly. The output from a strategic review today is more likely to take the form of a series of linked statements covering planning assumptions, strategic objectives, financial targets and project plans, all of which will be subject to regular scrutiny and updating as business circumstances and organizational visions change over time.

Environmental appraisal

There is a huge quantity of published literature on corporate strategy, strategic management and business planning, which offers numerous sets of acronyms and techniques that can serve as a helpful stimulus to thinking creatively about future service directions. Common examples include variants of the **SEPTEMBER formula** (introduced in the previous chapter) for assessing Sociological, Economic, Political, Technological and other factors influencing the operating environment, and **SWOT analysis** (see Chapter 10) – sometimes reformulated as **WOTS UP** (Weaknesses, Opportunities, Threats and Strengths Underlying Planning) in the context of strategic planning. These tools are also valuable in encouraging a systematic approach to assessing an organization's current situation or the past performance of a service.

Strategic focus

People often dispute the relevance of planning in uncertain times, and there has been a trend in recent years to shorten planning horizons (for example, moving from five-year to three-year plans) and to simplify planning processes. However, many proponents argue that it is during turbulent periods that organizations derive most benefits from having a shared view of their overall aims and constraints. If *strategic objectives* and *priorities* are understood by all concerned, day-to-day planning and decision-making become easier and more responsibility can be delegated to staff involved in frontline operations, who can then respond more quickly and flexibly at the customer interface. *Participative planning* encourages people to work together for a better future. As well as clarifying direction, establishing priorities and informing decision-making, strategic planning exercises can help people to think corporately, solve problems and develop expertise.

A crucial part of this process is to develop a strategic focus and profile for the organization. **Mission** and **vision statements** are often derided as empty platitudes, but some sort of statement of an organization's terms of reference is needed to inform stakeholders. This can take a variety of forms,

- **Values** – a statement of the beliefs and/or guiding principles that underpin organizational, professional and personal philosophies, and influence staff behaviour and attitudes, often stated as headings elaborated by two to three phrases or sentences.
- **Mission** – a concise summary in a few sentences or paragraphs of the organization's purpose or reason for existence, indicating its business area, customer base and distinctive contribution; sometimes incorporates values and/or objectives.
- **Objectives** – a short list of five to eight broad, general points indicating the continuing functions, main programmes or areas of activity of an organization, elaborating the mission statement (and often combined with it).
- **Vision** – a coherent description in narrative form depicting a preferred scenario or desired future state for the organization fulfilling its potential, frequently using powerful or dramatic imagery.
- **Positioning statement** – a pithy slogan or catchy 'soundbite' expressing the organization's strategic intent (aspiration) and/or summarizing its rôle, often in idealistic or challenging terms.
- **Strategic thrusts** – the major directions in which the organization must move to make the vision become a reality; can be equated with Key Result Areas (KRAs) where success is essential, improvement is necessary and/or concerted effort will bring most benefit.
- **Goals** – a list of new developments or improvements representing the directions in which the organization wants to move within a set timespan, grouped under broad headings, capable of translation into precise targets.
- **Tasks** – lists of specific targets representing the actions and actual deliverables required (of individuals) within specified timescales to achieve the goals; incorporated in project schedules and/or work plans/objectives of individuals.

Fig. 2.1   *The hierarchy of objectives*

and the formal terminology of planning is confused and inconsistent with a proliferation of terms used to describe how organizations wish to position themselves. 'Aims', 'goals', 'objectives', 'strategies' and 'targets' are used almost interchangeably to denote various levels in a hierarchy of statements about what an organization does, where it intends to go and how it will get there. The approach adopted here (see Figure 2.1) is only one of several possible interpretations. It does not matter which terms are used – they are all 'objectives' in the generic sense – but it makes sense to standardize on terminology within organizations to avoid misunderstandings.

Such statements are commonly publicized in strategic plans, promotional literature and annual reports. Few organizations have a complete set as suggested above, and some of these concepts can be combined in one statement. Mission/objective statements are the most widespread manifestation, but vision statements have become more popular recently. Separate statements of values are a lot more common among North American than British libraries. As an example of the latter, the University of British Columbia Library staff are committed to the following organizational values: Service, Integrity, Innovation, Effectiveness, Community, Well-being, Fun and Courage.[3]

The length and format of **mission statements** vary. It is difficult to achieve immediate impact and complete coverage in one statement, but a successful statement combines relevance and realism in a meaningful and memorable way. A convenient approach is to summarize the basic purpose in an opening sentence, and support this with a list of bullet-point statements, exemplified below by the National Mission Statement for the Public Library Service, developed by the (UK) Library and Information Services Council as a generic statement for library authorities to adapt to reflect their local needs and style of provision:

> The public library is a major community facility whose purpose is to enable and encourage individuals or groups of individuals to gain unbiased access to books, information, knowledge and works of creative imagination which will:
>
> • encourage their active participation in cultural, democratic and economic activities;
> • enable them to participate in educational development through formal or informal programmes;
> • assist them to make positive use of leisure time;
> • promote reading and literacy as basic skills necessary for active involvement in these activities;
> • encourage the use of information and an awareness of its value.

> The local and community nature of the service requires special emphasis to
> be placed on the needs and aspirations of the local community and on the
> provision of services for particular groups within it, while also providing
> access to wider resources through regional and national library networks.[4]

The fundamental purpose of most organizations remains fairly constant
over time, but formal statements should be revisited periodically to ensure
that they still look current in terms of their language and style, as well as
in the messages conveyed. Changes to other aspects of an organization's
strategic profile need to be followed through in its mission statement to
achieve consistency in focus and terminology (for example, in the prominence given to community involvement, or in the use of terms such as
'customer', 'client', etc). This sort of periodic check can be difficult if an
organization operates on a decentralized basis or pays little attention to formal articulation of its strategy, but should not be ignored.

ACTIVITY

Review the stated or implicit mission of your service, and its parent organization (if
applicable). If you cannot find a formal statement of this type, deduce the organization's
purpose from appropriate sources (eg annual report, publicity material, recruitment literature). Assess your findings for coherence and currency in relation to other verbal
statements and observed behaviour, and also compare your organizational/service
mission with those of your competitors or peers. Pay particular attention to clarity of
expression, consistency in vocabulary, and completeness of coverage. Unless you feel
there is no scope for improvement, draft a new mission for your service, taking account
of the points noted earlier. Revisit your draft after a few days and test your statement,
preferably with colleagues: is it meaningful? measurable? memorable? and distinctive?
If not, try again!

A successful **vision statement** embodies the tension between an organization's long-term ambition and its current capability in a compelling and
inspiring manner. In 1998, the Standing Conference of National and
University Libraries (SCONUL) which represents 135 services in the UK
and Ireland published a collective vision statement of academic information
services in the year 2002.[5]

One of the best known examples of a library **positioning** statement is the one formulated by the British Library in the early 1990s, 'The world's leading resource for scholarship, research and innovation' which also provided the title for the published version of the Library's strategic objectives, *For scholarship, research and innovation.*

For additional library examples, see the suggestions for further reading below, the collections of strategic plans published by the (US) Association of Research Libraries (cited above) or visit some information service websites. Common pitfalls in formulation include using jargon and wasting words by stating the obvious (for example, using words that are generally superfluous in this context, such as 'appropriate', 'quality' or 'relevant').

REFLECTION

Choose a few items from your work diary, timetable or 'to do' list (particularly things likely to take up quite a lot of time – for example, attending meetings, compiling reports). Consider how these activities or tasks relate to your service objectives, and whether you can see a direct connection between your day-to-day work and your organization's mission. Finally, think about the amount of time that you expect these items to require as a proportion of your working hours, and assess whether this reflects their strategic priority.

Strategic options

Strategies are the means of achieving the goals and objectives specified in this process. As there is likely to be more than one way of achieving each goal, strategy formulation involves identifying *options* and making *choices*, before reaching decisions on the action steps required. Among other considerations, strategies need to be assessed in terms of the risks involved and the knock-on effects for other areas; contingency plans and supporting strategies (for example, relating to staff training) follow on from this. Michael Porter, Igor Ansoff and other strategy 'gurus' offer a selection of tools and models to help people think about alternative strategies. While mainly concerned with securing competitive advantage in the business world, their relevance to non-profit information has increased with the environmental changes experienced in recent years. The strategy literature presents several **generic strategies,** applicable to various business situations, which can be used to stimulate thinking about the general approach to adopt.

One of the classic theoretical models of strategic choice is Ansoff's portfolio strategy matrix (see Figure 2.2), which suggests four generic strategies based on options related to products/services and missions/markets.[6]

Products Markets	Present	New
Present	**Market penetration**	**Product development**
New	**Market development**	**Diversification**

Fig. 2.2   *Ansoff's portfolio strategy matrix*

The four product-market strategies indicated in the figure and below represent different ways of developing the business. These and other strategies outlined below can be pursued in respect of the whole organization or specific services, individually or collectively:

- **Market penetration** involves improving the take-up of products or services within existing markets, referred to as increasing *market share* (eg increasing the number of active borrowers in a library population or the number of loans per borrower)
- **Product development** involves introducing new or modified products or services to existing customers (eg extending enquiry services to include in-depth research services, producing publications or organizing exhibitions based on library collections)
- **Market development** involves finding new customers or outlets for existing services (eg a university library offering services to local businesses or the general public, such as fee-based borrowing facilities)
- **Service diversification** involves both new products and new markets, and can take several forms, including expansion into related functions in the supply chain (such as setting up an on-site bindery or a publishing company)

- **Market segmentation** involves considering the demand for products and services in relation to particular market segments (eg libraries providing special services for ethnic groups or people with disabilities)
- **Product differentiation** involves distinguishing a product or service from rival offerings on the basis of cost/price or special features in the product/service itself or in the way it is presented (eg relaunching a service with a new name)
- **Service divestment** involves dropping non-core or low-priority services, usually to reduce costs or reallocate resources elsewhere (eg withdrawing an unprofitable priced service or closing down a branch library)
- **Consolidation strategies** involve maintaining the *status quo*, concentrating on serving existing customers with established offerings, and limiting changes to small incremental improvements. Consolidation can be a sensible strategy to adopt following a period of intensive development, but it is better to state this as a positive decision, rather than leaving people to deduce it!

Strategy implementation

Strategy implementation is often given less attention than it deserves: not following through properly from strategy to action plans (and related operating budgets) is one of the most common causes of failure, particularly not assigning personal responsibilities for making things happen. Other problems arise from not striking the right balance between development work and day-to-day service delivery, resulting in demotivated staff and/or alienated customers. Sometimes the difficulties are more fundamental – managers often fail to take account of underlying structural and cultural issues, and to acknowledge the extent of organizational development and change required in order to meet their strategic objectives. Unless a consolidation strategy is being pursued across the organization, implementing a strategic plan invariably involves managing change.

Managing change

The pace of technological and other developments in information services has made it commonplace for job advertisements to stress personal qualities and abilities associated with managing change. The capacity to innovate and act as a 'change agent' is assumed to be a prerequisite for senior management appointments, but similar capabilities are now also often sought in candidates for team leadership rôles and other professional positions. There are several reasons why the ability to handle change has apparently become more important. First, it is undoubtedly true that the service environment is more dynamic than it was even a decade ago. Secondly, the trend towards flatter structures and participative management has given more staff a direct involvement in both initiating and implementing change. Thirdly, organizations have experienced so many problems with change projects and programmes that they have been forced to pay more attention to their management.

There are numerous articles and books on the subject, offering various models and recipes. Despite the volume of published literature, this remains a difficult issue for most organizations. While managers will not find simple 'off-the-shelf' solutions to their problems in textbooks, reading about change can be a useful means of helping people to think before they act. Common themes which underpin current thinking on change include emphasis on the management of change as a *learning* process, more attention being given to *stakeholder* concerns, a move towards *bottom-up* and *open-ended* approaches, and stress on managing (and defining) the *transition* state, particularly in the context of large-scale long-term change. Much of what is written on the subject is dismissed by cynics as amounting to no more than common sense, but it is surprising how often basic mistakes are made – hence the need to state the obvious.

Experience suggests three things worth bearing in mind before you embark on the change process:

- **resources (time and money)** – everything always takes longer and costs more than originally estimated
- **fear of the unknown** – some people welcome and relish change as stimulating and exciting, but most are worried or disconcerted by it, and many find it quite frightening
- **evolution and revolution** – there is a significant difference between *incremental* and *discontinuous* change, which should be reflected in how you communicate and manage the process.

Think about your own experience of change in the workplace, and select an example of a change that you feel was implemented successfully, and also one that was less satisfactory. Compare and contrast the two experiences, and try to identify the critical factors in each case. For example, how was the change handled in respect of planning and resources? communication and involvement? flexibility and responsiveness?

Common causes of failure

Published writings and practical experience also provide some pointers to the most common reasons for the failure of strategic change initiatives, which reinforce the points made earlier:

- miscalculating costs and/or failing to secure proper budget provision
- under-estimating the time required, often by not thinking through all the tasks
- rushing over planning, and jumping too quickly to the action stage
- taking a compartmentalized view, and ignoring knock-on effects
- not involving middle managers/team leaders/supervisors early enough
- paying insufficient attention to training needs and related issues
- being unwilling to take tough decisions about individual people
- over-organizing, especially trying to plan in too much detail at the outset.

Tested tips for success

In addition to avoiding the above pitfalls, there are some factors that have proved critical in determining the likelihood of success in achieving change. The key issues are about having a strategic framework and taking an holistic view, putting people first and creating a supportive climate, which are all bound up with continuous carefully targeted **communication**, using a variety of methods and media (see Figure 2.3).

The first point is worth noting, as it is astonishing how often managers fail to explain the real reasons for change properly, with the result that staff often confuse *triggers* for change (like the arrival of a new boss or the recommendations of a service review) with the *root causes* – which are more likely to be related to environmental forces, such as financial pressures and

Strategic change is more likely to work if you have...

1   a good reason for change – a clear rationale, justified in business terms
2   a shared vision of the future – preferably with scenarios defining not only the end-point, but also intermediate states or stages
3   early involvement of key stakeholders – for example, staff, funders, and customers
4   effective liaison and trust – based on active communication, encouraging upwards feedback, with managers *listening* as well as talking
5   energetic and committed leadership – especially a strong senior team
6   support for individuals – including training, and explaining where they will fit in to the new organization
7   a strong external focus – with continuous consideration of the organization's position in the marketplace and wider environment
8   a perception of change as a natural ongoing process – rather than a disruptive *ad hoc* reaction.

Fig. 2.3   *Guidelines for managing change*

technological developments. This frequently leads to further misunderstandings later in the process, thus underlining how communication is undoubtedly the key to success in managing change. Sustaining momentum beyond the initial stages often proves difficult, and many organizations have chosen to pursue cultural change through formal programmes with an operational as well as a strategic focus, such as Total Quality Management.

REFLECTION

Consider whether your two specific examples confirm these general messages about managing change. What do they suggest about the personal qualities and abilities required by change agents? Review your own rôle in the change process. With the benefit of hindsight, is there anything you could have done in these cases to assist the change process more effectively? Do you feel that you have any particular strengths and weaknesses in relation to change management?

Quality management

'Quality' is another overused and poorly understood word in the vocabulary of management. It is a recurring theme in missions, goals and objectives, and often seems to add little of substance to such statements. However, while there is no single accepted definition of 'quality' in the management literature, there is some general agreement about quality, and its meaning in this context is quite distinctive from its use in everyday speech, where it has connotations of superiority, excellence, etc.

The quality gurus all have their own slogans or more formal definitions. For example, W Edwards Deming, the American best known for his pioneering work with Japanese companies, defined quality as 'a predictable degree of uniformity and dependability at low cost and suited to the market'. Another American, Joseph M Juran, who was also an important influence on quality improvement in Japan, offers the simpler definition of 'fitness for use'. A third American guru, Philip B Crosby, defines it as 'conformance to requirements' and sets a performance standard of 'zero defects' or 'right first time'. The British Standard definition (echoed by its international equivalent) is 'The totality of features and characteristics of a product or service that bear on its ability to satisfy stated or implied needs' (BS 4478:1978/ISO 8402:1986), which is just another way of saying 'fitness for use' or 'fitness for purpose'. At a practical level then, we can see that quality is about customer satisfaction, or meeting agreed customer requirements - every time.

It follows from this that in order to achieve quality we need to understand who our customers are, and what services they want. We also need to understand the difference between 'quality' and 'grade'. This distinction is critical, and it underpins the more precise way the term 'quality' is used today in management literature and practice, as opposed to previous associations with luxury, opulence, etc. The key point is that the grade or standard of a product or service depends on its purpose, so our choice may be high or low - but we always want perfect quality (to fit our purpose). To explain this in more concrete terms, to use the description 'quality press' as shorthand for broadsheet newspapers like *The Times* and *Daily Telegraph* is inappropriate, as customers may actually want a tabloid paper such as *The Sun* or *Daily Mirror*.

There are several different approaches to quality management which have evolved over many decades. These can be broadly categorized under three headings:

- **Quality Control** – the reactive detection of errors, through inspection after production (exemplified in a library by senior staff checking catalogue records created by others)
- **Quality Assurance** – proactive prevention of errors, through specification of procedures (for example, compiling a cataloguing manual to remove or reduce the scope for error)
- **Total Quality Management** – active improvement of the effectiveness and flexibility of the whole organization, through both cultural change and standardized systems (for example, recognizing that the effectiveness of a library catalogue depends not only on the accuracy and currency of the records, but also on the IT infrastructure and physical facilities, as well as the attitudes and competence of both library staff and library users).

There are other variants with different labels, for example *Total Quality Control*, *Process Quality Management*, and *Continuous Quality Improvement*. Morris Foster and Susan Whittle provide a useful summary with a comparative table in the *TQM Magazine*.[7]

Quality management has become a key issue for information professionals in the 1990s, particularly because of government interest in the subject. Various initiatives in the UK, including the promotion of BS 5750/ISO 9000, the launch of the Citizen's Charter and the Investors in People award, have required or encouraged organizations in the public and private sectors to pay more attention to customer needs, service standards and staff training, and generally to demonstrate efficiency and value for money. Many institutions have made explicit commitments to one or more forms of quality management, and this has generated debate about the relative merits of different approaches. Advocates of TQM often criticize the quality assurance approach, exemplified by ISO 9000, for undue emphasis on means rather than ends. Some commentators have drawn quite definite distinctions between these two approaches, but in practice, the situation is often not so clear-cut. Organizations, including libraries, often work towards ISO accreditation as part of a longer-term TQM programme.

Core concepts

TQM is generally distinguished from other methodologies on the basis of its more strategic and holistic approach. While it is associated with particular management tools, it is a management and organizational *philosophy*, rather than a system or set of techniques and procedures. Commentators use different permutations of words and phrases to describe the core concepts, but the guiding principles can be summarized as follows:

- **focus on the customer,** including the critical importance of supplier-customer relations (the 'quality chain') and the notion of 'internal' and 'external' customers – often referred to as '*big* C' and '*little* C'
- **process orientation** (rather than function), with processes being likened to the streams of work that flow through or across an organization, thus encouraging a *cross-functional approach*
- **management by fact and data** (rather than taking decisions on the basis of hearsay or intuition) through the use of standard tools for *process analysis* and *performance measurement*
- **people-based management,** with the emphasis on involving everyone, facilitated by training, and based on the view that people are needed to get results and *the expert in a job is the person doing it*
- **synergy through teamwork,** based on the assumption that collective thinking about a problem produces more and better ideas than individual thought, with good *vertical and lateral communication*
- **continuous quality improvement,** acknowledging that TQM must be an ongoing and total approach, covering all parts of the organization and for all time – *not a 'one off' or 'quick fix'*
- **commitment at all levels,** but above all commitment from *top management* expressed through leadership and a shared vision.

Cultural change is often included among the core concepts as most organizations have to make fundamental changes in the way they do things in order to sustain continuous quality improvement.

Tools and techniques

People are sometimes put off TQM when they hear others talk about formal problem-solving methodologies, the use of Statistical Process Control

(SPC) and the importance of training in quality 'technologies'. In practice, many of the quality tools and techniques are already familiar to information professionals. For example, the '7Q' (key tools for quality control) include flow charts and histograms, as well as the check sheets or 'tally charts' that are often used to record enquiries in libraries (and referred to as 'five-bar gates'). The basic tools for quality control and their uses are summarized below:

- **process flow charts** – what is done?
- **tick sheets** or **tally charts** – how often is it done?
- **histograms** or **bar graphs** – what do overall variations look like?
- **pareto analysis** – which are the big problems?
- **fishbone** or **Ishikawa diagrams** – what causes the problem?
- **scatter diagrams** – what are the relationships between factors?
- **run/control** or **Shewart charts** – which variations to control and how.

Brainstorming is another well-known technique, which is frequently used in TQM to generate ideas through group work. Further details of these techniques are given in many general TQM textbooks, and Di Martin's *Library and information briefing* on TQM includes illustrations of the different tools with library-related examples.[8]

Cynics frequently ask whether TQM is worth the effort. Some question the need to spend time on education and training in problem-solving methodologies when they feel staff are already hard pressed just keeping things going, or think they might benefit more from training in IT skills. Others suggest that TQM is no more than good management practice. This viewpoint is understandable, and indeed quality management has been described in the literature as 'applied common sense'. However, information services that have persevered with TQM have been able to point to significant **benefits** as a result of adopting a formal and more rigorous approach to managing services. As well as genuine improvements to products and services *per se*, managers have often seen important spin-offs from quality projects to 'business as usual'/day-to-day tasks – for example, staff who previously resisted performance measurement as something imposed upon them recognizing the need to monitor and measure operations, and others spotting the potential for applying tools introduced in the context of improvement projects to routine work (eg the use of control charts to monitor cataloguing throughput).

A sensible view of these and other concepts and techniques presented and discussed here is to see them as elements in the manager's toolkit. If they can help you to think about what you are doing more carefully, they will have served their purpose.

References

1 Cole, G A, *Strategic management: theory and practice*, DP Publications, 1994.
2 Bryson, J, *Strategic planning for public and nonprofit organizations: a guide to strengthening and sustaining organizational achievement*, Jossey-Bass, 1988.
3 Association of Research Libraries, Office of Management Services, Systems and Procedures Exchange Center, *Strategic planning in ARL libraries*, SPEC Kit 210, ARL, 1995.
4 Library and Information Services Council, Working Group on Public Library Objectives, *Setting objectives for public libraries: a manual of library objectives*, (Library Information Series 19, HMSO, 1991.
5 *The SCONUL vision: the academic library in the year 2002* prepared by . . . a task force convened by SCONUL's Advisory Committee for Information Systems and Services, SCONUL Briefing Paper, Standing Conference of National and University Libraries, 1998 (available at http://www.sconul.ac.uk/vision.htm).
6 Ansoff, H I, *Corporate strategy*, rev edn, Penguin, 1987, 108-9.
7 Foster, M and Whittle, S, The quality management maze, *TQM Magazine*, **1** (3), 1989, 143-8.
8 Martin, D, *Total quality management*, Library & Information Briefings 45, Library Information Technology Centre, 1993.

Suggestions for further reading
Strategic planning

Forsman, R, Incorporating organizational values into the strategic planning process, *Journal of Academic Librarianship*, **16** (3), 1990, 150-3.

Offers six ideas for drawing values into strategic (and day-to-day) management, including use of an assessment instrument in the planning process and alerting new employees to the relevance of values and philosophy to daily decisions, as well as using organizational values as a 'benchmark' of desired attitudes and beliefs for recruitment.

Brophy, P, The mission of the academic library, *British Journal of Academic Librarianship*, 6 (3), 1991, 135-47.

Explores the concept of mission with reference to both business and library literature, and reports on a study of UK academic libraries. Notes that statements focus on what business we are in (purpose) and/or how we do things (values), with overall similarity of content but different emphases (eg building collections, providing access, information skills).

Barrish, A and Carrigan, D, Strategic planning and the small public library: a case study, *Public Libraries*, 30 (5), 1991, 283-7.

Discusses experience of the Crawford Memorial Library in Monticello, New York (a summer holiday resort in the Catskill Mountains) of using the ALA Public Library Association manuals on rôle-setting and output measures, and relates this to the concept of strategy in the corporate world, referring to gurus such as Andrews, Ansoff and Porter.

Asantewa, D, *Strategic planning basics for special libraries*, Special Libraries Association, 1992.

A detailed practical guide (c60 pp) on how to organize, develop and manage a strategic plan, covering the composition and responsibilities of the planning team; situation analysis and survey methods; formulation of mission, goals/objectives, policies, rules and procedures; and use of the budget as a planning tool, concluding with a worked example.

Donlon, P and Line, M, *Strategic planning in national libraries*, Alexandria, 4 (2), 1992, 83-94.

Identifies distinctive aspects of planning for national libraries, including government influences, international responsibilities and diverse audiences. Discusses published examples, with particular reference to the National Library of Ireland.

Lee, S, Organizational change in the Harvard College Library: a continued struggle for redefinition and renewal, *Journal of Academic Librarianship*, 19 (4), 1993, 225-30.

Discusses the strategic planning process initiated at Harvard College Library, highlighting eight key factors critical to a successful outcome. Reproduces the library's vision statement (c400 words) referring to a complementary statement of its values.

Corrall, S, *Strategic planning for library and information services*, Aslib Know How Series, Aslib, 1994.

Concise guide (50 pp) covering the context and process of strategic planning, with separate chapters on environmental analysis, strategic focus, strategy development and documentation, concluding with annotated bibliography of 33 items arranged by subject.

Jajko, P, Visualizing the virtual library: an interview with Eugenie Prime, June 1991, *Medical References Services Quarterly*, **13** (1), 1994, 97–109.

The Manager of the Corporate Libraries at Hewlett-Packard Laboratories explains the paradigm shift required to visualize the library of the future, with reference to experience at HP. Discusses the difficulty of proving the value of information in the corporate environment, suggests managing change via pilot projects, and recommends a broadly top-down approach (while emphasizing the need to sell the vision to others).

Birdsall, D G and Hensley, O D, A new strategic planning model for academic libraries, *College & Research Libraries*, **55** (2), 1994, 149–59.

Describes a six-phase model which differs from other approaches in its emphasis on involving representatives from 'impact areas' in the planning team, ensuring acceptance of the agenda by partners/constituencies, and systematically securing adoption of the plan over five stages.

Hewison, N S, Achieving change in libraries: vision at the department, branch, and team levels, *Library Administration & Management*, 9 (3), 1995, 153–8.

Advocates a participative 'upstream' approach to creating vision statements, with reference to experience at Purdue University Libraries of using visioning techniques both for strategic planning and for planning shorter-term changes. Describes the 'focused conversation' technique of using predetermined questions to guide discussion and comments on the skills and attitudes needed by facilitators.

Himmel, E and Wilson, W J, *Planning for results: a public library transformation process: the guidebook*, American Library Association, 1998.

Practical guide (c125p) develops previous work of the Public Library
Association and describes a six-step planning process, with expanded
treatment of visioning and resource allocation. Part Two is devoted to
13 specific rôles or 'service responses', including community referral,
formal learning support, information literacy and lifelong learning.

Quality management

Riggs, D E, Strategic quality management in libraries. In Godden, I P (ed)
  Advances in Librarianship, Vol 16, Academic Press, 1992, 93-105.
  Argues that strategic planning and TQM are natural partners and mutually supportive. Summarizes key steps in strategic planning, outlines
  philosophies of quality gurus (Juran, Crosby and Deming) and then
  considers application of seven TQM principles in libraries: total
  commitment, customer driven service, rework elimination, teamwork,
  training, empowering and respecting people, and ongoing process.
Aluri, R, Improving reference service: the case for using a Continuous
  Quality Improvement method, *RQ*, 33 (2), 1993, 220-38.
  Criticizes previous approaches to reference evaluation for their lack of
  a systems perspective and long-term view. Discusses measures of service
  quality and illustrates the use of quality improvement tools, such as control charts, pareto charts, and cause-and-effect diagrams.
Brophy, P and Coulling, K, *Quality management for information and
  library managers*, Aslib Gower, 1996.
  Wide-ranging guide (c200 pp) combining a general introduction to quality management concepts, theories and systems with discussion of their
  relevance and application to LIS. Includes chapters on the quality gurus,
  the customer perspective, TQM, service mission, effectiveness and performance measurement, and a bibliography of 12 pages.

Part 2   Meeting information needs

3

Information sources

This chapter covers:

- collection policies
- selection factors
- acquisitions management
- cataloguing and processing
- collection maintenance
- deselection
- metadata.

Introduction

The organization and management of access to sources of information for a defined user community is the essence of a library or information service and a central concern for all information professionals. Collection development has become a more complex task in the networked environment with more choices for information professionals between paper-based and electronic formats and between purchasing, licensing and borrowing options. This chapter considers service policies and management processes for selecting, acquiring, organizing, maintaining and developing information resources to meet community needs. It also explores current issues and future directions for collection management, such as collaboration and metadata developments.

Collection management

Access to sources of information is what library and information services are all about. Ambience, helpful staff, user-friendly systems and value-added

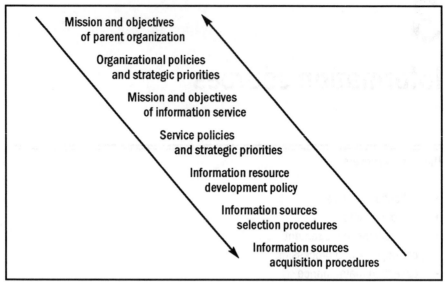

Fig 3.1   *Information sources: strategic and operational objectives*

tailored services are all important, but these are all essentially concerned with one thing – exploitation of the library or information unit's information resources.

Collection management today has to embrace both paper-based and electronically-delivered resources. Such management must be both efficient and effective. To achieve this, any policies regarding management of information sources – be they general collection management policies or more specific acquisition or disposal policies – must reflect the mission and objectives of the wider organization. We have already noted the significance of mission statements (in Chapter 2) and how the objectives of the parent organization should inform the mission and objectives of the library or information unit. These must in turn be translated and developed from top-level statements into day-to-day working procedures and practices. Just as operational plans and individual objectives must reflect the strategic priorities of the organization, so collection or information resource development policies must reflect the higher-level objectives, policies and priorities of the information service and the wider organization (see Figure 3.1).

Decisions can inform policy and strategy in both directions; for example, changes in teaching and research programmes will affect the levels and subjects of items required in an academic library, but bequests of special collections may also affect academic developments. As access to information is a fundamental need, effectiveness of the organization will depend (in part) upon the effectiveness of collection development policies. The establishment and review of such policies is therefore a key concern in managing access to information sources, but the extent to which policies are formally documented varies considerably from organization to organization, and there is no standard format for such statements. Examples range from broad statements of intent to specific criteria for selection/acquisition (covering subjects, formats, levels, etc) as well as for retention (preservation/replacement, relegation, withdrawal, etc). An example of a broad statement for an academic library is shown in Figure 3.2.

Collection Development Policy Statement

Our aim is to develop, maintain and make accessible collections of information resources that meet the learning, teaching, scholarship, research and development needs of the Library's user community.

We shall achieve this by:

- proactive liaison between Library staff and customers, particularly through our structure of Faculty Teams and Liaison Librarians
- informed selection (or production) of information content and formats that will support teaching, research and other programmes
- efficient acquisition of materials and/or rights of access for users through purchasing, licensing, borrowing and other means
- effective cataloguing and display/storage of items to provide users with convenient intellectual and physical access to our resources
- selective repair and replacement of items to maintain collections in optimum physical condition
- judicious stock editing/relocation programmes to maintain a 'living collection' to meet current needs
- strategic development of collections in line with the Library's overall strategy and the University's information strategy and academic plan.

Fig. 3.2   *Example of a policy statement for an academic library*

Find out what formal and informal collection development policies are in operation in your organization. Consider how general policy objectives can be translated into measurable operational objectives.

There is no standard format for collection policy statements, and the labels 'collection development policy', 'selection policy' and 'acquisitions policy' have been used for similar things by different libraries. Gorman and Howes suggest separating policy and principles from procedures and practices, and recommend three levels of statement: collection development policy; selection procedures statement; and acquisitions procedures statement. In this model, the latter (which can also be described as 'manuals') cover specific practices, including how the process is organized and who carries it out, with examples of forms used. The **collection development policy** statement contains *general principles* for the collection as a whole and also specifies *collection levels* by subject and/or form.[1] The detailed contents might include the following:

- **philosophy of the institution and the collection** – overall purpose, overview of needs and priorities
- **parameters of the collection** – user groups, subject boundaries, material types, form restrictions, cooperative arrangements
- **collection levels**, subject-by-subject, typically arranged by a classification scheme, showing collection *density* – the extent of existing collections; collection *intensity* – the extent of current collecting activity; and collection *policy* – the desired level for future collecting (using defined codes or terms such as 'comprehensive', 'research', 'study', 'basic', 'minimal').

Selection and acquisitions

Selecting items for acquisition is a potential minefield. Shortage of resources and space means that we must invest in stock wisely, hence the need for policy guidelines, which should stipulate priorities (for example, the balance between research and teaching materials in a university library; or the relative importance of business and technical information in an industrial library) and preferred formats (for example, hardback or paperback) as well as any constraints (such as limits on prices or numbers of copies) and guidance on when not to purchase, but to rely on access to external collections. Policy decisions also need to be taken on rôles and responsibilities in the selection process. There are various forces which impact on the process, which can be broken down into 'supply' and 'demand' elements.

Supply factors

In order to select information artefacts for our collections, we need information on what is potentially available. This information typically comes from several sources, for example:

- **publisher information** – hard-copy catalogues, CD-ROM catalogues, web listings with online ordering facilities
- **supplier information** – hard-copy catalogues/stocklists, enhanced CD-ROM catalogues (including jacket and title-page details), individual title slips, online databases, booksellers on the web, approval collections, representatives, showrooms and 'stock pick' options
- **reviews and listings** – media, professional, subject and trade journals, publication databases
- **invisible college** – colleagues, notices in the professional press, discussion groups.

Demand factors

Policy on who selects items (information professionals or other stakeholders) will vary from organization to organization. There are often several players involved, for example:

- **information specialists** – a member of information service staff may be responsible for selecting in a specific subject or medium/format, or on behalf of a particular customer group (for example, a local history librarian, reference librarian or children's librarian in a public library; a liaison librarian in a university library)
- **customer representatives** – a member of the user community may be responsible for selecting (or coordinating selection) on behalf of col-

leagues (for example, a teacher/researcher in an academic institution; a research scientist in an industrial organization)

- **individual customers** – a proportion of acquisitions may be purchased as a direct result of specific requests from customers, which may be routed through either information specialists or customer representatives for a second opinion and/or to check compliance with policy guidelines
- **specialist suppliers** – a bookseller may be asked to select material on behalf of the library against a collection profile under a 'blanket ordering' or 'outsourcing' arrangement, usually for particular categories of material (for example, minority-language fiction collections in public libraries).

In the USA, the most widely discussed instance of outsourcing has been Hawaii State Public Library System, which outsourced materials selection to book wholesaler Baker & Taylor, as well as acquisition, processing, cataloguing and distribution for the system's 49 libraries, as a response to massive budget cuts.[2] The level of professional interest and concern generated by this case is evidenced by the subsequent establishment of an Outsourcing Task Force by the American Library Association, to consider the impact of such practices on library and related services in the context of professional values and the Association's Code of Ethics and other policies.[3] In the UK, more recently, Westminster and Hertfordshire Libraries announced collaborative projects to experiment with 'supplier selection'.[4]

REFLECTION

Who is responsible for stock selection in your information service? Is it predominantly information professionals or other stakeholders? Why? Are different materials selected in different ways?

What do you consider to be the benefits/drawbacks of this model? How do collection development policies inform decision making? Do you think that informed suppliers could select on your behalf?

Another element that affects demand is the **time of year**. Public libraries are influenced by the *publishing cycle*, which has peaks just before Christmas and the summer holiday season. Academic libraries often see increases in demand at the beginning of the *academic session* (or the start of modules) and at the end of the financial year. The acquisitions manager has to balance such pressures of demand with a need to manage the workflow for suppliers, as well as for acquisitions, cataloguing and processing staff.

Media factors

Information professionals today are less obsessed with format than their predecessors, but there are particular points to bear in mind for different kinds of information artefacts, for example:

- **monographs** – status/reputation of the author, status/reputation of the publisher, currency, edition, binding, value for money
- **serials** – status/reputation of the publisher, editorial board/refereeing policy, impact factor, indexing availability, currency and frequency, cost-effectiveness
- **multimedia** – suitability of format to user needs, copyright restrictions, longevity (of style and medium), storage and security, playback facilities, cost/income implications.

For all prospective purchases today a key issue is whether the expected level of use justifies acquisition or demand can be met by occasional access (via document supply/interlibrary loan or visit to another collection). For multimedia items, off-air recordings or in-house production may be viable alternatives to purchasing. For sources available in electronic format, assessing cost-effectiveness can be complicated by the range of options (such as standalone or networked CD-ROMs, single/multi-user licences, unlimited access or pay-per-search online databases) and the need to take account of equipment and training costs.

We also need to learn from past mistakes and to be wary of new or 'transient' technologies. Libraries that invested heavily in videos in Betamax (rather than VHS) format can probably afford not to worry too much about the security of their collection, but their customers probably see few benefits in such a collection. Having issued this warning, we should not be constrained by the fear that today's (tried and tested) technologies will soon be superseded. Tony McSean and Derek Law's article, 'Is CD-ROM a transient technology?' sounded the death knell for CD technologies in

November 1990, but the popularity of this medium has hardly declined.[5-6] Although electronic technologies *are* transient by their very nature, we should not ignore the needs of *today's* customers. Online, DVD or other options will probably replace CD-ROM sooner rather than later, but we must satisfy current customers, as well as plan for future service provision.

Selection criteria

Gary Gorman's comprehensive overview of this area cites other authors providing very detailed guidance for evaluating material, in one case identifying seven criteria broken down into 50 sub-categories. Gorman offers a more manageable set of six criteria, which can be concisely expressed as the **ASTAFS** formula:

- **Authority** of creators
- **Scope**
- **Treatment** and level
- **Arrangement**
- **Format**
- **Special considerations** or special features.[7]

Acquisitions management

Traditionally, acquisitions has been seen as a backroom job for retiring individuals: selection was passive acceptance of decisions by colleagues; acquisitions was routine dealings with time-honoured suppliers; and cataloguing was the exclusive preserve of the Cataloguing Department. Today, this picture could not be further from the truth! The environmental changes outlined in Chapter 1 and elsewhere have made this one of the most dynamic areas of information services management, where booktrade knowledge, financial acumen and teamwork need to be effectively applied to get the best deals for the organization. The *real* qualities required by **acquisitions managers** today are quite different from the stereotype. You need to be a:

- **professional** – you must be accountable, ethical, knowledgeable . . . in other words, a professional

- **corporate animal** – you must develop policies which reflect the wider policies of your organization; you must also be a team player, bringing together the work of acquisitions staff, cataloguing staff and collection management staff, with front-line and client liaison staff. You will be working in partnership with information services staff, finance staff, suppliers and other stakeholders
- **specialist** – you may not be a subject specialist, but you are the *supply* specialist, with knowledge, understanding and contacts in all areas of the information supply chain, and you will need to communicate your expertise to colleagues at all levels
- **financier** – you must invest budgets wisely, investing funds in the best *overall* deals
- **manager** – you will need to manage effectively your budgets, your human resources, your equipment and yourself!
- **politician** – you need to be a diplomat at all times; you must know how your organization works and use this knowledge to the best advantage of your department
- **communicator** – you will be dealing with support staff, fellow professionals, senior management and other stakeholders, staff in allied departments in your organization and external suppliers: different people at different levels with different backgrounds and different needs. This is no job for the shrinking violet, but one for the Great Communicator!
- **visionary** – you need to keep your eye on the future as well as the present, and you will need a flexible approach to balance current and future directions.[8]

The acquisitions process is best depicted as a flow chart (see Figure 3.3). Although steps in this process are increasingly being automated, the key to the whole process for the acquisitions manager lies in successful liaison with selectors, acquisitions staff, finance and accounts colleagues, and external suppliers (and also systems staff).

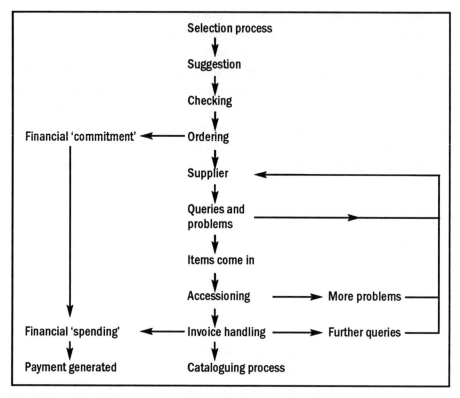

Fig. 3.3   *Acquisitions process*

Supplier policies

Once a suggestion for stock has been checked and is ready for ordering, a supplier must be selected. Several factors have to be taken into account here, for example:

- **Supplier portfolios.** What can the supplier offer in terms of ordering options, stock coverage, speed of supply, discounts and 'value added' services (for example, cataloguing and processing)? You need to consider your needs and priorities in relation to supplier offerings, and also whether you wish to use different suppliers to satisfy particular subject/language/format needs.
- **Organizational policy.** Does your parent organization have a formal policy on purchasing with a list of preferred suppliers (for example, through membership of a purchasing consortium)? Information service

priorities may have to be tempered by other factors, including policies and procedures laid down by your parent body's purchasing, finance and audit departments.

- **Specialist suppliers.** Is it best to place some orders with publishers/producers or specialists (for example, designated agents for official publications, firms specializing in multimedia items)? You need to consider the 'trade-offs' between speed of delivery, volume-related discounts and staff time.
- **An equitable balance.** Some suppliers are far more expert and accommodating than others, but it is desirable not to give all the 'difficult' orders to one supplier, but to aim for a fair balance in your sourcing. (It is also good practice to spread your orders among several suppliers to reduce business risk.)

Underpinning your dealings with suppliers you should have a **customer specification**, setting out practical details such as your invoice address, delivery address, contact names, reporting requirements, automatic cancellation arrangements, allowable price differences, binding preferences, servicing requirements, and discounts. Some documents of this type are more formal and binding agreements, which also cover the level of expected financial commitment, and as such must be carefully drafted (and preferably vetted by your organization's legal advisers).

ACTIVITY

What supplier policies inform decision-making in your information service? How is supplier performance monitored?

Supplier problems

One of the benefits of dealing with a (good) supplier is that most of the day-to-day problems of order administration will be dealt with by your supplier, working to the information given in your customer specification and in close liaison with the (named) contact staff. Despite this, some problems are inevitable, and to solve them successfully the acquisitions manager will need recourse to the skills indicated earlier. Anticipating problems and establishing policies in advance helps to minimize such difficulties. The following checklist give examples of areas where problems often arise and policy guidelines will make things easier:

- **approvals** – do you ever order items 'on approval', or is this likely to prove impracticable with some media . . . or selectors?
- **out-of-print items** – do you have a policy on items reported out of print, for example using specialist suppliers or tracking agencies?
- **pre-payment** – do you have an established procedure for dealing with 'pro formas' from (small) suppliers who want payment in advance?
- **standing orders** – are these treated as monograph or serial orders, and are they manageable in times of financial constraint?
- **unordered items** – what is your policy on free/donated items, and has this been properly communicated to key stakeholders?
- **urgent orders** – do you have a preferred supplier and/or a 'fast track' for urgent needs, and how is this managed from both supplier and requester perspectives?

Information service financial policies and procedures will need to follow organizational regulations and guidelines. It is *essential* that you fully understand both principles and practice to inform your dealings with stakeholders and colleagues, as well as with finance staff, suppliers and auditors.

Cataloguing and processing

Once an item is acquired, it needs to be made accessible to the information service customer. This requires two backroom processes, cataloguing and processing, which are considered in this section. Cataloguing is often seen as one of the defining characteristics of a library, the process which gives *organization* and *order* to a collection, and thus distinguishes it from similar objects stored in a random arrangement. Jennifer Rowley summarizes its purpose thus: 'the objective of the organization of knowledge is to permit that information or knowledge to be found again on a later occasion . . . Poor organization makes it difficult to find something later'.[9] It is not our purpose here to cover cataloguing procedures in depth, but rather to consider some management and policy questions related to the cataloguing process, and in particular to consider the human resource aspects of cataloguing.

In recent years, many information services have reviewed their organizational structures and allocation of tasks among professionally qualified, paraprofessional and support staff in the light of service demands and system developments. Some libraries have moved away from functional specialism in the form of a central cataloguing unit in order to focus better on customer needs through client-oriented teams. Others have delegated cataloguing responsibility to paraprofessional staff and/or library assistants in order to devote more professional staff time to contact with customers. These options are explored below.

Centralized cataloguing versus decentralized cataloguing

The centralized option (which is common in larger libraries) generally involves **specialization,** with specialist cataloguers devoting all or most of their time to cataloguing. The perceived benefits and drawbacks of this model are as follows:

BENEFITS

- Individuals develop an in-depth knowledge of cataloguing techniques and the working of the library's catalogue
- Individuals immersed in cataloguing with few interruptions to their routines can often catalogue very quickly.

DRAWBACKS

- Excessive specialization can lead to a situation where cataloguers get wrapped up in the minutiae of cataloguing regulations and lose sight of the priorities of the organization
- Insufficient task rotation can lead to task alienation and a fall in productivity.

Alternatively, in the decentralized model of **multi-tasking,** all or most professionally qualified staff are involved in cataloguing alongside other functions, including frontline work and client liaison. This model also has perceived benefits and drawbacks:

BENEFITS

- The workload is shared
- There is a growth in team spirit and understanding of wider service pressures
- Job enlargement/task rotation helps to avoid task alienation
- There is a spin-off between frontline and backroom duties – cataloguing staff gain understanding of catalogue user needs, liaison staff will be better equipped to teach information skills if they fully understand the workings of the catalogue.

DRAWBACKS

- More staff require training in cataloguing procedures
- Cataloguing can take more time per unit because staff are less knowledgeable about rules and routines
- There is more scope for time being lost between tasks with more fragmented job descriptions
- Cataloguing may be disrupted by demand for 'more urgent' duties.

Deprofessionalization of cataloguing

Another school of thought asks whether the 'cataloguing' carried out in most libraries and information units today is a professional task at all. With the move to flatter management structures and more emphasis on frontline liaison work, is it sensible to employ professional staff on what has increasingly become an editing task to clean up bought-in records? The contrary view asserts that 'the death of quality cataloguing' is going to cause long-term problems for both information service staff and their customers; it is a false hope that we can leave it to the machines to overcome the problems caused by sub-standard cataloguing. As Harmon (amplifying the concerns of Rowley) argues, 'the more work catalogers do behind the scenes, the more efficient the work on the front lines. If a cataloger does not put the data in the record, the machine is not going to pull it out.'[10]

But *where* should this cataloguing be carried out? Quality cataloguing, fit for its purpose (see Chapter 2) is part of the quality service we offer our customers. But *who* should be generating these quality records? How can we guarantee standards of bought-in records? Should we be editing to meet local needs or merely to rectify basic cataloguing mistakes? Another contemporary management approach is **team cataloguing**, which uses both professional and paraprofessional/support staff working together in subject/language/format teams, dividing descriptive and subject cataloguing tasks.[11] The perceived consequences of this model are as follows:

BENEFITS
- Improved cost-effectiveness from reallocation of tasks to different categories of staff
- Specialization by subject/language/format builds expertise and facilitates faster throughput
- Team structure encourages division of work which utilizes individual strengths
- Reskilling at all levels: new cataloguing skills for paraprofessional/support staff; new supervisory skills for professional staff
- Greater interaction between professional and paraprofessional/support staff
- Paraprofessional staff have instant access to professional colleagues for advice
- Professional staff are freed up for other activities.

DRAWBACKS
- A considerable amount of time is required for training at all levels
- Standards can be sacrificed to throughput
- Shared work processes can prove very time-consuming
- Changes in work patterns can have a negative effect on morale
- Professional staff can feel that their cataloguing skills are being underutilized
- Professional staff may not want to be cataloguing supervisors instead of cataloguers

- The team structure can be divisive for the service as a whole if not properly managed.

PROCESSING

Before an item of stock can be circulated, it needs to be processed. Ownership stamping, stock labelling, security triggering and increasing durability are the daily concerns of staff involved in processing, but there are also significant management questions here. As with cataloguing, we need to ask how much should be done, and who should do it, bearing in mind that the answers to these questions will affect not only processing staff, but also acquisitions and circulation colleagues. The following are examples of points to raise in considering *how much* processing is necessary:

- Do you reinforce paperbacks?
- Do you buy hardbacks where possible?
- What level of security triggering do you employ?
- Do you de/resensitize?
- How do you deal with non-book materials or multi-part items?

The question of *who* processes often leads to more radical decisions. For most public libraries processing is carried out by library suppliers, whereas in the academic sector it has more often been performed in-house, and a few university libraries still have their own on-site binderies, enabling complete self-sufficiency in this area. In the UK, since the demise of the Net Book Agreement in 1995 and the rise of discounts, chargeable 'value added services' have been promoted by suppliers as a way of defending their (declining) profit margins. With changes in cataloguing practices, increased expertise on the part of suppliers, and continuing pressure on library staff time, many academic library managers are now reconsidering the situation, with a view to some form of outsourcing.

ACTIVITY

In anticipation of continuing pressure on staffing budgets, you have been asked by senior management to produce a discussion paper outlining strategies for reducing the involvement of staff – especially professionally qualified staff – in technical services. Consider the strengths and weaknesses of identified options for reorganizing cataloguing and processing services in your own organization. Conclude your report with your recommendations, perceived benefits and strategies for tackling foreseeable problems.

A living collection

Getting the stock on the shelves and ready for use is not the end of the story. We need to ensure that we have a 'living collection', and indeed stock does have a 'life cycle'. As well as the obvious life events, such as conception (selection), birth (acquisition) and death (deselection), there are many other stages and phases in the lives of our collections, including opportunities for rejuvenation and development, as well as questions about conservation and relegation of stock to stacks (closed access or remote storage areas). There are many ways to keep our collections alive, and these are just some of the issues to consider:

- **Promotion.** Many information services start off well by producing lists of new acquisitions and/or displays of new stock, but fail to promote stock after this initial effort. Suggested methods include subject-based displays (which can be linked to organizational events) and printed or electronic guides to specialized areas.
- **Circulation.** Loan periods and privileges can have a significant impact on stock usage and items can often be given a new lease of life or a death sentence by changing circulation parameters. For example, putting essential reading material for mature, part-time students into a four-hour loan collection is unlikely to encourage widespread use.
- **Physical state.** Stock can look tired and dated long before its content is obsolete if thought is not given to how it looks on the shelves, and physically ageing material detracts from its neighbours. Public libraries sometimes acquire spare book jackets to double the lifespan, but university libraries frequently prefer to discard colourful covers. (A related issue to consider here is the upgrading of formats to maintain attractiveness, such as replacing vinyl recordings with compact discs.)
- **Stock editing.** Some information professionals view weeding as a negative task that takes up valuable time and irritates stakeholders, while

others see it as a positive process to enliven collections. Too many out-of-date texts on the shelves can frustrate and deter users as they struggle to pick out current items wedged between old volumes.

ACTIVITY

Concentrating on a few selected areas of your stock, consider how you would revitalize collections. What parameters and policies would you employ for stock editing/relegation? Consider appearance, content, level, medium and circulation factors.

Deselection

In his review of relegation practice in UK university libraries, Geoffrey Ford identifies five main types of so-called 'objective' criteria for weeding:

- usage
- obsolescence
- age
- death
- decay.[12]

Other factors often considered include:

- duplication (of the item or its contents)
- availability in collections elsewhere.

The main area where most research libraries encounter deselection is not in monographs but in serials collections. Each year, *American Libraries* and the *Library Association Record* publish inflation figures for periodical titles in various disciplines, and each year prices rise on average by around 10%.[13-14] In a world where general inflation rates are far below this and index-linked resources budgets are rare, information service managers face an obvious problem. The common response now is to cut subscriptions, most libraries and information units having already cut back in other areas of the budget over the past decade.

There is a prolific supply of articles on **periodical cancellation programmes,** many of which offer step-by-step guides to 'cuts without chaos'. You will find advice in the suggestions for further reading at the end of this chapter, but experience suggests the following points merit special attention.

SEVEN SUGGESTIONS FOR SUCCESSFUL SERIALS REPROFILING

- **Start early.** This is a time-consuming process. Lists will go back and forth to (busy) research staff to establish interest, degree of interest (as titles are seldom the preserve of one group or department) and degree of need (vital/useful/dispensable/etc). If working backwards from subscription renewal dates, give yourself a very long lead-in period, usually of not less than six months.
- **Be thorough.** If you fudge a review one year, you are only storing up more work for the next. Inflation will not go away and neither can reviews. As the research environment changes, so does need, but a thorough programme to establish individual and/or group interests in subscriptions to be maintained (as well as those to be cancelled) in Year One will save considerable time in Year Two, and so on.
- **Appoint a project manager.** A thorough, complex and time-consuming task needs one overall manager to act as coordinator, push the project forward and provide a much needed focus/contact point for both information service staff and research colleagues, though it is desirable for staff normally responsible for liaising with particular client groups to handle negotiations with their clients. A relatively senior appointment will stress the importance of the project.
- **Automate the process.** Save time by using easily manipulated databases and consider the use of project management software if you have a large-scale operation to manage. Spread workloads by using a shared directory, and if possible make your title and price data available to stakeholders via your intranet.
- **Think strategically.** Encourage everyone to weigh up all the costs and benefits of each title (see Chapter 8) bearing in mind that some very expensive titles may still be 'worth the price' in terms of the use made of them on a day-to-day basis, and always act in line with the strategic priorities of the organization.

- **Be positive.** Market your project: are you just suffering cuts or reprofiling your collection? A sensible review will allow researchers to go beyond the prescribed savings to reallocation of funds for new titles to reflect changing needs. In thoroughly reviewing your collection, you are ensuring that limited budgets are being invested wisely: publicize this positively in newsletters, on your website and at committees and other meetings. Remind colleagues that this is a global concern – not a symptom of *your* financial mismanagement! Be transparent and accountable. Do not be ashamed.
- **Learn from the experience.** Reflect on how your experience can be used for long-term planning, and use insights gained from projects of this sort to inform your client liaison and communication strategies.

The electronic imperative

The environmental factors outlined in Chapter 1 – social, economic, political, technological, educational, market, business, ethical and regulatory factors – look set to affect our management of information sources, just as they will have impacts on other elements of service provision. The literature is full of warnings of 'the rocky passages ahead'.[15] Economic forces have brought the 'serials crisis' and emphasis on academic research output has resulted in the 'crisis of scholarly communication'. Copyright is still a problem, especially in relation to electronic media. Archiving of non-book materials has already been impeded by legal and technological constraints, and the situation is likely to become more problematical as items traditionally produced in hard copy move to electronic formats.[16] Just as publishers do not now keep copies of unprofitable monographs or runs of serials, the archiving of electronic information resources will probably fall to libraries, which then raises questions about maintaining software, hardware and playback facilities.[17] These problems become magnified when we consider electronic files which are constantly being amended, and how to archive *dynamic* databases. Such questions are currently occupying the Research Libraries Group (RLG) and the Commission on Preservation and Access (CPA) in the USA and the Consortium of University Research Libraries (CURL) in the UK. But not all is doom and gloom, and we can point to exciting and promising developments in some areas.

Metadata management

One challenge already being faced by many information professionals is the mismatch between the constraints on our time, the demands of IT-literate customers and the chaos that is cyberspace. This is a big problem and there is no quick solution. As Stephen Hearn has warned,

> It is not enough simply to stack new kinds of information together in our menu displays like bricks in a wall. One of the major challenges facing librarians charged with organizing this new information environment is that of integrating and linking these disparate kinds of information into efficient, workable systems. We are only beginning to explore the optimum ways of representing our various databases and services in terms of categories, hierarchies, and relationships. As the new systems become more familiar to users, rising expectations are driving the need for greater integration. Once periodical indexes have been included in the online system, the desirability of active links between the article citations and the library's serial holdings becomes apparent. Once online access to electronic texts is offered by the system, the desirability of online catalog records with active links to the online texts becomes clear. As users encounter multiple indexing vocabularies in different parts of the system, the desirability of greater coordination between these vocabularies becomes an issue of growing concern.[18]

As information professionals, we know that what the Internet needs is organization. Cyberspace needs an index. If Rowley's warnings about poor organization impeding retrieval ever needed a specific example, here it is. The problem is likely to get worse as multimedia developments take us from text-based to image-based data, or viewed more positively, the opportunities for information professionals will be even greater than at present: a new age has been heralded for librarians, when the meek cataloguers look set to inherit the Earth![19]

Some colleagues argue that Internet resources should be selected, added to stock and properly catalogued, just like 'old fashioned' media.[20] Others acknowledge it is a bit more complicated than that, and indeed new models and standards for metadata – data about data – are already emerging to facilitate access to networked resources, notably the Dublin Core Element Set, which has given rise to a number of high-profile international projects covering a range of disciplines and domains.[21] Metadata is one of the buzzwords of the 1990s: a lot of ground-breaking work has been done, much of it through international collaboration, but there is a great deal more to be done at the local level within libraries and information units before the levels of bibliographic control that have been achieved for paper-based resources apply to electronic resources. Professional cataloguers should not feel threatened by the 'deskilling' of their traditional work, but welcome the opportunity offered to apply their knowledge and skills in the new environment as metadata managers. As well as technical aspects, there are policy issues to address, such as just how much effort to invest locally in creating resource descriptions for subject-based information gateways ('niche portals') on your own website, when ready-made descriptions may be available elsewhere and accessible to your customers.

Collaborative management

> Where once-upon-a-time academic research libraries pursued the proud goal of a comprehensive stand-alone collection of resources that would meet most (if not all) needs of local patrons, it is now necessary to begin the collective migration to a more streamlined post-modern 'collection of collections' mediated by new electronic networking technology that connects scholars across space and time. In other words, economic forces and technological advances have combined together to create a new environment, one where access to collective scholarly resources that no one library could ever afford supersedes the historic quest for the great comprehensive collection.[22]

As Harloe quite rightly points out, the coming together of economic challenge and technological opportunity means that we should be looking to force the 'access versus holdings' debate beyond the bounds of mere rhetoric. In this environment, we can expect renewed interest in Conspectus and other systematic approaches to collection assessment, as a basis for resource-sharing and collaborative collection management.[23] Once strengths (supply) and interests (demand) have been established, mutually beneficial information resource networks can be set up, facilitated by information and communication technologies. Convenience will no longer lie solely in the monograph or periodical part on the shelf, but in easy access to electronic text and images through subject gateways, user empowerment through effective information skills development programmes and document delivery in cost-effective formats. In this model, the library can finally be viewed as a logical concept rather than an architectural conceit – assuming the intellectual property rights and institutional politics don't get in the way! Predicting the future is a hazardous pastime, but we can all agree that for the information professional it is going to be both challenging and exciting.

ACTIVITY

Utilizing environmental scanning, identify the key factors which you think will affect the management of information sources in your information service over the next five years. Talk with colleagues involved in collection management to assess strengths in your own organization's collection(s). Consider the scope for resource-sharing locally, nationally, or internationally. How could this most successfully be pursued? What would be the short-term and long-term implications of such schemes?

References

1   Gorman, G E and Howes, B R, Form and content of collection development policies. In their *Collection development for libraries*, Bowker-Saur, 1989, 27–84.

2   Angry Hawaiian librarians denounce B&T outsourcing, *American Libraries*, 28 (1), 1997, 12.

3   Outsourcing Task Force to meet at Midwinter, *American Libraries*, 29 (1), 1998, 9.

4   Hall, C, Valentine, S and Fletcher, S, Into the age of supplier selection, *Library Association Record*, 100 (9), 1998, 476.

5   McSean, T and Law, D, Is CD-ROM a transient technology?, *Library Association Record*, 92 (11), 1990, 837–41.

6   East, H and Leach, K, The continuing prominence of CD-ROMs in academic libraries: the findings and evaluation of a survey, *Aslib Proceedings*, 51 (8) 1998, 208–14.

7   Gorman, G E and Howes, B R, Selection principles and practices. In their *Collection development for libraries*, Bowker-Saur, 1989, 185–246.

8 Based on a presentation by Frank Edwards at the NAG Acquisitions School, 1997.

9 Rowley, J E, *Organizing knowledge: an introduction to information retrieval*, Gower Publishing Company, 1987, 3.

10 Harmon, J C, The death of quality cataloging: does it make a difference for library users? *Journal of Academic Librarianship*, 22 (4), 1996, 306.

11 Schuneman, A and Mohr, D A, Team cataloguing in academic libraries: an exploratory survey, *Library Resources & Technical Services*, 38 (3), 1994, 257-66.

12 Ford, G, A review of relegation practice. In Corrall, S (ed) *Collection development: options for effective management: proceedings of a conference of the Library and Information Research Group*, University of Sheffield, 1987, Taylor Graham, 1988, 71-87.

13 For example, Alexander, A W and Dingley, B, U.S. periodical prices – 1998, *American Libraries*, 29 (5), 1998, 82-90.

14 For example, Annual periodical prices for 1998, *Library Association Record*, 100 (7), 1998, 363.

15 Harloe, B and Budd, J M, Collection development and scholarly communication in the era of electronic access, *Journal of Academic Librarianship*, 20 (2), 1994, 86.

16 Weston, M, Half inched video, *Viewfinder*, 30, 1997, 14-15.

17 Duckett, B, If you can't access it, does it exist? *Library Association Record*, 99 (4), 1997, 207.

18 Hearn, S, Bibliographic control in the electronic age, *Journal of Library Administration*, 22 (2/3), 1996, 128.

19 Shimmon, R, [Editorial], *Library Association Record*, 100 (1), 1998, 1.

20 Demas, S, McDonald, P and Lawrence, G, The Internet and collection development: mainstreaming selection of Internet resources, *Library Resources & Technical Services*, 39 (3), 1995, 275-90.

21 *Dublin Core metadata initiative* (available at http://purl.oclc.org/dc/).

22 Harloe, B and Budd, J M, Collection development and scholarly communication in the era of electronic access, *Journal of Academic Librarianship*, 20 (2), 1994, 83.

23 Mosher, P H, Collaborative interdependence: the human dimensions of the Conspectus, *IFLA Journal*, 16, 1990, 327-31.

Special Interest Groups

These groups bring together individuals and organizations from all stages of the supply chain (producers to users). They offer information and advice to members in various forms, including annual conferences, seminars and workshops, e-mail lists, regular journals/newsletters and other publications. The annual NAG Acquisitions School provides an intensive overview of the processes and problems practitioners are likely to encounter.

National Acquisitions Group
NAG Administrator
Lime House
Poolside
Madeley
Crewe CW3 9DX, UK
Tel/Fax: (01782) 750462
http://www.nag.org.uk/

United Kingdom Serials Group
UKSG Business Manager
114 Woodstock Road
Witney
Oxfordshire OX8 6DY, UK
Tel: (01993) 703466
Fax: 01993 778879
http://www.uksg.org/

North American Serials Interest Group Inc
NASIG Treasurer
P.O. Box 54362
Cincinnati, OH 45254-0362, USA
http://www.nasig.org/

Suggestions for further reading
Collection management

Tezla, K E, Reference collection development using the RLG conspectus, *Reference Librarian*, **29**, 1990, 43-51.
> Argues that reference collection development should be managed as an integral part of the overall management of research library collections, and identifies potential components of a collection development policy statement based on the RLG Conspectus methodology.

Carrigan, D P, Collection development - evaluation, *Journal of Academic Librarianship*, **22** (4), 1996, 273-8.
> Argues the need for explicit evaluation of collection development in a library - as distinct from the evaluation of a library collection - and discusses how to set about achieving this.

Jenkins, C and Morley, M (eds), Collection management in academic libraries, 2nd edn, Gower, 1999
> Substantial volume (c300 pp) containing ten contributions from the UK and North America providing an overview of current issues and concerns. Topics covered include organization and staffing; finance and budgeting; performance measurement; electronic information; serials management; document delivery; stock revision; preservation; and future directions.

Russell, J, Collection profiling, *SCONUL Newsletter*, **16**, 1999, 26-30.
> Explains the purpose and benefits of collection assessment and then describes a project at the University of Birmingham using the Conspectus method. Covers profile format, staff involvement, assessment criteria, validation methods and implementation issues; also includes references to other articles, and URLs for policy document and profile examples (see **http://www.is.bham.ac.uk/cm/colldev.htm**).

Selection

McSeán, T and Law, D, Is CD-ROM a transient technology? *Library Association Record*, **92** (11), 1990, 837-8, 841.
> Considers the limitations of CD-ROM as a database medium, speculates about technologies that may supplant it and concludes that it is only a step on the way to something else. A seminal article which initi-

ated a debate in the features and letters columns of the *LAR* over several months, raising several questions about future directions for sources and services.

Jenkins, P O, Working with faculty to build collections, *College & Research Libraries News*, **56** (5), 1995, 322.

Advances the view that effective collection development is part of the academic liaison function, with examples of ways to maintain good working relations with faculty members.

Acquisitions

Chapman, L, *Buying books for libraries*, Library Association Publishing/Clive Bingley, 1989.

Provides a step-by-step account of the book acquisitions process and the rôles of those involved from pre-order checking to receipt, highlighting the importance of communication between libraries, users, booksellers and publishers. Although out-of-date in places (notably, in relation to the Net Book Agreement) many of the main points are still valid. Publisher's note: this title is currently being updated.

Lacey, S and Cameron, J, Consolidation services – a view from the National Library of Australia, *Serials*, **10** (1), 1997, 49-52.

Describes trials undertaken by National Library of Australia for supply of US serials, and later other titles, concluding use of such services has improved reliability of supply.

Gray, R, Evolution or extinction: the current state of library supply, *Public Library Journal*, **13** (5) 1998, 70-2.

Provides supplier perspective of library supply chain processes (select and order, deliver and receipt) and suggests future changes to reduce time and cost of supply, including supplier selection and various Internet-based services. Argues the need for quality guarantees, fault-tolerant systems, and mutual trust for such changes to work effectively.

Cataloguing

Schuneman, A and Mohr, D A, Team cataloguing in academic libraries: an exploratory survey, *Library Resources & Technical Services*, **38** (3), 1994, 257-66.

Reports on team organization of librarians and paraprofessionals in eight US academic libraries, and the perceptions of team members of its impact on productivity and morale.

Harmon, J C, The death of quality cataloging: does it make a difference for library users? *Journal of Academic Librarianship*, 22 (4), 1996, 306-7

Entertaining defence of 'quality cataloguing' which concludes that quality MARC records are part of quality service to our customers, and we should not input sub-standard records in the hope that one day 'the machines' will be able to rectify cataloguing shortcomings.

Libby, K A and Caudle, D M, A survey on the outsourcing of cataloging in academic libraries, *College & Research Libraries*, 58 (6), 1997, 550-60.

Based on literature review and questionnaire survey of 187 American libraries: 28% of respondents had outsourced and 14% were considering doing so. Comments on factors influencing decisions, choice of vendors, range of coverage and the success of projects.

A living collection

Williams, R, Weeding an academic lending library using the Slote method, *British Journal of Academic Librarianship*, 1 (2), 1986, 147-59.

An extensively referenced case study of a project at Humberside College of Higher Education, based on Stanley J Slote's concept of the 'core collection' determined by 'shelf-time periods' (length of time between circulations). Describes how 20,000 volumes were removed from the library within nine months, using this simple, flexible and cost-effective method.

Harloe, B and Barber, H M, Managing the reference collection: the practice of pruning, *Reference Librarian*, 29, 1990, 159-73.

Looks at the management of stock editing processes in an academic collection, covering criteria for weeding and how to deal with reference serials in both print and electronic formats; highlights the need for a planning cycle approach and effective communication. (Contribution to an issue devoted to the weeding and maintenance of reference collections.)

Metz, P, Thirteen steps to avoiding bad luck in a serials cancellation project, *Journal of Academic Librarianship*, 18 (2), 1992, 76-82.

Describes six-month project at Virginia Tech where 1250 serials were cancelled with minimal damage to the collections and minimal impact on library-faculty relations, and identifies 13 critical factors for successful cancellation exercises. Also provides list of references to published literature on serials cancellations, use studies and related issues.

Zappen, S H, Are the methods working? Where do we go from here? *Collection Management*, **19** (3/4), 1995, 171-83.

Based on experience of a US academic library, offers a set of precepts for dealing with the problem of rising subscriptions, and forecasts changes in journal provision for the future.

Kiger, J E and Wise, K, Auditing an academic library book collection, *Journal of Academic Librarianship*, **22** (4), 1996, 267-72.

Describes techniques used at the University of Tennessee Library, claiming that a reliable estimate of interest can be obtained from a relatively small amount of 'attribute sampling'.

Smith, A, Preservation in the digital age: what is to be done? *American Libraries*, **30** (3), 1999, 36-8.

Argues that preservation is a basic responsibility for information professionals in all communities and considers the challenges of preserving the growing amount of content stored on fragile materials and in digital form. Identifies seven common strategies used, emphasizing the need for techniques that are fully reversible and properly documented.

The electronic imperative

Harloe, B and Budd, J M, Collection development and scholarly communication in the era of electronic access, *Journal of Academic Librarianship*, **20** (2), 1994, 83-7.

Argues that IT developments enable us to move beyond merely talking about access and ownership and to take a more radical look at the concept of the library. Suggests provision of local gateways to information stored physically close at hand and external gateways to remote information sources available electronically or via document delivery services.

Demas, S, McDonald, P and Lawrence, G, The Internet and collection development: mainstreaming selection of Internet resources, *Library Resources & Technical Services*, **39** (3), 1995, 275-90.

Suggests methods for systematically identifying, evaluating and selecting Internet resources, arguing that established principles and practices of collection development can be used to integrate Internet resource selection into day-to-day activity. Identifies key policy issues and provides extract from a collection policy statement and a taxonomy of resources.

Hearn, S, Bibliographic control in the electronic age, *Journal of Library Administration*, 22 (2/3), 1996, 123-32.

Suggests that pressures from users will force us to reassess bibliographic control and the way that our systems are linked. Identifies staff development and hardware development as particular areas where libraries will have to make additional investment in this context.

Miller, P, Metadata for the masses, *Ariadne*, 5, 1996 (available at **http://www.ariadne.ac.uk/issue5/metadata-masses/**).

Introduction to the concept of metadata, which sets out the background to current developments, itemizes the 13 elements which at that time constituted the Dublin Core, considers future developments, and concludes with an extensive list of useful references.

Lyon, E, A moving performance, *Library Technology*, 1 (5), 1996, 97.

Reports progress of the eLib Performing Arts Resources Online (Patron) project which aims to deliver music and dance materials (audio, video, graphics and text items) to students on-demand as part of a digital short loan collection at the University of Surrey, discussing technical requirements, copyright and licensing issues, and project evaluation.

Fox, P, Access versus holdings: a new perspective from an ancient university, *Relay*, 44, 1997, 3-7.

Two-part article which looks at the problems of archiving electronic formats (partly in relation to legal deposit) and then comments on three options put forward for information sharing: digitizing stock will take too long; circulating stock will increase wear and tear on decreasing resources; and circulating customers to collections will incur other costs.

Crawford, W, The danger of the digital library, *The Electronic Library*, 16 (1), 1998, 28-30.

Warns against thinking that all libraries will become digital, and argues that we must strive for a balance between print and electronic alternatives, dependent on what best meets the needs of libraries and their customers. Notes some potential benefits and drawbacks of digital distribution and speculates about issues for information professionals in the future.

Owen, C, Metadata for music and movies, *Audiovisual Librarian: Multimedia Information*, **24** (1), 1998, 47-50.

Lists the 15 elements of the Dublin Core metadata set and explains how the Performing Arts Data Service at Glasgow University is using metadata to describe and organize digital sound and moving image resources in the areas of film, video, broadcast arts, theatre and dance.

Webb, J, Managing licensed networked resources in a university library, *Information Technology and Libraries*, **17** (4), 1998, 198-206.

Provides overview of current issues and concerns: advocates involvement of systems staff in collection development; suggests web-based databases of licence conditions; considers pros and cons of aggregators and consortia; and raises questions about cataloguing policy, multiple access points, printing facilities, archiving agreements and academic integration.

Dublin Core metadata initiative (available at **http://purl.oclc.org/dc/**).

The official website for the Dublin Core content description model for electronic resources outlines its distinguishing characteristics (simplicity, semantic interoperability, international consensus, extensibility, metadata modularity on the web) and defines the core elements. Other sections cover news and publications, projects, schemas, tools and working groups.

4

Information services

This chapter covers:

- trends in service provision
- breadth of service portfolios
- emerging models for reference services
- value-added services
- service level agreements
- service quality
- performance indicators.

Introduction

Various environmental factors have influenced information service strategies in recent years, the most obvious examples being information and communication technologies, financial and human resources, and managerial and political policies. Information services are interpreted here as covering the total array of services, products and facilities offered by libraries, information units and other forms of resource centres. This chapter covers trends and developments in service provision and management thinking. It also introduces concepts and tools to assist with identifying added value, defining service levels and assessing service quality, with practical guidance and examples drawn from recent practice in library and information services.

Trends in service provision
Service and product portfolios

The range of products and services potentially available from the networked information centre differs significantly, both qualitatively and quantitatively, from that offered in the past. Technological developments have given information service managers a wider set of options from which they can select the best mix to meet the needs of their customers. Historically, the quality of a library was usually judged on the size of its collections of books, periodicals and other materials. Today, the emphasis has shifted from *collections* to *services*, and to the delivery of documents and other items to customers irrespective of their location. In future, service quality will be equated more with staff competence than with collection strength, even though in some cases they may have a less visible rôle in the supply of electronically mediated information and document delivery. Another significant point to consider is how the balance of staff effort expended in libraries on loans/document supply and reference/information work may change in the longer term.

Information and communication technologies have enabled services to develop in ways that offer improved choice, convenience and customization for individual users and groups:

- **Self-service facilities** have moved on from open-access collections and customer-operated photocopying to self-issue, returns and reservations/booking, as well as 'end-user' database searching, downloading and printing
- **Distributed delivery** of centrally managed services has progressed from loans and document supply to desktop access to databases and instructional material, 'virtual' library tours, reference desks and suggestions boxes
- **Tailored services** (often with tiered levels of provision) have been developed to meet the specific needs of particular groups, such as people with physical disabilities or learning difficulties, and distance-education students
- **Partnership provision** is becoming more common, especially for 'boundary-spanning' activities, where library staff work alongside other specialists or host facilities managed by a third party (such as IT centres or bookstores) with the shared goal of providing a 'seamless service' experience for users (also known as 'one-stop shopping').

Library service portfolios are generally characterized by a tendency to retain all or most of their traditional offerings in addition to newer elements; library managers seem to be rather reluctant to drop products and services, even when budget pressures might suggest it. Failure to face up to such issues strategically often means that services deteriorate and the portfolio of offerings is altered operationally without a proper decision being taken to withdraw or modify the service (for example, by limiting its availability or redefining levels of provision). Situations of this kind can create resentment and resistance to change among both staff and customers, which could be avoided if more attention were given to deciding priorities at the outset, enabling better management of stakeholder expectations. Many customer care programmes have not delivered anticipated benefits for this reason: managers have concentrated on interpersonal skills for frontline staff without pursuing customer focus at the strategic level, as an integral part of the overall service strategy.

Despite financial constraints, the range of services offered by libraries and information centres is impressively broad. A survey of UK public libraries conducted in the early 1990s identified more than 30 distinct service elements, of which approximately one-third were offered by more than half of the 139 respondents.[1]

Figure 4.1 reflects the public library's traditional commitment to education, information and recreation (which are not mutually exclusive categories) and also indicates how some services tend to be described in terms of their content or format, while others are defined in relation to their users. Missing from this list are the basic service components of general reference and lending collections, which form the core provision for most service points. Public libraries have the challenge of trying to meet the needs of all members of society, and indeed the (UK) 1964 Public Libraries and Museums Act places a statutory duty on them to provide a 'comprehensive and efficient' service; but this is not formally defined, which makes it difficult for service heads to decide the breadth and depth of offerings. Other types of libraries and information centres face less extreme but similar problems in determining an accessible, affordable and appropriate mix of services, products and facilities, which underlines the importance of having an agreed statement of the mission, objectives and priorities for the service and its parent body, and reviewing it regularly.

Examples of public library services and facilities

Business information	Services to the housebound	Exhibitions
Foreign literature	Mobile libraries	Room for meetings
Online bibliographic searches	School library services	Holiday activities
Viewdata	Hospital library services	Film shows/plays/music
Teletext/television	Services to ethnic groups	Lectures
Local history/genealogy	Prison library services	Arts events
Community information	Instruction in schools	Museums
Publications	Open learning	Festivals/fairs
Tourist information	Writers' workshops	Authors in residence
Local government information	Toy library	Galleries

Fig. 4.1   *The range of services and facilities offered by UK public libraries*

Rethinking reference

Many libraries have been rethinking their reference and information services in the context of the electronic environment, with a noticeable shift away from the traditional undifferentiated all-purpose enquiry desk (staffed by a professionally qualified librarian) to tiered levels of provision, employing different categories of staff for particular purposes. William Whitson reconceptualizes reference as a composite model of five distinct but interrelated services:

- **directional and general information** (typically about services, hours, and locations), requiring no specialized knowledge, staffed by student assistants/lower-level support staff – or replaced by audiotext messages, online screens, automated kiosks, etc
- **technical assistance**, requiring technical skills/knowledge of specific reference tools, provided by trained students/support staff (or professional librarians) based at desks and/or 'roving' the online catalogue/CD-ROM area in a proactive manner
- **'information lookups'** for the client, taking in questions via telephone, fax, e-mail or desk, and handling them on-demand or in batch mode, using a mix of experienced reference staff and apprentices learning on-the-job

- **research consultation** or advisory assistance, involving a systematic interview before devising a research strategy and suggesting reference tools/other resources, offered by professional-level staff on a drop-in, sign-up, appointment or clinic system
- **library instruction,** for both individuals and groups, provided by those staff working as technical assistants or research consultants (as defined above) on an organized basis and as a natural part of their encounters with clients.[2]

Choosing staffing configurations to optimize customer convenience/satisfaction and service efficiency and effectiveness is difficult in a transitional situation where there are so many possible permutations. The model above offers several options, which could be elaborated to include research consultation office hours in 'outreach' locations; consultation covering software advice as well as traditional research assistance; use of other categories of staff, such as 'reference technology assistants' – specialist sub/paraprofessionals to deal with printer jams, disk installations, etc - or combined staffing for library/computing help desks. While on-demand assistance, instruction and consultation can be separated conceptually, in practice the distinctions are often blurred on the ground, though the trend toward round-the-clock self-service access will surely continue to move the professional rôle away from information provision to facilitation via information skills transfer and systems design. Chris Ferguson and Charles Bunge picture the future thus:

> For example, an alternative to a branch library system . . . might be the large-scale proliferation of some combination of an electronic integrated library system that emphasizes direct-user access to both full-text and bibliographic resources, a high-quality document delivery service, reference and instruction services delivered over the network, and a research consultant located in an office within appropriate departments and schools. Various of these elements have been developed or prototyped in recent years, but not yet have they come together in a way that enables continued use of paper as needed while affording flexible and proportionate adaptation to increasing use of digital resources, all the while providing personal, value-added services in situ.[3]

Collaborative provision

Service models of the above sort are applicable to all types of library and information unit. The digital era offers the opportunity to combine 'global reach' and 'local touch' in enticing and exciting ways, notably through the creation of local gateways to global resources, offering customers simple and rapid access to networked information organized on a thematic basis and tailored to community needs. 'Push' technology – also called 'webcasting' – puts cost-effective *customizable* information services within reach of public libraries, to support the business, education or leisure interests of their clientele (for example, communicating new title alerts or offering other forms of SDI – Selective Dissemination of Information).

Network technologies also facilitate **partnerships** with other service providers, internally and externally, enabling comprehensive 'seamless' services and 'one-stop shopping' on an unprecedented scale – particularly in the context of community education, citizen reskilling and lifelong learning (for example, cross-sectoral cooperation between public and academic libraries involved in community learning initiatives). Intra-organizational strategic alliances might include not just computing/IT services, but also careers advisory services, photographic/design studios, printing and publications units. Working with other providers enables managers to experiment with new services without investing in additional infrastructure support.

Commercial intermediary services are often keen to collaborate with academic and public libraries on very favourable terms to showcase their CD-ROM/online products and reach new markets. As well as minimizing risks and lowering costs, potential benefits to libraries include attractively packaged services, standard user interfaces and technical/helpdesk support. In due course the technical aspects of these developments will require less attention, but regulatory and legal issues (including copyright and data protection) will remain a major concern for the foreseeable future. While skills levels are on course to improve and end-users are set to become more independent, the much trumpeted demise of intermediary services is unlikely, as there will still be a need for both the infrastructure services and the interpersonal contributions which information specialists should be equipped to supply:

* helping people to articulate and focus their information needs
* identifying and locating resources to meet customer requirements

- negotiating rights and designing systems to make information and related technology accessible and useful.

Delivering documents

The shift from holdings to access combined with the migration from print to electronic provision has complicated document supply services with new players entering the arena, services aimed at individuals as well as institutions, and packaged deals linking document delivery with online journal contents lists. Periodical subscription agents are repositioning themselves in anticipation of continuing cutbacks in periodicals holdings and offering bundled services, including automated systems, current awareness and individual articles, in addition to traditional provision. Library consortia and libraries with specialized collections have become suppliers as well as customers, competing with longer established library cooperatives, regional systems and national centres.

Service managers are therefore taking a more critical look at current suppliers, and reviewing their strengths and weaknesses with reference to the relative priority and value attached by their users to issues such as convenience, cost, simplicity and speed. Organizations are moving away from concentration on a few suppliers and adapting approaches similar to those adopted for purchasing or acquisition of other goods/materials, including devising decision matrices showing preferred suppliers to satisfy particular types of request.

Value-added services

The concept of 'added value' (or 'value added' – the terms are used interchangeably) acquired particular significance in the information services sector in the 1980s as information gained more importance as a tradable commodity with the opportunities for service development and improvement offered by advances in information technology. People often associate 'value-added services' with fee-based information provision, but the concept is more generally applicable to information and library services, although it is especially useful when considering charging and pricing policies. In the discipline of economics, 'value-added' has a specific meaning in the context of *wealth creation*, but in other contexts it is used variously to

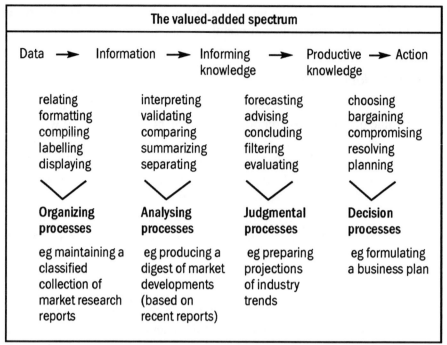

Fig. 4.2   *Value-adding activities and processes (adapted from Taylor 1986)*

denote the *characteristics* or *attributes added* during a process; the *'exchange value'* or *'apparent value'* attached to the process or its end-product by the recipient; or the *benefit* which ultimately accrues to the recipient as a result.

In his classic study of the subject, Robert Taylor offers a model illustrating the spectrum of **value-added processes** in information systems, which shows four general processes – from initial data gathering, through various transforming operations, to final use in action – and provides some examples of *value-adding activities* associated with each stage or part of the spectrum.[4] Figure 4.2 is based on Taylor's model. He argues that document-based systems, such as abstracting and indexing services and libraries, are value-adding entities operating principally at the *organizing* level, whereas data analysis centres and research services operate at the *analysing* and *judgmental* levels. This line of thinking is reflected in the approach taken by some library managers towards charging for 'value-added' information services, when they introduce a charge on the basis of the service provided involving an element of analysis (in addition to organization) of information. A British Library-sponsored research study into the business information needs of science park companies at Aston University, developed a 'levels of service' model, defining eight types or levels of enquiry, which provides a practical illustration of Taylor's basic model at the organizing, analysing and judgmental levels.[5]

Enquiries at different levels
1   Queries about the library
2   Quick reference requests
3   Basic presentation of results
4   Reformatting to requirements
5   Some interpretation of results
6   Arrangement of internal information
7   Information consultancy
8   Business consultancy

The Aston researcher concluded that there was significant value added between levels 3 and 4 (moving from Data to Information) while level 5 represented progression to data analysis (moving from Information to Informing Knowledge). Other libraries simply describe chargeable enquiries as 'extended', 'difficult' or 'complex' enquiries, and define them by the length of time required for research (for example, queries taking more than 30 minutes). The latter approach thus puts a premium on staff *input* (ie competence/expertise) rather than on the service process or *output* (ie the end-product) and is typically associated with a fees policy based on staff costs per hour, which is a convenient way of dealing with pricing services whose outputs (and outcomes) are difficult to quantify. Robert Taylor goes on to develop his basic model into a more complex one which translates these simple value-adding activities into 23 values, which he relates to various value-added processes and six user criteria of choice. These models show how all library and information services add value through basic operational processes and also offer a rationale for chargeable services or (service increments) in the context of fee-based services. The models also have potential value in helping service managers to analyse and define their service offerings in the context of customer charters or *service level agreements*.

ACTIVITY

Choose some examples from your existing service portfolio, and consider how you could add value for customers. (Think about the perceived problems or common complaints of your current users.) List some service increments that might be offered as premium services, privileges that might be granted to customers who paid to join a 'priority club' and any other options for generating new income. What are the operational implications of a strategy based on differential provision for different categories of paying/non-paying customers?

Service level agreements

In common with other service managers, information and library service managers are now often required to draw up and implement detailed formal agreements with clients or customer departments about the services which they will provide. Service level agreements (SLAs) were introduced in the IT services sector as a means of dealing with concerns about the performance and cost of central computing/IT departments. They have subsequently spread to other service areas, and are particularly associated with organizations committed to formal quality systems and those operating an 'internal market' for services with systems for *cross-charging* users of centrally provided services or facilities. SLAs are now widely used for a range of interdepartmental services in business and industry, in local and central government, and in the academic and health sectors. They are frequently implemented to manage *partnership* or *outsourcing* arrangements, as well as for more conventional customer-supplier relationships. In the UK library and information services community, examples exist in all sectors, and also cross-sectorally – notably between university and National Health Service clients, booksellers/library suppliers and individual libraries, and subscription agents and library consortia.

Definitions and variants

As the words suggest, SLAs can be described as *agreements* between the provider and client, which define not only the *service* to be provided but also its *level*, normally expressed in quantifiable terms representing a minimum acceptable standard (with estimated costs). Andrew Hiles defines a service level agreement as 'an agreement between the provider of a service and its customers which quantifies the minimum quality of service which meets the business need'. Hiles also uses the phrase 'quantified availability, serviceability and reliability', but acknowledges that both public bodies and commercial organizations often find it difficult to specify precise business targets.[6] In addition to service targets, SLAs generally specify client obligations, reporting procedures and negotiating mechanisms. SLAs have been described as 'proxy contracts' in the sense of being formal agreements entered into in good faith but not having the full status of a formal legal obligation. Other names used by information and library services for similar documents include 'service codes', 'service definitions', 'service standards', and 'service targets'. Service specifications in general are viewed as a means of improving both the quality of service delivery and the accountability of the provider to the customer. Among the benefits cited are the prevention of overprovision, by identifying actual needs and priorities – the real current service requirement – and imposing discipline, on both the provider and the customer.

SLAs are typically (re)negotiated annually to fit in with organizational reporting and budgeting cycles, which can result in excessive focus on unit costs and other quantifiable aspects of service at the expense of a longer-term strategic perspective. In organizations where strategic management is absent or weak, service managers need to make a particular effort to place SLAs in a business context beyond day-to-day operational transactions, which means having a strategic plan or framework to inform negotiations. One possible approach is to present service costings for three to five years ahead which make explicit provision for 'strategic initiatives' throughout the period, while accepting that only the first year's funding may be formally agreed. An alternative strategy is to take account of planned strategic developments in estimating annual costs and try to incorporate them in the budget. Creative thinking is required here as funders tend to be reluctant to approve budget lines labelled as 'unallocated' or 'contingencies'.

Cost, time and *quality* are thus key parameters for SLAs, and the relative importance given to each dimension will vary according to circumstances. Some of the terminological variants of SLAs (for example, 'service definitions', 'service standards') are especially concerned with quality and specify performance targets for different service components, but do not break down service costs to the same level. Other approaches require cost data for each component service, which often necessitates a shift from functional-based to service-based budgeting – a major task to undertake in addition to other work involved in the introduction of SLAs. One feature of SLAs which often appeals to service managers is having the chance in turn to specify the responsibilities of their customers. For example, university libraries can require academic staff to liaise with them over proposals for new programmes, to provide reading lists by a specified period in advance of the start of a course, and to notify them before recommending a text as essential to their students.

Benefits and pitfalls

Although the decision to introduce SLAs is more often taken by organizational top management than by information service staff, many service managers have found the process beneficial in aligning service provision to organizational priorities and strengthening links with clients. In this sense, they can be viewed as marketing and communications tools that can help to improve service quality and customer satisfaction, as well as demonstrating value for money. Developing a dialogue with users enables better management of their expectations and provides the opportunity to agree both the level or standard of service required and the criteria for measurement of performance.

However, it is often hard to predict the level and nature of demand, especially for services based on developing technologies. Monitoring can also be problematic: continuous monitoring is very expensive for some types of service, but periodic sampling or 'snapshot' monitoring does not necessarily provide a true picture of service performance. Problems often arise with documentation and negotiation, which can take up a huge amount of time and effort, and also undermine good relations. In addition, 'over-specified' agreements may restrict what library staff can do (and how) and service descriptions may appear to trivialize some library activities.

Preparation

SLAs vary significantly in their content, format and length. In some organizations, managers are expected to draft SLAs in a prescribed format; in other cases, they have more flexibility and freedom to determine the size and style of the document, and the headings used. It is worth remembering that even if you are working within an established formal system, you are probably the only person (or one among a small group) charged with documenting information and library services, which puts you in a strong position to influence how the SLA process is adopted – and adapted – in your particular service area. In addition, even where content is tightly defined, there will usually be scope for including other information as annexes or appendices to the specified documentation.

Among the issues to consider are whether to negotiate separate agreements with different client groups or opt for a blanket agreement for all customers, and how many service elements or increments to document as discrete entities. One approach, used at Aston University, is to divide services into 'standard' ones, offered to all users on the same basis (for example, online public access catalogue, general reference collection, photocopying facilities) and 'tailored' ones, designed to meet specific needs of particular groups (such as current awareness or information skills programmes) and then to negotiate a single agreement on standard services with representatives of the whole community, and a series of agreements on tailored services with different client groups.[7] Much of the documentation can be re-used (which reduces the intellectual effort) but holding separate meetings with each group acknowledges their differing needs and priorities, allows the discussion to focus on their concerns, and conveys positive signals about customer-orientation.

Documentation

The information and data required to document services effectively in this context falls naturally into three categories. Some is of a general nature and can usefully be separated out from the more specific details related to each particular service component; this general information can be further subdivided into background information about the information/library *service*, and what amounts to the standard terms and conditions of the *agreement*. The core part of the documentation will be the detailed specification and any supporting data showing the *level* of provision for each service component or category. Items to consider for each part of the documentation include the following:

- **background information** – edited/condensed extracts from existing strategy documents; assumptions about the internal and external service environment; copies of organization charts showing reporting lines; a summary of all the services covered, with brief scope notes; policy and procedures for obtaining user feedback.
- **core specification** – service definition, scope and objective; customer entitlement, obligations and communication; quality standards, performance indicators and targets; costing method, cost elements and estimated service costs; charges, charging basis and chargeable service increments.
- **'contractual' information** – definitions of key terms; purpose and scope of the agreement; benefits expected for both parties; timetable and mechanisms for negotiation and review; responsibilities of both parties; monitoring and liaison arrangements; costs/charges with billing methods (if applicable); procedures for complaints, disputes and variation of requirements; dependencies on third parties; contingencies or caveats ('escape clauses' to cope with unpredictable events).

Irrespective of whether you are obliged to agree statements of service levels with clients – or suppliers – it is essential to have a shared understanding among information service managers, staff and other stakeholders about what you offer, to whom, and why; the rôles and responsibilities of those involved; and how performance will be monitored, evaluated and reviewed. The following checklist (which is based on the quality management standard ISO 9002) indicates the key points to consider.

SEVEN STEPS TOWARDS ESTABLISHING SERVICE LEVELS

1   Define what you do.
2   State who your clients/customers are.
3   Say how you evaluate what you do and describe quality assurance mechanisms.
4   State operational objectives within the context of overall strategic objectives.
5   Establish standards of performance for your service and for your customers.
6   State the expected constraints on meeting these standards.

7   Indicate proposed service improvements (with timetable if possible).

ACTIVITY

Choose a specific service in which you are directly involved on a regular basis. Write two or three short sentences, in simple non-technical language, summarizing its scope and purpose. (Imagine you are describing it to a first-time user from another country.)

Service quality

The current decade has seen a heightened interest in service quality in the library and information services sector, as in the wider business and public service environment. The UK Citizen's Charter has imposed formal requirements on libraries in central and local government control (including the British Library) and programmes of Quality Audit and Quality Assessment in the higher education sector have posed similar challenges for university libraries. Government-sponsored reviews of academic and public libraries have recommended the development of a standard set of **performance indicators** for their sectors.[8-9]

Information service managers have adopted a variety of approaches to defining and measuring quality. Some have introduced comprehensive sets of measures as part of SLAs, others have added selected performance indicators to the service statistics traditionally recorded in their annual reports. Quantitative usage data can be derived from library management systems which now offer quite sophisticated report generation facilities; qualitative data can be gathered from customer comments, simple quality check forms distributed with products/documents supplied, suggestion schemes, and *ad hoc* or regular user satisfaction surveys, often involving focus group discussions and questionnaires, and sometimes individual interviews. Among other issues, managers need to decide whether to opt for continuous monitoring or snapshot surveys (for example, sampling enquiry activity at fixed times during the year, rather than keeping records of every query handled). It is also important to ensure that well-intentioned efforts to obtain customer feedback do not result in survey fatigue for the user population – and staff – of the information service.

Many service managers are now turning to 'off-the-shelf' solutions for their **survey methodology**. In the UK, following pioneering work by the University of London Library, academic libraries are increasingly adopting the methodology and software offered by the company Priority Search – an approach which offers various levels of consultancy support, as well as a user group facilitating exchange of experience among practitioners.[10] In North America and Australia, academic, public and special libraries have adapted the PZB 'SERVQUAL' model, based on extensive research in the United States across five different service industries.[11-14] Parasuraman, Zeithaml and Berry identified ten dimensions (represented by 97 individual issues) that consumers use in forming expectations and perceptions of services, which transcend different types of services.[15] They subsequently reduced and refined the original multiple-item scale to 22 items spread among five dimensions, known as the RATER criteria:[16]

- **Reliability** – ability to perform the promised service dependably and accurately
- **Assurance** – knowledge and courtesy of employees and their ability to inspire trust and confidence
- **Tangibles** – physical facilities, equipment, and appearance of personnel
- **Empathy** – caring, individualized attention the firm provides its customers
- **Responsiveness** – willingness to help customers and provide prompt service.

REFLECTION

For each of the five RATER dimensions, consider the key words in the accompanying descriptions and think about where you would place your service on a seven-point scale (where 7 is extremely good and 1 is extremely poor) – think about comparable or competing operations to form a view of an appropriate standard for your service. Consider the relative importance of these five dimensions to your customers, and in what order they would rank the dimensions. Should staff pay more attention to or place more emphasis on any of the areas indicated?

The SERVQUAL model is designed to be applicable across a broad spectrum of services and provides a basic skeleton that can be adapted or supplemented to fit the needs of particular organizations. The authors argue that it is most valuable when used periodically to track service quality trends and when used in conjunction with other measurements. The actual survey instrument is in two sections, with 22 separate questions for customer expectations (what they feel the service *should* provide) and their perceptions (what they feel it *does* provide). It is reproduced in full in their article, with instructions for use.[16]

Performance measurement is not an end in itself but should be seen and used as a management tool to support planning and decision-making – at both strategic and operational levels – by checking progress against objectives and identifying problems. **Quantitative indicators** are easier to deal with than qualitative data and tend to receive more attention irrespective of their value. The performance indicators proposed by the UK Public Libraries Review are all of this type, for example, under Access and Usage:

- book issues per capita
- percentage of requests supplied within seven and within 30 days
- reference enquiries per capita. (Note that it is questionable whether a high number of enquiries is a positive sign!)

In contrast, in *The effective academic library*, 'the proposed indicators range from hard factual statistical data to forms of assessment not involving numerical measures'. The latter include indicators to assess the degree of integration between the objectives of the library and its parent institution, as well as indicators of service quality/user satisfaction, delivery, efficiency and economy. Quantitative indicators include some similar to those above, eg:

- enquiries answered per student
- enquiries answered/FTE library staff numbers
- total library expenditure/enquiries answered.[17]

The **service context** is a critical factor that must be taken into account in both determining performance indicators and interpreting data. For example, there are many reasons why enquiry numbers might rise – a larger/more demanding user population, service publicity and promotion, a smaller/less up-to-date reference collection, poor signage and guiding – so raw data must viewed in relation to other relevant information. Other measures worth considering as alternative indicators of enquiry service performance include the number of complaints received, and queuing and turnaround times. Performance indicators agreed as part of the process of formulating SLAs have the advantage of being set in a specific context, where the service objective is explicitly stated and quality standards, performance indicators and service targets can be developed within a coherent framework. Examples for some common library operations are shown in Figure 4.3.

Electronic library developments have prompted consideration of additional indicators covering issues such as satisfaction with the IT infrastructure, availability of workstations, and quantities of data downloaded and pages printed from electronic information sources (as a parallel to book issues). It is also much more difficult to define the boundaries of library and information services in an electronic environment, for example provision of study facilities might include access to networked resources from PCs in a library building, on other parts of a campus and at student residences. Finally, as a report from the Management Information for the Electronic Library (MIEL) programme points out, we need to think carefully about our interpretation of data in this context.

> Indeed, some of our traditional management information and performance measures may be turned on their head. For example, the fact that a user comes into the Library may be a sign of failure (poor service) rather than success – she could not find what she wanted via the network, either because it had not been provided or because it was difficult to find and use. In such cases the Library itself was a poor second-best to the direct access the user had first sought.[18]

It is particularly difficult to fix performance measures and targets in this arena as the range of service offerings is constantly changing, including the mix of print and electronic provision, and it is hard to predict the shape of future services. Information service managers have to be alert to such issues, and ensure that both their service portfolios and their quality criteria reflect environmental developments and current needs.

Shelving	
Quality standards	• Shelving to be carried out accurately and quickly • Shelf guiding to be accurate, clear and self-explanatory
Performance indicators	• Accuracy of shelving • Time delay in returning items to shelves • Number of requests for guidance to shelves
Service targets	• Shelve all items in the correct location • Reshelve 100% of returned items within 24 hours • Maintain shelf occupancy rate at no more than 80% • Tidy shelves systematically – all areas annually – all heavy-use areas at least termly • Review guiding for all shelves annually

Interlibrary Loans	
Quality standards	• Staff to be thoroughly trained in procedures, knowledgeable about regulations and entitlements, and have good interpersonal skills • Service to be quick and accurate, providing timely supply of items requested • Staff to be helpful and courteous at all times
Performance indicators	• Speed, accuracy and timeliness of delivery • User satisfaction, as measured in general survey
Service targets	• Supply 85% of requested items within 8 working days from receipt of request • Achieve average overall assessment score from users of at least 5 (on a scale of 1 to 7)

Fig. 4.3   *Examples of standards, indicators and targets for a university library*

REFLECTION

Using the service previously selected, consider how its success is judged, by staff? by users? by managers? Do they have different criteria? What indicators would you use to monitor performance. (Think about satisfaction, timeliness and utilization.)

References

1 Kinnell, M and MacDougall, J, Marketing public library services – opportunities for change, *Library Management*, **13** (4), 1992, 22-32.
2 Whitson, W L, Differentiated service: a new reference model, *Journal of Academic Librarianship*, **21** (2), 1995, 103-10.
3 Ferguson, C D and Bunge, C A, The shape of services to come: values-based reference service for the largely digital library, *College & Research Libraries*, **58** (3), 1997, 252-65.
4 Taylor, R S, *Value-added processes in information systems*, Ablex Publishing, 1986.
5 Orminski, E, *Business information needs of science park companies*, Library and Information Research Report 81, British Library, 1991.
6 Hiles, A N, Service level agreements: panacea or pain, *The TQM Magazine*, **6** (2), 1994, 14-16.
7 Corrall, S M, The access model: managing the transformation at Aston University, *Interlending & Document Supply*, **21** (4), 1993, 13-23.
8 Joint Funding Councils' Libraries Review Group, *Report*, The Councils, 1993 (Chairman: Professor Sir Brian Follett).
9 Department for National Heritage, *Reading the future: public libraries review*, Department for National Heritage, 1997.
10 Robinson, E, Studying user satisfaction: why do it? how to do it? where next? One library's experience, *The New Review of Academic Librarianship*, **1**, 1995, 179-85.
11 Coleman, V, Xiao, Y, Bair, L and Chollett, B, Toward a TQM paradigm: using SERVQUAL to measure library service quality, *College & Research Libraries*, **58** (3), 1997, 237-51.
12 Hebert, F, Service quality: an unobtrusive investigation of interlibrary loan in large public libraries in Canada, *Library and Information Science Research*, **16** (2), 1994, 3-21.
13 White, M D and Abels, E G, Measuring service quality in special libraries: lessons from service marketing, *Special Libraries*, **86** (4), 1995, 36-45.
14 Armstrong, B, Customer focus: obtaining customer input, *Australian Library Journal*, **43** (2), 1994, 108-17.
15 Parasuraman, A, Zeithaml, V A and Berry, L L, A conceptual model of service quality and its implications for future research, *Journal of Marketing*, **49**, 1985, 41-50.

16 Parasuraman, A, Zeithaml, V A and Berry, L L, SERVQUAL: a multiple-item scale for measuring consumer perceptions of service quality, *Journal of Retailing*, **64** (1), 1988, 12–40.

17 Joint Funding Councils' Ad-hoc Group on Performance Indicators for Libraries, *The effective academic library: a framework for evaluating the performance of UK academic libraries*, The Councils, 1995.

18 Brophy, P and Wynne, P M, *Management information systems and performance measurement for the electronic library*. University of Central Lancashire, Centre for Research in Library and Information Management, 1997 (available at http://www.ukoln.ac.uk/dlis/models/studies/mis).

Suggestions for further reading
Trends in service provision

Sykes, P, Liability for information provision: spectre or reality, *Aslib Proceedings*, **43** (5), 1991, 189–98.
  Discusses the (UK) legal context of information service provision and assesses risks for the information professional. Provides advice on record-keeping, exclusion clauses, insurance cover and written contracts, concluding the risks are lower for information intermediaries than for primary producers (but greater with increase in fees charged).

Whitson, W L, Differentiated service: a new reference model, *Journal of Academic Librarianship*, **21** (2), 1995, 103–10.
  Discusses and tabulates the advantages and disadvantages of traditional undifferentiated reference service and an alternative composite model, identifying five types of service. Comments on skills required and implementation strategies, concluding that on balance the differentiated model delivers more effective service and flexible, better use of staff.

Ward, S E, Document delivery: the perspective of industrial information services, *Interlending & Document Supply*, **24** (2), 1996, 4–10.
  Explains background and objectives of comprehensive review of document delivery at Glaxo Research and Development; indicates weaknesses in existing provision, provides examples of services currently used or under test and identifies issues for further study.

Brunskill, K, *CASIAS services: a critical evaluation of the functionality, costs, impact and value*, British Library Research and Innovation Report 4, British Library Research and Innovation Centre, 1996.
Includes review of literature and research on Current Awareness Services/Individual Article Supply and related areas with details of 30 projects and programmes in the UK, Europe and US. Discusses services on offer and views of users and providers, in context of a survey at Aston University; provides checklist for evaluation of services.

Pearson, K M and Jarvis, D J, Drumming up business, *Special Libraries*, 87 (3), 1996, 163-8.
Case study showing growth of a small special library with limited resources from a 'document dump' (collection-centred archive) to a 'personalised information agency' (customer-centred virtual library) enabled by IT developments and entrepreneurial activities/advertising linked with corporate Continuous Improvement/TQM programme.

Price, S P, Morris, A and Davies, J E, An overview of commercial electronic document delivery suppliers and services, *The Electronic Library*, 14 (6), 1996, 523-42.
Surveys 21 commercially-available document delivery services with an electronic element under three broad headings: collection-based, specialized collection-based and others. Includes descriptions of each service and comparative tables showing contact details, charges, subject fields, delivery times and whether intermediary or direct provider. Highlights difficulties of assessing cost-effectiveness in rapidly changing marketplace.

McKee, B and Nankivell, C, IT Point, *Public Library Journal*, 12 (2), 1997, 33-6.
Describes demonstration project at public library in Solihull, West Midlands, offering a range of IT-related services, including computers for public use, Internet access, CD-ROM and other information sources, and self-teaching facilities. Argues such services should be integrated (not 'add-ons'), combining information and computing resources.

Ferguson, C D and Bunge, C A, The shape of services to come: values-based reference service for the largely digital library, *College & Research Libraries*, 58 (3), 1997, 252-65.

Argues the need to develop and deliver high quality reference service and instructional support through the network and in person, at remote locations and around the clock. Discusses different service elements and staffing configurations, and concludes that collaborative working and integrating technologies will maintain values and aid success.

Lagerborg, K, Self-service in libraries: an overview, *VINE*, **105**, 1997, 3–7.

Places the concept of self-service in its social, economic and technological context, and tracks developments in libraries with examples; concludes with a formal definition and short list of published literature and web links. (Introductory article of thematic issue containing eight other articles and contact details for suppliers of self-service products.)

Morrow, V, To serve or not to serve, that is the issue, *Library Association Record*, **99** (6), 1977, 312–14.

Discusses introduction of self-service issue and return systems, drawing on examples from academic and public libraries, covering both management and technical aspects, and providing details of system suppliers, published reports and review articles.

White, M, Market prospects for consumer online services, and implications for library and information services in the future. In Raitt, D (ed), *Libraries for the new millennium: implications for managers*, Library Association Publishing, 1997, 219–39.

Describes the development of mass-market commercial online services, with particular reference to the educational and business content of America Online and Compu-Serve. Considers their potential rôle in expanding the resources of public libraries to reach off-site users, teach information retrieval skills and create electronic user communities.

Chepesiuk, R, Internet college: the virtual classroom challenge, *American Libraries*, **29** (3), 1998, 52–5.

Discusses online resourcing and library support for distance learning students with reference to developments at six US universities. Notes difficulties such as content digitization, copyright permissions, network security, novice faculty and student skill-levels, but argues that problems are soluble. (Provides web addresses for sites covered.)

Clegg, S, Converged enquiry/help desks: rhetoric or reality, *Relay*, **45**, 1998, 7–10.

Describes experience at South Bank University of developing a multi-skilled workforce capable of supporting basic information searching,

general software applications and other media/equipment (video, satel-
lite, printing). Offers list of success factors and problem areas drawing
on other UK and US initiatives, and comments on future directions.

Service level agreements

Ford, G, Service level agreements, *The New Review of Academic
Librarianship*, 2, 1996, 49-58.
Explains various reasons for introducing service level agreements, and
discusses format and content (including related background material).
Provides examples of specific services covered and gives sample targets
for a few key activities. Outlines benefits and risks, and offers some
solutions to problem of multiple constituencies.

Pantry, S and Griffiths, P, *The complete guide to preparing and implementing service level agreements*, Library Association Publishing, 1997.
A compact introduction (c130 pp) to service level agreements for
library and information services: provides definitions, outlines contents
and suggests wording for service descriptions, their availability and turnaround times; also covers monitoring, charges, communication, and
SLAs between LIS and their internal and external suppliers.

Performance indicators

Abbott, C, *Performance measurement in library and information services*,
Aslib Know How Series, Aslib, 1994.
A wide-ranging practical guide (c50 pp), which explains the purposes
and benefits of performance measurement, clarifies terminology, and
provides a comprehensive listing of different types of performance indicators for 13 generic library functions.

Alston, R, Performance indicators in Bromley: purpose and practice,
Library Management, 16 (1), 1995, 18-28.
Explains the rationale for introducing PIs for Bromley public libraries,
and the criteria for their selection, and discusses their fitness for purpose. Describes the two main sets of indicators for branch libraries and
bibliographic services and their different purposes, as well as others
used for comparisons among five South East London Boroughs.

Tuck, J, Operational planning and performance measurement in the John Rylands University Library of Manchester, *The New Review of Academic Librarianship*, **1**, 1995, 15-31.
Discusses use of surveys and evaluation as means of implementing and monitoring the Library's strategic plan, concentrating on four key areas and concluding with proposals for adoption of operational planning and performance indicators throughout the Library.

5
Information skills

This chapter covers:

- information literacy
- learning and teaching
- programme benefits
- stakeholder partnerships
- delivery methods
- programme evaluation
- presentation skills.

Introduction

Training people to find and use information effectively has become a key rôle for information professionals in all sectors. Information skills teaching is no longer concentrated in school and college libraries, and delivery methods have also developed in line with technological changes. This chapter examines the concept and components of information literacy and shows how the ability to manage information productively is now viewed as an essential skill for life. It also considers the rôles of information professionals and others in teaching information skills, and the processes of planning and evaluating information skills programmes, with references to published examples and case studies.

Information literacy

Despite pessimistic colleagues bemoaning the 'death of librarianship' and computer firms running advertisements depicting libraries as dark menacing places to be avoided, the future for information professionals looks

remarkably bright, as the ability to handle information is at last acknowledged as a key skill for the 'information age' of the 21st century.[1-2]
Information professionals have known this for a long time, as have enlight-
ened educationalists, evidenced by the report of a working party set up by
the British Library and the Schools Council two decades ago:

> Individuals today have an increasing need to be able to find things out. Never
> before has so much information been available to so many, and never before
> have our lives depended so much on our ability to handle information
> successfully. We need to be able to search out what we require, to assess crit-
> ically the ideas and facts offered to us, and to make use of our findings.
> 'Learning to learn', which begins at school, continues in our adult lives – in
> our work, in our leisure activities, and in any further education.[3]

The difference today is that this message is being promoted more actively
and more widely than ever before, and it is being promoted by people
beyond our professional community. In the UK, the Fryer Report on lifelong learning gives public libraries a central rôle in information provision
and information skills education,[4] and in the nursing sector, the Libraries
Access Campaign of *Nursing Standard* has demanded access to information *and training* so that 'every nurse should be educated in systems and
services to support evidence-based practice'.[5] In the USA, a popular Texas-
based website reinforces this message and restates more forcefully the
potential benefits of information skills:

> As the 21st century rapidly approaches, the Information Age is considered
> well underway. Over the past decade, certain groups of people have already
> started to enjoy more success, including increased compensation, better job
> opportunities, and a higher quality of life. Likewise, some students (whether
> in grade schools or in major national universities) are moving ahead of their
> counterparts and creating a new benchmark for academic achievement. The
> advantages bestowed upon these groups largely spring from one source: their
> ability to manage information productively.
>
>   How, then, can you survive the Information Age, much less thrive in it?
> Clearly, you must develop a comprehensive and well-thought out strategy for
> dealing with Information Overload. Obviously to succeed in the Information
> Age, you must have access to Information. But it's not enough to merely have

access. You must learn how to convert raw data into knowledge, to communicate it effectively to others, and to use it to meet your personal objectives or the objectives of your firm. Only by using Information to generate and provide value can you rise above the crowd and excel.[6]

Defining information skills

Traditionally, information skills have been taught very much within the library context. Terms like *bibliographic instruction*, *library orientation* and *user education* are often used without clear definition, though the emphasis is usually on *literature searching* and *information retrieval*. This limited view has been compounded by restrictions on time (of the libary user and library staff) and a lack of clarity about the rôle of the library in such processes. Figure 5.1 is based on Michael Marland's model of information skills derived from his ground-breaking work in secondary schools in the 1980s, and provides a convenient starting-point for discussion. Despite its age, this pamphlet remains a standard text for those new to information skills programming, and is applicable to a variety of settings.[7]

Increasingly, in recent years, libraries (however described) have been viewed as educative institutions in their own right, and programmes have extended well beyond the traditional separate 'user ed' events to more comprehensive courses, more closely related to participants' study, research or

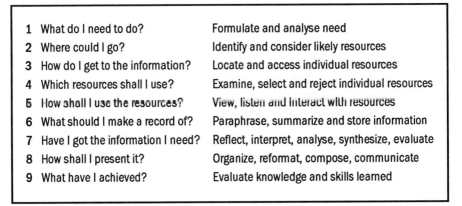

1	What do I need to do?	Formulate and analyse need
2	Where could I go?	Identify and consider likely resources
3	How do I get to the information?	Locate and access individual resources
4	Which resources shall I use?	Examine, select and reject individual resources
5	How shall I use the resources?	View, listen and interact with resources
6	What should I make a record of?	Paraphrase, summarize and store information
7	Have I got the information I need?	Reflect, interpret, analyse, synthesize, evaluate
8	How shall I present it?	Organize, reformat, compose, communicate
9	What have I achieved?	Evaluate knowledge and skills learned

Fig. 5.1 *Information skills: the nine-step model (adapted from Marland 1981)*

employment needs. The impact of computing and telecommunications technologies on information systems and services has highlighted the need for skills development, not just in finding and using information, but in evaluating its quality. The proliferation of material available via the world wide web and superficial similarities in formats can mask crucial differences in its provenance, reliability and validity: people need to be able to detect bias and other influences on content, and to distinguish between information that has been subject to conventional quality assurance processes (such as academic peer review) and sources whose accuracy and authority is questionable.

The shift towards electronic information sources has further confused the terminology employed, with many stakeholders not properly differentiating content-related *information* skills from conduit-related *technology* skills. Computer literacy is only one aspect of true **information literacy**, which requires a combination of knowledge and skills, and recognition that information is not confined to things stored in a computer. In practice, information professionals are often involved in imparting information technology skills as well as information handling skills. A real concern for us all here is to ensure that the importance of content-related skills is acknowledged by stakeholders, and that people do not just equate information skills with e-mail and 'surfing the Net'.

Broadening the framework

Over the past decade there has been much discussion (particularly in the USA) about the critical role of information literacy not only in relation to educational and business success, but also in the context of wider social and policy issues. In 1989, the final report of the American Library Association (ALA) Presidential Committee on Information Literacy highlighted the need for all people to become information literate, and thereby to become 'empowered for effective decision making, freedom of choice, and full participation in a democratic society'. In this context information literacy has been defined as the ability both 'to recognize when information is needed' and 'to identify, locate, evaluate, and use effectively information needed for the particular decision or issue at hand'. The report points out that these abilities have always been important to success and quality of life, but the volume and variety of information now available – not only from books, journals, newspapers, radio, community experts and government offices, but also from television, CD-ROMs, online databases, multimedia packages, the Internet and digitized government documents – means that the abilities required have become more complex and more important.[8]

Substantial developments have taken place during the 1990s, as shown by a recent report of progress towards the ALA's goals, which notes various local and national initiatives in the USA and elsewhere. Some of this work has been coordinated by the (US) National Forum on Information Literacy, whose membership grew in ten years to more than 65 national organizations, representing business, government and education. This progress report also flags up the need for further research and demonstration projects related to information literacy, identifying the following research questions as priorities:

- How can we *benchmark* information literacy abilities and progress?
- How can we *measure* the effectiveness of information literacy programmes on *individual performance*?
- How is information literacy manifested in work settings and how does it enhance *workplace productivity*?

The report also includes an explicit statement on the contribution of information literacy to **business performance**:

> The workplace of the present and future demands a new kind of worker. In a global marketplace, data is dispatched in picoseconds and gigabits, and this deluge of information must be sorted, evaluated, and applied. When confronted by such an overload of information, most workers today tend to take the first or most easily accessed information – without any concern for the quality of that information. As a result, such poorly trained workers are costing businesses billions of dollars annually in low productivity, accidents, absenteeism, and poor product quality. There is no question about it: for today's and tomorrow's workers, the workplace is going through cataclysmic changes that very few will be prepared to participate in successfully and productively unless they are information literate.[9]

The significance of information literacy in both organizational life and a democratic society has been cogently articulated by Jeremy Shapiro and

Shelley Hughes in their seminal article, 'Information literacy as a liberal art'.[10] Shapiro and Hughes ask what an individual needs to know today to be a fully-fledged, competent and literate member of the information society. They argue that information literacy involves more than accessing and using information and information technology effectively (and adapting to their constant changes) but includes a critical perspective on the contemporary world of knowledge and information – reflection on the nature of information itself, its technical infrastructure, and its social, cultural and even philosophical context. Their broad interpretation of the abilities required for **educated citizenship** is thus much more ambitious than librarians' traditional definitions, adding liberal and humanistic dimensions to technical and professional competencies. The seven dimensions of the 'new curriculum' of Shapiro and Hughes are summarized in Figure 5.2.

Developments in *student-centred learning*, the concepts of *organizational learning* and the learning organization, and the promotion of continuing professional development and *lifelong learning* mean that information professionals in all sectors can expect to become more actively involved in facilitating and supporting such skills development, in areas ranging from basic IT, 'network literacy' and study skills to Internet-based research and knowledge management. There are as yet no standard definitions of 'information skills' and 'information literacy', but many examples are available in both conventional textbooks and organizational websites, which vary significantly in their breadth and length. Figures 5.1 and 5.2 offer two potentially useful models, and you will find others in the suggestions for further reading at the end of this chapter.

REFLECTION

Two definitions of information literacy are given in Figures 5.1 and 5.2. From your own experience, how would you define a portfolio of information skills? What skills are taught or otherwise imparted in your organization? What skills should be taught?

Teaching rôles

Before embarking on any activity that will use up scarce resources we must always ask *why* we should deploy them in this manner. With limited

Seven dimensions of information literacy

- *Tool literacy* — the ability to understand and use the practical and conceptual tools of current information technology, including software, hardware and multimedia, that are relevant to the education, work and professional life expectations of the individual.
- *Resource literacy* — the ability to understand the form, format, location and access methods of information resources, especially daily expanding networked information resources, including concepts of the classification and organization of such resources.
- *Social-structural literacy* — knowing how information fits into the life of groups, knowing about the institutions and social networks that create and organize information and knowledge, and about the social processes through which information is generated.
- *Research literacy* — the ability to understand and use the IT-based tools relevant to the work of today's researcher and scholar, including discipline-related computer software for quantitative analysis, qualitative analysis and simulation as applicable.
- *Publishing literacy* — the ability to format and communicate research and ideas electronically, in textual and multimedia forms, and to introduce them into the electronic public realm and to disseminate them among the electronic community of scholars.
- *Emerging technology literacy* — the ability to adapt to, evaluate and use the continually emerging innovations in information technology so as not to be a prisoner of prior tools and resources, and to make intelligent decisions about adopting new ones.
- *Critical literacy* — the ability to evaluate critically the intellectual, human and social strengths and weaknesses, potentials and limitations, benefits and costs of information technologies, including historical, philosophical, sociopolitical and cultural perspectives.

Fig. 5.2   *Information literacy: proposals for a new curriculum*

resources, it is easy to find reasons why we should not organize formal programmes to teach information skills. It can be argued (given the lack of widespread formal programme evaluation) that there is little evidence of tangible benefits. Many undergraduates, for example, seem quite happy to restrict their information gathering to items on reading lists and/or in short loan collections, so why should we teach them how to develop elaborate search strategies? Another more persuasive argument suggests that libraries are unnecessarily complex and we should devote more effort towards making them easier to use – after all, we are not taught how to use supermarkets!

The **benefits** of teaching information skills can be considered from various perspectives:

- **Information service customers.** 'Give a man a fish and he eats for a day; teach a man to fish and he eats for life.' This Chinese proverb points to the main benefit, namely that our customers become empowered for life with transferable skills, skills which are increasingly important in today's educational, business, vocational and social environment.
- **Information service staff.** Our human resources are more effectively deployed. Time invested 'upfront' in induction/instruction sessions generally means time saved later on at the enquiry desk, for both staff and customers.
- **Other stakeholders.** Our customers will be more effective community members. Teachers, employers and society in general all stand to benefit from the development of information skills among students, employees and citizens in every capacity.
- **Information resources.** Our expensive stock is more effectively exploited. Customers are more likely to make good use of our full range of hard-copy and electronic resources if they are given the right encouragement.
- **Information service generally.** Our whole service is perceived more positively. We should not overlook the public relations potential of information skills programmes, and in particular the value of induction events, which should be primarily concerned with providing a welcoming introduction and a friendly face, especially for customers who may have damaging preconceptions about libraries.

REFLECTION

Consider various programmes of information skills training that you have encountered. Who or what were the main beneficiaries and how did they benefit? Have you encountered any elements that have not proved cost-effective, and if so how has this been tackled?

Teaching partnerships

A further question is whether information service staff are the best people to teach information skills, particularly in educational institutions where there are trained teachers who are also subject specialists. As with so many elements of information service provision, successful information skills programmes are based on successful **partnerships**. We need to think about the **stakeholders** in this enterprise:

- **Information service customers.** Understanding the needs of our customers (in terms of content, coverage, level, style, timing and venue for delivery) is a fundamental requirement, and should include some assessment of existing competence (especially in relation to computer literacy) and may involve subdividing groups to meet special needs. Some libraries are taking their programmes out to customers, rather than expecting them to visit the library, for example by offering online tuition or providing a mobile service, such as Hertfordshire County's Rolling Zone mobile CD-ROM/Internet service offering instruction at point of need for 'remote' users.[11] Managers also need to clarify whether customers actually want information skills training: in a special library/business setting, it may actually be more cost effective for library staff to search rather than, say, engineers.
- **Information service staff.** Most information skills teaching/training tends to be carried out (or at least led by) information professionals, but there is significant variation among services in the range of people involved. Managers need to consider whether all professionally qualified staff should be involved, or does teaching require special talents, suggesting it should be left to keen volunteers? Many services now also involve paraprofessionals and library/information assistants in training customers, thus posing a further set of questions.[12]
- **Allied staff.** Some programme elements may be best covered by specialist colleagues from within (or even outside) the organization, particularly IT specialists and teachers with subject expertise. For example, in academic institutions, both library and computing staff may be involved in introducing students to networked information resources, with the former concentrating on the information and the latter on the technology aspects. With convergence (formal and informal) of previ-

ously distinct operations, boundaries are being redrawn and collaborative provision is common.

- **Sponsors.** Some people may not be directly involved in programme delivery, but have sufficient interest in the process to make them key players, whose support and cooperation is critical. For example, in educational institutions, teachers may play an important rôle in ensuring the relevance of courses to particular assisgnments, assisting with *authoring* of materials, *evaluating* event outcomes and *marketing* the programme. Similarly, information professionals need to secure support from managers at all levels so that time spent attending training events is considered a worthwhile investment.

REFLECTION

Consider the stakeholders involved in information skills training in your organization. How do you cater for customers with special needs, eg isolated users or infrequent customers, such as part-time students? How could service provision be improved? Who is involved in delivering information skills programmes, and why? How does information skills training fit into your wider relationship with your sponsors?

Learning and teaching

The 'theory' side of the education process tends to get little coverage in our initial professional education. It seems to be assumed that librarians can 'just teach', which is obviously not the case! In the UK higher education sector, the Electronic Libraries Programme included several projects to help information professionals in their teaching and training rôles, including the EduLib and Netskills projects (which provided a national programme of workshops and have also produced training materials for local use) and electronic magazines such as *Ariadne* and *DeLiberations*.[13-16] The (UK) Library Association has also recently introduced workshops on learning, teaching and training into its Continuing Professional Development programme, with events aimed at trainers and managers, school library staff, and staff in further and higher education.[17] In addition to numerous practical guides to teaching aimed at a more general readership, there are also various electronic resources available, such as the US-based World Lecture Hall.[18]

REFLECTION

Consider the instruction you have received on teaching or training. Are there any other elements of your life (eg experience in amateur dramatics) that could prove useful in preparing you for teaching? Are any of your colleagues particularly expert at teaching? What instruction have they received? What can you learn from them?

For information professionals who have not been formally trained in the education process, Geoffrey Squires provides an excellent user-friendly introduction covering the theory of learning and teaching, the preparation of individual sessions and the production of full-scale course programmes.[19] According to Squires, learning incorporates four points:

- Learning involves **change**
- That change is fairly **permanent**
- It may be a change in **consciousness** (how we think) or **behaviour** (what we do) – but usually both
- It comes about through some **interaction** with our **environment** – information, people, events, experiences, including (but not confined to) teaching/training.

For this process to be effective, we require a positive, open-minded person with the ability to *process* meaningful and relevant *information* in an *environment* which is both supportive and stimulating. Obviously, much of the onus on learning comes from the individual, and (in real life) much of the time people do not need 'proper' teachers and trainers because they are doing this themselves. The real rôle for the teacher/trainer, then, is to do for the learner what they *cannot* do for themselves. Squires suggests that the **teacher** has **ten key functions**, namely to:

- **motivate** – stimulate, enthuse, get and keep interest
- **audit** – assess needs, pre-test, explore initial expectations
- **orientate** – guide, set objectives, give a sense of direction
- **inform** – tell, show, demonstrate
- **explain** – clarify, relate, amplify
- **explore** – open up, debate, discuss
- **develop** – encourage problem solving, critical thinking, learning to learn
- **exercise** – set tasks, practise, experiment

- **appraise** – feedback, comment, criticize
- **reinforce** – emphasize, encourage, reward.

Consider your own experience as a teacher or trainer. How do you carry out these ten elements? Which do you find easiest to carry out? Which are the most difficult? Why?

Developing programmes

The foundation of any properly planned programme of training or development is the **training cycle,** which is illustrated in Figure 5.3. This underpins the practical aspects of planning considered below.

Assessing needs

We have already considered library customers and their needs. Any planning of sessions must consider both content and practical (who? what? when? where?) organizational needs. Much valuable planning information

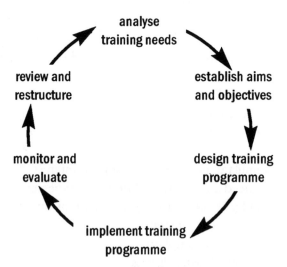

Fig. 5.3   *The training cycle*

will be available from your sponsors. If a departmental manager is request-
ing sessions for secretarial support discuss planned learning outcomes. In
an educational setting, teaching staff will be able to supply expected attendance numbers, at least a notion of IT experience and relevant assignment
details. Public librarians are faced with less easily defined client groups but
some needs (eg needs of Open University students) can be assessed with a
bit of detective work. When information cannot be supplied in advance, an
informal interview or more formal skills and outcomes questionnaires could
prove useful.

REFLECTION

Consider a group you have taught in an information skills programme. How did you
assess needs initially? Was the needs assessment an ongoing element of the course?
If so, how did this work? How did this affect the structure of the course? What problems did you encounter with group tuition?

Setting objectives

If we are to get away from the vague notions of the traditional user education programmes mentioned above we must establish precise objectives for
our programmes. Stating our objectives brings many benefits: it gives the
course a structure; it explains the purpose to customers and sponsors; it
gives the programme direction; and it enables us to evaluate it. Such statements can be used also as the basis for course handbooks or service level
agreements. Objectives can vary in scope and detail. General statements like
'to enable researchers to handle information efficiently' or 'to enable students to study effectively' are easy to write, but what do they really mean?
We need to invest time and effort in formulating effective aims and objectives. Morris and Webster's seminal work, *Developing objectives for library
instruction*, remains useful as a model.[20] An example based on their work
is shown in Figure 5.4.

Overall aim of programme	Students will have the information skills necessary for independent study by the time they leave this college.
General objective of course	By the end of their first year, students will have the information skills necessary to plan, research and write class assignments and projects at a level acceptable to their teachers.
Terminal objective of unit	At the end of the two-hour unit on information search strategies, first-year students given a suitable topic will be able to retrieve enough relevant information from the learning centre's reference resources to handle an assignment based on that topic.
Enabling objective of unit	At the end of the two-hour unit on information search strategies, first-year students will be able to use *Encyclopedia Britannica* to provide an agreed number of references for an assignment.

Fig. 5.4   *Objectives for an information skills event at a college (adapted from Morris and Webster 1976)*

Programme form

Having determined the scope and level of the information skills to cover, we are now in a position to design our training programme. We need to decide which overall methods of teaching to employ, and what modes of teaching/formats of support materials to use. The overall *method* chosen will depend largely on the culture of the organization. There is probably more scope for varied approaches in the academic sector than in national or public libraries or specialized information services, but even in academic institutions the nature of relationships with sponsors, as well as budget/staffing constraints, often restrict options. These typically include:

- **Formal standalone events.** Separate self-contained courses are often offered by services with diverse customer bases that cannot be easily segmented for teaching or training purposes (such as national and public libraries). Such events are usually quite comprehensive, but are often seen as rather abstract and lacking relevance to the particular needs of participants, creating problems in audience attraction and retention.

- **Task-related or programme-related instruction.** Modular courses, broken down into units covering defined components, can be linked to the task needs of participants (such as undertaking a research assignment or writing a business plan) and spread over an appropriate period of time. This approach is increasingly used in academic institutions, but is also applicable in other sectors.
- **Integrated programmes.** Programmes or courses which integrate information skills with other learning or development activities are the next stage in the evolutionary spectrum. In this model, information skills are treated as an integral part of the course; documented aims and objectives, a commitment to evaluation, and a very close working relationship between information professionals and other partners are essential here.
- **Point-of-need instruction.** Traditional forms, such as enquiry-point or help-desk support, are increasingly being supplemented or replaced (during 'unsocial hours') by various types of self-help and self-paced learning. Examples of the latter include printed guides, user documentation, workbooks and multimedia packages, which can be designed for general use or tailored to the needs of particular groups.
- **Surgery support.** Timetabled periods when information professionals are available for one-to-one tuition, either on an appointment or 'drop-in' basis, can be a cost-efficient, staff-centred approach. In the early 1990s some librarians chose this solution to the growing problem of constant calls for help with CD-ROM searching which were taking up a disproportionate amount of their time.

For *modes* of teaching, the choice is even wider, and most people combine several elements in a programme. Choice is usually informed by our own *ability* (to use or produce various modes), the *cost* of materials (including hidden costs, like staff time), the *time* required for preparation (in mastering and/or producing materials) and the *culture* of the organization (which will affect how particular teaching modes are received).

ACTIVITY

Consider the following teaching modes:

- formal lectures
- workshops
- demonstrations
- games/simulations
- audio cassettes
- video cassettes
- interactive multimedia kits
- web-based tuition
- workbooks
- internally produced guides
- externally produced guides.

Write down the benefits and drawbacks you see for each of these in relation to your own organization.

Marketing your programme

The marketing of courses demands special attention. The best designed courses can go unattended (or, at least, under-attended) without proper marketing and explicit support from **sponsors**. Even in the higher education sector, mandatory timetabled sessions may be the only way to guarantee attendance. Joyce Levant and David Cleeton have identified three types of customer for the training manager: *the direct customers* (the trainees); *the backers* (people of influence who can pull strings – both political and financial – who can make or break your operation); and the *agents* (champions who will spread the good word and encourage attendance).[21] Sponsors will probably carry out all three rôles at some time, but in the long-run will be acting primarily as your backers and agents.

For non-mandatory sessions you need to rely on general marketing techniques (see Chapter 10). You need to establish what are the aims of your campaign; who is your target audience; whether it is more efficient to target the backers and agents than the direct customers; and which are the best channels of communication. A public library may choose a poster campaign, whereas the Open University has used web-based advertising and booking facilities.[22]

How do you market your information skills programmes at present? Investigate how other information services in your sector promote their training programmes. In the light of this, consider how you could improve your marketing.

Evaluation

Evaluation is the area most often neglected by information professionals involved in the management of information skills programmes. There are several possible reasons for this:

- not knowing what to do – we have not been trained to teach . . . or evaluate
- not having the properly constructed programme objectives necessary for evaluation
- not having the time and/or money to carry out meaningful investigations
- not wanting to risk the pain of adverse comments about our teaching
- not wanting to dwell on the event – just being happy to get it finished with.

This is hardly adequate justification: if resources are limited, we should be especially keen to ensure they are being effectively utilized; and if we feel so insecure as teachers, perhaps more self-assessment should be mandatory. There are other positive reasons for formal evaluation of information skills programmes:

- It is an important part of the training cycle: constant evaluation and re-evaluation is essential to provide training that is effective and remains so in the changing political, social and technological environment.
- It is an integral part of quality management: performance measurement and assessment is vital to identify problems for resolution and to find

opportunities for improvement, and is increasingly a formal requirement.

- It can provide feedback on other aspects of service operations (for example, comments on the user-friendliness of the online catalogue).
- It can provide evidence of our professionalism to our sponsors.

As already indicated, an effective information skills programme should benefit several parties. One of the problems with evaluation here is clarity about what is being evaluated – the development/performance of the trainees or the development/performance of the trainer? We need to consider carefully the *objectives* of evaluation before embarking on this part of our programme. In general terms, the questions to consider are:

- Were learning outcomes achieved? This can only be monitored effectively if we have detailed objectives in the first place.
- How satisfied were the participants? This can cover several aspects (such as the content, level, timing, location and delivery).
- How well did we perform as teachers?
- How effective was the programme as a whole?

There are various *methods* of evaluation available. The most common are:

- questionnaires, interviews or discussions
- pre- and post-testing
- documentation of skills development
- observation by colleagues/videoing sessions
- management information or anecdotal evidence (for example, perceived effects on enquiry services).

Evaluation is not easy, not least because it is time-consuming for trainees as well as for trainers, so we need a method which we can persuade our customers to use. It is also difficult generally to assess effectiveness of teaching programmes: if Student X does show marked improvements in skills A, B and C, is this because of the teaching, or the individual's efforts, or other external factors? In a scientific environment, the scientist typically employs a control group, but would it be fair for us to have a control group who were deliberately given no information skills training at all?

Timing is another problem. Often the benefits of an information skills programme will not be fully realized until some time afterwards. At the University of Reading, students on the MA programme in social work are invited back six months after the end of their course to be interviewed about the whole programme and its benefits. The students enjoy this as a class reunion, and the academics have found it a useful addition to their quality assessment programme; should information professionals use similar approaches?

Activity

Bringing all the points covered so far in this chapter together, prepare a ten-minute presentation for colleagues on how to plan a training programme on world wide web resources in a particular subject discipline. Although you may wish to refer to some of the sources covered, this presentation should be concerned with the design and development of a programme, not a version of the programme itself.

Consider the following areas and outline decisions made:

- objectives of your programme
- needs of your customers
- liaison with sponsors
- content, level and format of the programme
- practical planning considerations (location, timing, etc)
- evaluation procedures.

In order to help you focus on the principles, do not carry out this exercise with your usual environment and customers in mind. Instead, choose one of the scenarios below that is least like your present and past experience:

- a school librarian producing a programme for a group of teachers (for staff development purposes)
- a public librarian producing a programme for members of the local business community (in a sector of your choice)
- a healthcare information specialist producing a course for a group of community nurses
- a university librarian producing a course for part-time MA students in a humanities discipline.

After your presentation, discuss this topic as a group, highlighting any differences in approach between these case studies and also with your day-to-day practice.

Presentation skills

It is essential for information professionals to develop good presentation skills. This is not only so that you can perform effectively in the teaching/training arena, lead by example and train your colleagues; presentation skills will also assist your professional and personal development, helping you in transactions with both current colleagues and *potential* employers. It is therefore sensible to invest a significant amount of time and effort in developing this side of your professional portfolio.

Numerous guides have been produced on presentation skills, ranging from advice columns in broadsheet newspapers and popular books on management skills to more serious studies of teaching techniques. It is beyond the scope of this book to provide in-depth coverage, but you will find some practical pointers below, with additional guidance on these and other aspects in the suggestions for further reading at the end of this chapter and in Chapter 12. Our top tips for professional presentations are as follows.

Thirteen top tips for professional presentations

1   **Plan well ahead.** The more you know in advance, the less there is to go wrong on the day. Know your material inside out. Use triggers as reminders (bullet points on cards, headings or images on overhead transparencies) and be prepared to 'ad lib'. Produce support materials on which you can rely: they provide variety for your audience and comforting familiarity for you.

2   **Get to know your room and equipment.** Assess the size of the room to address the size of your performance. To move freely you should know where everything is located . . . down to the power button for the OHP. Test-drive equipment before your group arrives: asking how to switch on the video does not look professional! Where possible, carry spare bulbs for projectors. Try (where appropriate) to 'play on home ground'.

3 **Be properly introduced, or introduce yourself.** Establish your authority in your subject area without pomposity. Develop authority also in the management of your audience, especially when dealing with side discussions, unresponsive groups and over-responsive individuals. Consider how *you* want to deal with questions and discussion activities.

4 **Think about the structure of your session.** Always prepare and learn your opening line and closing line, even if the rest of the session is less strictly planned. Use signposts, structure and summaries.

5 **Do not try to pack too much in.** Information specialists often want to tell everybody everything on Day One. (This probably comes from a history of trying to find any time at all for information skills teaching.) Resist this temptation – a well structured programme will make this easier.

6 **Put detailed information in handouts, but refer to key points.** Consider the relationship between handouts and the session. Will giving out handouts at the beginning of the session add to or detract from the session?

7 **Employ variety in sessions.** Break up talks with demonstrations or activities. Consider the attention span you can expect, given the nature of your group and subject matter!

8 **Use technology you are happy with.** The effectiveness of using overhead projectors, flip charts or online demonstrations is dependent largely on how comfortable the presenter feels, which in turn depends on your competence and confidence.

9 **Develop your act.** When presenting (or indeed, carrying out other professional functions) it often helps to regard this as acting a part. This is a good defence mechanism. Develop a *persona* you are happy with, and stick with it.

10 **Develop vocal techniques.**

11 **Consider your body language.**

12 **Use humour with your audience – not against it.**

13 Remember that there is **no one best way** to present a training session.

Presentation skills develop over time. The more you perform, the happier you will feel 'on stage'. Always expect to be nervous – indeed, you should worry if you are not nervous – but learn to direct those nerves in a constructive way. Watch other 'performers' (be they librarians, teachers or television personalities) and learn from their techniques. Practise in front of a mirror and you will develop in front of your group.

Presentations are not easy – if they were, everyone would be up there doing them – but presentation techniques can be learnt and developed, and once you get a real 'buzz' from a good session, you will find yourself volunteering for more.

ACTIVITY

In a group with colleagues (with whom you feel at ease and with whom you can be honest!) discuss how you have each developed your presentation skills. Consider the highs and lows of performing presentations. Observe willing colleagues to see what you can learn about presentation techniques, and then reflect on your own style.

References

1   Fisher, D, A few notes on the death of librarianship, *Assistant Librarian*, 85 (2), 1992, 22-3.
2   Saatchis' ad shows nightmare library, *Library Association Record*, 98 (12), 1996, 605.
3   Marland, M (ed), *Information skills in the secondary curriculum: the recommendations of a working group sponsored by the British Library and the Schools Council*, Schools Council Curriculum Bulletin 9, Methuen Educational, 1981.
4   Fryer, R H, *Learning for the twenty-first century: first report of the National Advisory Group for Continuing Education and Lifelong Learning*, The National Advisory Group for Continuing Education and Lifelong Learning, 1997 (Chairman: Professor Bob Fryer).
5   *Nursing Standard*, 6 (12), 1997, 25.
6   Information skills for the 21st century (available at **http://www.wwguy. com/InfoPreneur/K-Base/K-Base2/info-skills.html**).
7   Marland, M, op cit.
8   American Library Association, *American Library Association Presidential Committee on Information Literacy: final report*, American Library Association, 1989.

9   American Library Association, *A progress report on information litera-cy: an update on the American Library Association Presidential Committee on Information Literacy final report*, 1998 (available at http://www.ala.org/acrl/nili/nili.html).

10 Shapiro, J J and Hughes, S K, Information literacy as a liberal art: enlightenment proposals for a new curriculum, *Educom Review*, **31** (2) 1996 (available at http://www.educause.edu/pub/er/review/reviewArticles/31231.html).

11 Hampson, A, Information skills: time to transfer, *Assistant Librarian*, **90** (10), 1997, 150.

12 Turner, D J and Grotzky, M E, They teach too: a role for paraprofes-sionals in library instruction, *The Reference Librarian*, **51/52**, 1995, 181-93.

13 EduLib: educational development for higher education staff (available at http://www.hull.ac.uk/edulib/).

14 Netskills: network skills training for users of the electronic library (avail-able at http://www.netskills.ac.uk).

15 Ariadne: the web version (available at http://www.ariadne.ac.uk).

16 DeLiberations on teaching and learning in higher education (available at http://www.lgu.ac.uk/deliberations/home.html).

17 For example, New approaches to learning; Effective information skills: teaching and learning for schools; Teaching skills. See http://www.la-hq.org.uk/directory/training/trtt.html.

18 Available at http://www.utexas.edu/world/lecture/.

19 Squires, G, *A new model of teaching and training*, The author, 1994.

20 Morris, J M and Webster, D F, *Developing objectives for library instruction*, Library Instruction Clearinghouse, 1976.

21 Levant, J and Cleeton, D, *Marketing the training function*, Kogan Page, 1993, 34.

22 See http://oulib1.open.ac.uk/lib/train.htm.

Suggestions for further reading
Information literacy

Sutton, A, Newton, R and McConnell, M, Open learning and the Internet in public libraries: an information skills approach [1998] (available at http://www.south-ayrshire.gov.uk/blric/project.htm).

Research update on a British Library-funded project to integrate open
learning collections in South Ayrshire Libraries with Internet resources
and user support offered via a web-based information skills tutorial,
based on a six-step cyclical model of information handling (defining
and planning; identifying and selecting; searching and retrieving;
analysing and organizing; presenting and communicating; reviewing and
learning) accessible via this site.

Grassian, E and Clark, S E, Information literacy sites: background and ideas
for program planning and development, *College & Research Libraries
News*, **60** (2), 1999, 78–81, 92.

Notes huge number of Internet resources available to professionals
interested in information literacy and reviews a representative selection
of websites offering relevant content and/or links. Sections include
directories/megasites; guidelines and reports; programmes; tutorials;
discussion groups; electronic journals; articles; and organizations.

Teaching rôles

Downard, K, User education in academic libraries, *Library Management*,
13 (3), 1992, 29–38.

Provides an overview of user education, covering the reasons for doing
it, arguments for and against, and its different forms – library orientation, bibliographic instruction, information skills teaching, online
instruction and course-related instruction. Offers guidance on planning
and implementing a programme, with good coverage of evaluation.

Clinch, P, The skills revolution: the challenge for librarians, *The Law
Librarian*, **23** (4), 1992, 200–6.

Considers the nature of legal research skills and how they should be
taught, drawing on results of a questionnaire survey of higher education
law librarians in England and Wales, noting the absence of formal evaluation and importance of working with academic staff.

Pacey, P, Teaching user education, learning information skills; or, towards
the self-explanatory library, *The New Review of Academic
Librarianship*, **1**, 1995, 95–103.

Argues that traditional approaches to library/bibliographic instruction
were misconceived, and librarians should create user-friendly libraries,

which are well signed and guided, and then help academic staff to rein-
tegrate information skills into the student curriculum.

McFadden, T G and Hostetler, T J, Introduction, *Library Trends*, **44** (2),
1995, 221-36.

Introduction to a special issue devoted to information skills/biblio-
graphic instruction; considers the changing rôle of librarians and the
particular need for library staff to teach information handling skills in
the age of the Internet. (Other articles in this issue cover relationships
with sponsors, examples of good practice and views of the future.)

Mendelsohn, S, Keeping up with expectations, *Library Manager*, **18**, 1996,
19-21.

Looks at environmental changes and how information professionals
have responded to increased demand for information skills and IT
teaching, giving examples of projects in the higher education sector and
providing details of materials and other support available.

Developing programmes

Malley, I, *The basics of information skills teaching*, Clive Bingley, 1984.
Despite dated examples, offers a good overview of how to develop an
information skills programme.

Duff, A S, Bibliographic instruction for nurses: a programme outline, *Nurse
Education Today*, **14**, 1994, 322-5.
Outlines programme delivered to students at Glasgow College of
Nursing and Midwifery.

Dubber, G, *Teaching information skills*, SLA Guidelines, School Library
Association, 1995.
Practical guide to planning information skills programmes (in schools
and in other sectors).

Francis, B W and Fisher, C C, Multilevel library instruction for emerging
nursing roles, *Bulletin of the Medical Library Association*, 83 (4), 1995,
492-8.
Discusses the multilevel programme developed for undergraduate, post-
experience and postgraduate nursing students at Florida University,
which is academically integrated and has objectives for each stage of
learning, and describes several methods used to evaluate it.

Winship, I R, Workbooks for information skills teaching at the University of Northumbria at Newcastle, *The New Review of Academic Librarianship*, 1, 1995, 105-18.

Describes the use of self-teaching subject-based workbooks for first-year students, introduced to replace seminar-based teaching as a way of dealing with increased numbers. Covers workbook content, academic involvement and project evaluation; concludes with nine lessons learned from the experience, and four sample pages from various workbooks.

McNamara, D and Core, J (eds), *Teaching for learning in libraries and information services*, University of Hull/University of Abertay, EduLib, 1998.

Comprehensive practical compendium (c275p) of training materials for library and information service staff involved in information skills programmes. Well documented with references and case studies, the topics covered include planning events, assessment methods, large audiences, small groups, individual differences, open and distance learners.

Presentation skills

Rawlins, K, *Presentation and communication skills: a handbook for practitioners*, Macmillan Magazines Ltd, 1993.

User-friendly introduction, well laid out with many activities. Provides extensive coverage of planning presentations (more than half the book) as well as delivery and evaluation.

Thompson, A H, Guidelines for more effective OHT production, *AVL: Multimedia Information*, 22 (4), 1996, 248-62.

Explains different techniques of using overhead transparencies (OHTs), lists 18 benefits for speaker and audience, and notes how OHTs add value through illustration and structure. Provides eight design guidelines to avoid common errors, and concludes with detailed step-by-step guidance for producing hand-drawn and computer-produced OHTs.

For additional references see the suggestions for further reading at the end of Chapter 12.

6

Information systems

This chapter covers:

- electronic library developments
- website and intranet design
- Internet filtering
- strategic planning for IT
- automation and systems migration
- convergence of library, computing and related services
- human aspects of IT developments.

Introduction

Computer-based systems for the management of library operations have evolved from mainframe-based batch processing to real-time client-server systems running on industry-standard hardware and software, with networked access and self-service features. Systems for database searching have similarly evolved to facilitate desktop access for end-users, with web technologies enabling seamless integration of information systems and services. This chapter provides an overview of developments in IT-based information provision. It also covers planning for library automation or systems migration, the convergence of information services and related services, and the human dimensions of IT-based provision, including the changing rôles of staff with specialist systems responsibilities.

Technology trends

Previous chapters have indicated the dramatic impact of IT on both information services and society at large. IT can be seen as both an *enabler* and *driver* of change.[1] It is also often promoted (by suppliers and paymasters) as a 'solution' to problems such as expanding demand and reduced unding. The interaction of technological developments with other environmental forces (political, economic and especially legal) poses particular management challenges. The pace of technological change is an added challenge, and we have to accept that new technologies will continue to emerge, as noted by Douglas Coupland: 'A good piece of technology dreams of the day when it will be replaced by a newer piece of technology. This is one definition of progress.'[2]

In the UK higher education sector, various government-funded initiatives have promoted the use of IT in management and administration, in teaching and learning, and also in libraries, with the **Electronic Libraries Programme** (eLib) covering areas such as document delivery, electronic journals, access to network resources, digitization, on-demand publishing and hybrid libraries.[3] The new Labour Government has given further impetus to such developments by promoting technology-assisted learning in the context of its lifelong learning and social inclusion policies, thus bringing together the University for Industry, the National Grid for Learning and the New Library/People's Network initiatives. Libraries have also pursued IT-related developments individually and collectively; a collaborative project to provide Electronic Access to Resources in Libraries (EARL) established in 1995 now has more than 150 public library authorities in membership.[4]

In the USA, the **Digital Libraries Initiative** (DLI) was established in 1994 by the National Science Foundation, the Department of Defense Advanced Research Projects Agency and the National Aeronautics and Space Administration, with the overall goal of dramatically advancing the means to collect, store, organize and use globally distributed knowledge resources of diverse information type and content stored in a variety of electronic forms. There are six university-led projects, which involve almost 100 separate organizations, including major US computer and communications companies, academic institutions at all levels, libraries, publishers, government and state agencies.[5] The DLI differs in emphasis from the eLib programme, in that the former is essentially high-risk basic research, which may take years to translate into products available for general use, whereas the main aim of eLib has been 'to engage the higher education community in developing and shaping the implementation of the electronic library'.[6]

Individual academic, public and special libraries have also exploited IT to improve services, redesign processes and streamline administration. Examples range from self-service facilities and networked access, through electronic data interchange (EDI) with suppliers, to the use of standard business applications, such as e-mail, word-processing, spreadsheets, desktop publishing (DTP) and project management software. In addition, the content of libraries and information services continues to migrate to digital formats: reference works, such as abstracts and indexes, dictionaries and encyclopedias, are now well-established in online and CD-ROM formats; electronic journals and newsletters are growing in number; and 'e-books' seem ready to be launched on the mass market, after a long gestation period, but with many unanswered questions about copyright control and technical standards.[7]

It is beyond the scope of this book to explore the use of such information systems in depth; there are many examples of textbooks covering both the library field[8] and the business world.[9] It is also not possible to cover more than a selection of IT-related developments in information services. Our purpose here is to focus on key issues in managing information systems and services, by selecting a few themes reflecting contemporary trends and concerns.

Hybrid libraries

The terminology of IT-based library developments is confusing, with some commentators appearing to use the terms *digital library, electronic library* and *virtual library* almost interchangeably. Other labels used include *gateway library, logical library* (as distinct from a physical library) and *networked library*. The eLib programme has now adopted the term *hybrid library* to describe a situation where electronic resources (or 'digital artefacts') are used alongside paper resources (or 'legacy materials') and eLib Phase 3 includes five hybrid library projects aimed at developing and demonstrating workable models of this concept. **The hybrid library** is a useful concept as it acknowledges that most information services will comprise a mixture of traditional and newer media for the foreseeable future. Moreover, even if electronic publication and retrospective digitization spread rapidly, many libraries will never become 'all-digital' so the hybrid library should not be seen as 'an uneasy transitional phase', but as 'a worthwhile model in its own right, which can be usefully developed and improved'.[10]

However, even the term 'hybrid library' can be misleading as it may not convey to everyone the scale and scope of **integration** that is envisaged. For example, the Agora hybrid library project aims to demonstrate *cross-domain searching* for *mixed-media resources* (for example, not only conventional publications and audio-visual materials, but also archival holdings and museum objects) thus enabling an 'end-to-end' service for heterogeneous media from a variety of different curatorial traditions.[11] Other issues being addressed by these projects include the *interconnectivity* and *interoperability* of systems, and automatic procedures for *authentication* and *authorization* of information users (establishing the identities of individuals and their access rights and restrictions) to deal with the growing problem of multiple logins and passwords for different dataset services.

The development of the **electronic library** can be traced back over more than three decades. Ten years ago, Michael Buckland offered a simplified model of computer development in libraries, along the lines shown below.[12]

	Library operation	*Library materials*
Phase I	Paper-based	Paper-based
Phase II	Computer-based	Paper-based
Phase III	Computer-based	Computer-based

REFLECTION

With reference to Buckland's model, consider what stage of development has been reached by your information service. How far do you see your service becoming an electronic library?

Networked provision

The key to the electronic library is its networking technology, which enables information provision to be decentralized and provides the opportunity for end-user empowerment. Information service managers are increasingly concerned with the management of networked information systems. All aspects of networked provision - CD-ROM networks, electronic journals, online datasets, staff intranets - need to be managed using our familiar planning cycle. We need to ask *why* we are adding services, and how they *fit* with our strategic objectives and priorities. We should also assess customer needs beforehand and thereafter – by monitoring, evaluating and reviewing provision, as an ongoing process of service development and improvement. Networked provision poses particular challenges for managers, in areas such as the security of information, protection of intellectual property rights and acceptable use of the network. We also need to ensure that our user community has the competence and confidence to use the network facilities provided. The following sections outline current developments and concerns for information professionals.

WEBSITES

Librarians and information scientists were among the first groups to see the benefits of using websites for providing information and promoting services. There are several **advantages** in developing a world wide web presence as part of your networked provision, for example:

- Publication of information is relatively simple
- Distribution of information is very inexpensive
- The web provides an exceptionally large potential audience
- It offers the opportunity to utilize multimedia applications
- Editing and updating information is easy and inexpensive
- The web's use of non-proprietary standards gives sites a long life expectancy.

There are also potential **problems**, for example:

- Network access can be slow, especially at certain times of the day
- Copyright can be troublesome, particularly in a global context
- Some multimedia applications have limited capabilities.

One of the main challenges for information professionals is making their websites relevant and encouraging target audiences to use them. Website design is not as easy as it appears! Examining successful sites and consulting expert colleagues can help, but the best way is to get direct feedback from your users and act on it.

INTRANETS

Increasingly web technology is being utilized by organizations for internal purposes. An intranet uses similar technology to form an information system restricted to users within a company or other type of organization. Intranets can fulfil various rôles, from digital filing cabinet to electronic company newspaper. Information stored ranges from archived information (meeting minutes, organization charts, policy documents) to news items updated daily (service changes, staff appointments, training courses). An intranet is often a key component in **knowledge management** initiatives, where it can be used to store customer data, competitor intelligence, and client presentations, as well as recording internal procedures and capturing *lessons learned* and other forms of intellectual capital. They can also provide links to other sources of information (including in-house databases, such as *directories of expertise*, as well as external sources) and they offer a more user-friendly alternative to e-mail attachments as a means of document delivery.

Typical library and information service applications include their use for publicizing duty rotas, maintaining procedures manuals, communicating project reports and supporting information work (for example, by recording frequently-asked questions and storing database guides). Intranets can also promote Continuing Professional Development by providing links to online journals and details of professional meetings.

The use of an intranet as the main method of staff communication and primary source of information can have many **advantages**, for example:

- Information can be easily and cost-effectively distributed to a wide group
- People can become better informed about a wider range of activities
- Individuals do not need to duplicate and store information separately
- Communication is improved, especially for part-timers working unsocial hours
- All staff can develop and practise basic IT skills, assisting with multi-skilling
- Staff can be encouraged to author pages, leading to further upskilling.

In practice, intranets do not always deliver all their expected benefits. Possible disadvantages include further dependency on the IT infrastructure and additional responsibilities placed on individual staff.

ACTIVITY

Consider the introduction of an intranet within your own organization. What difficulties do you see in making the intranet the preferred means of communication for all staff? How could these problems be overcome?

FILTERING

Networks enable information to be distributed more easily and cheaply than ever before, but this has created as many problems as it has solved. Complaints about 'information overload' have become routine, as have comments on the difficulty in finding 'quality resources' among the huge numbers of websites now accessible from most desktop PCs. The creation of *subject-based information gateways* by specialists committed to **quality control** has enabled researchers in those areas to target their searches more effectively.[13] Another challenge facing information service managers, especially those working in public libraries, is the question of what constitutes 'acceptable use' of their networks. Public opinion is divided on whether public libraries (and other information services) should sift, filter or block access to sites disseminating pornographic or offensive material, particularly in the context of increasing Internet access for children. Some people advocate use of **filtering software** (such as *Net nanny* and *Cybersitter*) but others champion freedom of expression and argue that such filters are often blunt instruments which block useful sites, or even sinister vehicles for software providers to pursue their own hidden agenda.[14]

The American and UK Library Associations have both made statements outlining rights of access, but pressure groups continue to push for restrictions.[15-16] Information professionals have to consider such issues in the context of the guidelines and policies of both their professional bodies and their parent organizations. In the UK higher education sector, the JANET Acceptable Use Policy provides a definition of what constitutes *unacceptable* use of the network, and could serve as a model or starting-point for managers in other sectors considering the formulation of similar policy statements.[17] Further guidance in this area can be found from the websites referenced and items in the suggestions for further reading.

REFLECTION

Consider the arguments for and against the use of Internet filtering packages. Do you feel that they have a rôle to play in your own organization?

Strategy and planning

As with all aspects of management, a strategic approach is essential when managing information systems and technology. Although many libraries and information services have established planning and budgeting processes, few have developed formal information technology or information systems strategies to underpin their service development plans at the level of detail necessary to support financial planning of ongoing investment in the IT infrastructure. With the replacement cycle for equipment shortening all the time, most services need to plan for a rolling programme of replacement and upgrading, as well as budgeting for regular commitments (such as maintenance contracts and computer consumables) and making provision for larger 'one-off' purchases (such as a new automated system or a CD-ROM network) within a medium-term timeframe of three to five years. For examples and guidance on IT **strategy**, see the suggestions for further reading at the end of this chapter.

REFLECTION

How is the development of the IT infrastructure represented in your service strategy? Do you have a plan for replacing and upgrading equipment in the medium to long term?

Planning the installation of a new computer system is a daunting task first time around, but information and advice is readily available through specialist exhibitions and short courses, published guides and case studies, and the 'invisible college' of fellow professionals. Exhibitions (such as the

Library and Information Show and Libtech) provide the opportunity for demonstrations and discussions with supplier representatives, and the UK-based National Acquisitions Group offers a module on automating acquisitions at its annual school. *Library Journal* publishes regular reviews of the automated systems marketplace and the Library Information Technology Centre has published a guide to library systems with a comprehensive checklist of functions, as well as a range of introductory packs and reports on planning, choosing and evaluating automated systems.[18] The (UK) School Library Association has also produced a publication specifically for its sector.[19] The invisible college of fellow professionals can be accessed via e-mail discussion lists or personal contacts – many people are willing to share lessons learned from their own experience and even to provide copies of their own procurement documentation.

Automation

Although first-time automation is less common now than system migration, small special libraries (especially those in the voluntary sector with large collections of non-book materials) are often in this unenviable position, and even some larger libraries with established systems have not fully automated all their functions.

As with any service development, the first question to ask is 'Why?' This is particularly important with automation as the process will inevitably be time-consuming and people often have rather simplistic (and silly) notions of what automation can accomplish. It is essential to consider the potential benefits and drawbacks in relation to *your particular library*, as textbook benefits might not apply, and it is important to be honest! If you over-sell the project to your funders, your stakeholders will probably be disappointed with the outcome and your credibility will have been damaged as a result. You need to weigh up long-term benefits against short-term upheavals and stresses, and the visible and hidden costs. It makes sense to start with the objectives of your library and translate them into system requirements; this ensures relevance and helps weighting of required and desired functionality. Once you have established what you want in general terms, you can begin to identify and investigate systems (using the sources suggested above). The invisible college can prove particularly useful at this point as visits to other libraries as 'reference sites' allow you to talk with colleagues (rather than sales people) about the true strengths and weaknesses of systems. But you must also beware of choosing a system just because it is favoured by colleagues, as their needs might be very different to yours.

Migration

Migration from one system to another is a similar process in many respects, but has other complexities and the potential benefits/drawbacks are often less clear. For large libraries, systems have traditionally had an effective lifespan of about seven years. Planning and managing the migration may take between one and two years, depending on the scope and scale of the exercise, and any timetabling or other organizational constraints.

As with first-time automation, the first question to ask is 'Why?' Suffolk County Council Libraries and Heritage had four main **reasons** for replacing its system in 1995:

- **Technological advances.** The existing programme was based on software design features that had been superseded by more powerful, more reliable and cheaper to maintain systems.
- **Political changes.** Local government reorganization was on the horizon, which in effect set a time limit for installation of a system that could easily communicate with other systems.
- **Interoperability issues.** The county was keen to extend its interlibrary networking and to allow remote access to the system more generally, which required a system using open standards.
- **Public perceptions.** Customers had become used to colourful user-friendly Windows interfaces at home and at work, and were beginning to view library terminals as 'old-fashioned'.

At a more specific level, Suffolk sought improvements in *efficiency, functionality* and *management information* to inform decision-making; and also wanted *industry-standard* hardware, communications technology and database management systems.[20]

Another key aspect of planning automation or migration is **timing** (the 'When?' question). Large purchases necessitate formal tendering procedures which may impose significant constraints on the timetable. The availability of key stakeholders also needs to be taken into account, and managers must also consider the impact of the project on day-to-day service operations. Academic libraries generally plan to have the change-over to a new system during the long summer vacation to minimize disruption to users, and public libraries similarly often try to schedule the 'cut-over' during their quietest periods. An example of a migration timetable for a large library is shown in Figure 6.1. This timetable assumes that in-principle approval and funding have already been secured! In addition, the timetable omits some of the tasks and activities which would be going on throughout the project, such as progress reports to library staff, senior management and internal com-

Ongoing	consult stakeholder groups
Spring	form project team identify potential systems develop preliminary checklists formulate project plan
Summer	visit major suppliers contact reference sites
Autumn	draft operational requirement initiate tender process
Winter	receive supplier enquiries despatch operational requirement receive formal tenders shortlist potential suppliers
Spring	conduct on-site evaluations select preferred system negotiate contract terms finalize implementation timetable
Summer	convert existing data install test system customize system features train service staff revise staff procedures update user documentation
Autumn	Implement live system launch new system
Ongoing	Educate service users

Fig. 6.1 *Milestones in a system migration timetable*

mittees, and also targeted communication and consultation with key stake-holders (including IT specialists and library customers).

Involvement of as many **stakeholders** as possible in the selection process is recommended, both to ensure that the new system meets their needs and to gain their support during a disruptive period. Information service staff working at different levels in different areas will all have different demands and different expectations of the system. Information service customers will be even less homogeneous! Managers have used a range of methods to con-sult users (staff and customers) about what they want from a new system, including e-mail, focus groups, posters and questionnaire surveys. Asking people what they think are the best and worst features of your current sys-tem can be a useful starting point. The consultation process should be continuous, allowing views to be fed in to initial 'wish lists' as well as informing the formal specification or 'operational requirement', and ideally also involving a cross-section of staff and customers in evaluating or 'test-driving' short-listed systems on site. Customers (particularly students) can be encouraged to participate in the process with offers of free refresh-ments. Timetabling library assistants and other support staff for evaluation sessions makes it clear that the project is important and that their opinions really matter; providing them with copies of suppliers' literature and includ-ing them in site visits further underlines this.

System **specification documents** vary considerably. Some libraries pro-duce very *detailed* lists of requirements (for example, the Reading University Library 1996 operational requirement contained 300 points cat-egorized as 'mandatory', 'highly desired', 'desired' or 'interesting'). Others (such as Suffolk) are more *strategic*, concentrating on the purpose of the service and how a system should respond to these aims, giving suppliers the opportunity to come up with a more imaginative response. Most libraries will need to draw on the expertise of specialist IT staff in specifying tech-nical requirements and assessing tender responses (for example, in relation to networking) and many have found it useful to include one or more IT colleagues in the membership of their project teams.

The choice of system is only the first part of the exercise: **implementa-tion** is the next stage. Issues to consider here include how much of your existing data (such as borrower records) you wish to convert, the method of change-over (for example, the 'big bang' of a direct cut-over versus a phased introduction of different modules or parallel running for a given period) and the timing and content of training and education for staff and customers. It is worth thinking about formally launching the new system with a party for those who have contributed, or a more public event for profile-raising and/or customer relations purposes. As with any planning cycle approach, new/migrated systems must be monitored, evaluated, reviewed, upgraded and (eventually) replaced. On top of this, everyone who has gone through this process – especially anyone who has made use of the invisible college – should in turn become active in the rôle of 'informed consultant' to colleagues elsewhere.

ACTIVITY

Assume your organization is planning to upgrade its management/housekeeping system. Which stakeholders would you involve in the planning process? What rôles do you envisage they would play, and how would you encourage active participation? Do you anticipate any difficulties with stakeholder involvement in the planning process?

Service convergence

Another aspect of information systems management that requires continuous review is the relationship between the library/information service and other service providers, specifically IT support agencies. As libraries and equivalent units increasingly take on IT-related rôles, with pressure for efficiency gains and improved services, greater cooperation between allied services becomes inevitable.

The trend for **convergence of libraries and IT departments** (mirroring earlier partnerships between libraries and educational technology units) has been most publicized in the UK higher education sector, but similar reconfigurations are evident in the business and industrial sectors, notably where corporate libraries have been replaced with knowledge centres. No one model for merger has triumphed. Bruce Royan's survey of convergence – prompted by Follett's recommendation that each higher education institution should formulate an integrated information strategy – showed that (for the 76 institutions surveyed) there were five broad patterns of managerial change, with the converged service under the control of an executive director as the most dominant model. The second most common approach was at the other end of the management spectrum – a day-to-day working partnership based on 'goodwill and commonsense', rather than formal restructuring.[21] The Fielden report usefully distinguished two main types of convergence – *'organizational* or formal' and *'operational* or informal'.[22] Most organizations fit somewhere between the two poles.

There are many good reasons and **purposes** quoted for pursuing convergence:

- **Customer need.** Changes in teaching and learning have placed new demands on support services: customers are not concerned with organizational structures, but want and demand a seamless service or 'one-stop shopping'.
- **Strategic management.** Overlapping service rôles are more effectively managed together: convergence allows and encourages a single view of strategic priorities.
- **Resource efficiency.** Economies of scale and resource synergy can be achieved by bringing services together and pooling staff expertise.
- **Technology dependence.** Technological change (particularly the move to networked information) has shifted the focus and priorities of 'computer centres' and libraries so past structures may no longer be appropriate.

There are also more *ad hoc* or expedient causes, such as the opportunity to save a large salary arising from the departure of either service head, or just the desire to follow the crowd.

Convergence can bring several clear **benefits.** As library enquiries and information skills teaching programmes take on a greater IT emphasis, it is particularly useful to have IT expertise at hand. Staff from both backgrounds can play to their strengths and also gain from opportunities for information sharing and skills development. There is obvious value in having dedicated IT staff in a systems planning team, and this benefit extends beyond major procurement exercises to the increasing number of service development initiatives with an IT dimension. At a more strategic level, a larger service unit should have more influence within the organization and enable more holistic planning across functional boundaries.

There are also potential **drawbacks.** On the downside, it has been argued that multi-tasking dilutes specialist expertise and results in the loss of professional identities, and the cultural differences between (people-orientated) library staff and (technology-centred) IT staff give rise to tensions and conflict. How much this is based on outmoded stereotypes or fact is open to debate, but any change must be justifiable, properly explained and carefully managed. Appropriate training for all parties is essential and the extent *and limits* of overlap need to be clearly defined if rôle confusion (for customers and staff alike) is to be avoided. Larger units may provoke charges of 'empire-building' within organizations. A combined service is also vulnerable to bias reflecting the background of the service head: for example, most library/information specialists see the need to invest significant sums in the 'conduit', but it is questionable whether most computer/IT specialists have the same appreciation of 'content' needs.

REFLECTION

What is the relationship between the information service, IT support and other service providers in your organization? How has this developed over the last five years? What problems have been encountered and how were they addressed?

The human element

One aspect of information systems development that is often overlooked or not given sufficient attention is the human dimension. This may be partly attributable to an anxiety to get the technical side of developments right, but it is clear that we should be devoting more effort to considering human resource implications. An astonishingly small proportion of the literature on library automation covers human aspects, even though the vast majority of reported problems in automation projects are concerned with human and organizational aspects. Managers need to be sensitive to the staff concerns that frequently arise from technological change, particularly among support staff who may not have had much previous involvement with such systems. Some concerns may be specifically technology-based – such as apprehension about using or damaging the system, fears about health-related issues, and worries about **deskilling** or redundancy – whilst others will be more general symptoms of organizational change.

In practice, *staff* rarely become redundant as a result of library automation or systems migration, but managers often forget to give staff the necessary reassurances. Some *skills* may become redundant (for example, sorting and filing catalogue cards) but others may need further development (for example, the interpersonal skills of assistants expected to help or train customers to use self-service systems which were previously mediated). **Reskilling** is the norm, but it is essential that managers make development and training plans clear to everyone. With the move to service convergence, formal or informal, **multiskilling** for both information and IT service staff has become a central concern. In the UK, Follett/Fielden and the *New library* reports (referred to previously) have all emphasized the criticality of IT skills in the migration to electronic information provision, and have in turn spawned various training and development projects and studies. Recent reports have specified information and communication technology tasks and skills for various groups of staff in both academic and public libraries.[23-4]

Systems specialists

While technological change has affected all information service workers, its impact is most keenly felt by staff with special responsibility for systems within information services. Over the past three decades the job of the **systems librarian** or equivalent has evolved and developed from an *operational responsibility* for the library 'housekeeping' system to a more *strategic rôle*, encompassing all aspects of the service's information technology infrastructure. Library systems have progressed from mainframe-based batch processing for separate functions to the current generation of integrated real-time client-server systems, with networked access for service staff, customers and suppliers. The remit of the 'head of systems' or equivalent in an information unit today often covers everything from traditional library management operations through specialist electronic information sources to standard business applications packages, and includes the hardware, software and network.

Historically, the library systems specialist was often based in the 'bibliographical services' or 'technical services' department, but today the information service systems supremo is more likely to be a member of the senior management team, leading a **specialist systems team** as well as coordinating the work of other staff with substantial rôles in systems management and support (such as the functional managers of acquisitions, cataloguing and circulation). In larger information services the systems team is likely to include both information specialists and IT specialists, who have particular specialisms. The move to library systems running on standard hardware and software platforms enables more efficient and better integrated systems management alongside other organizational systems. This is often mentioned as a potential benefit of formal convergence of library and IT services, but has also been successfully pursued through service level agreements between a library and its IT counterpart, thus enabling the library to draw on a wider range of specialist expertise than would probably be possible within its own staffing establishment.

The pace of change is so rapid that information service managers need to keep staffing arrangements in this area under continuous review. New technologies often necessitate the creation of **new specialist rôles** to provide a focus of expertise until applications become embedded in practice and are no longer seen as a specialism. Many libraries had individuals or units specializing in online searching in the 1980s, and then disbanded them when this came to be regarded as a basic skill for most information professionals. Today some information services have designated individuals to develop, coordinate and promote access to electronic journals and multimedia resources, but we can expect these to be considered standard offerings for all but a few services in the very near future. Another example of a new IT-related rôle emerging both within information services and in other parts of organizations is the 'webmaster' or **web manager**, a job which demands a mix of 'content' and 'conduit' skills, and is thus often hard to place within existing organizational and service structures. Suggested duties for this 'new player in the information centre's online team' include the following:

* designing and maintaining service homepages, including links to essential sources, such as relevant subject-based information gateways or 'niche portals'
* providing technical back-up (and training) for web-based researchers, including awareness of new developments, advice on search engines, etc
* assisting information service colleagues with management of personalized information/alerting services, including the use of 'push' technologies

- leading a team to manage the development and upkeep of an intranet, serving as an electronic noticeboard and repository for news, instructions, procedures, etc
- managing local web-based databases.[25]

Crystal-gazing is always a dangerous pastime, especially where technology is concerned. However, we can be confident that IT-based systems will continue to grow apace, and also hopeful that information will receive just as much attention as technology, and that the human dimension (which is fundamental to all information systems) will be more carefully considered as the use of such systems becomes an accepted part of everyday life.

REFLECTION

How has the rôle of information systems staff changed in your organization? What changes can be anticipated for the next five years?

References

1   Lester, R, IT is the driver! *Ariadne*, **12**, 1997, 8 (available at http://www.ariadne.ac.uk/issue12/minotaur/).

2   Coupland, D, *Microserfs*, Flamingo, 1996, 179.

3   eLib: electronic libraries programme. See http://www.ukoln.ac.uk/services/elib/.

4   Earl: the consortium for public library networking. See http://www.earl.org.uk/index.html.

5   Griffin, S M, Taking the initiative for digital libraries, *The Electronic Library*, **16** (1), 1998, 24–7. For more information on the initiative, the projects and related work, see Digital libraries initiative: available research at http://dli.grainger.uiuc.edu/national.htm.

6   Brophy, P, The eLib programme, Relay, **47**, 1999, 5–7.

7   Dorman, D, The e-book: pipe dream or potential disaster? *American Libraries*, **30** (2) 1999, 36–9.

8   For example, Rowley, J E, *The electronic library*, 4th edn, Library Association Publishing, 1998.

9   For example, Laudon, K C and Laudon, J P, *Management information systems: new approaches to organization and technology*, 5th edn, Prentice Hall International, 1998. See also http://www.prenhall.com/laudon.

10 Pinfield, S and others, Realizing the hybrid library, *D-lib Magazine*, October 1998 (available at http://www.dlib.org/dlib/october98/10pinfield.html) or (for UK readers) at http://mirrored.ukoln.ac.uk/lis-journals/dlib/dlib/dlib/october98/).

11 See http://hosted.ukoln.ac.uk/agora/.

12 Buckland, M, Foundations of academic librarianship, *College & Research Libraries*, 50 (4), 1989, 389-96.

13 Pinakes: a subject launch pad (available at http://www.hw.ac.uk/libWWW/irn/pinakes/pinakes.html).

14 *Faulty filters: how content filters block access to kid-friendly information on the Internet*, Electronic Privacy Information Center, 1997 (available at http://www.epic.org/reports/filter-report.html).

15 American Library Association, Intellectual Freedom Committee, Statement on Internet filtering, 1997 (available at http://www.ala.org/alaorg/oif/filt_stm.html. See also Minow, M, Filters and the public library: a legal and policy analysis, *First Monday*, 2 (12), 1997, 7 (available at http://www.firstmonday.dk/issues/issue2_12/minow/index.html).

16 The Library Association, *Library and information services and the Internet: a statement by The Library Association*, The Library Association, 1995.

17 Day, R A (ed) *JANET acceptable use policy*, United Kingdom Education and Research Networking Association (on behalf of the Higher Education Funding Councils), 1995 (available at http://www.ja.net/documents/use.html).

18 Leeves, J and Russell, R, *Libsys.uk: a directory of library systems in the United Kingdom*, South Bank University, Library Information Technology Centre, 1995. See also http://www.sbu.ac.uk/litc/.

19 Butterworth, M, *Preparing for automation in the school library*, SLA Guidelines, School Library Association, 1991.

20 Pachent, G, Network '95: choosing a third generation automated information system for Suffolk Libraries and Heritage, *Program*, 30 (3), 1996, 213-28.

21 Royan, B, Are you being merged?: a survey of convergence in information service provision, *SCONUL Newsletter*, **1** 1994, 17-20.
22 John Fielden Consultancy, *Supporting expansion: a report on human resource management in academic libraries, for the Joint Funding Councils' Libraries Review Group*, Joint Funding Councils, 1993, paragraphs 2.25-31.
23 Garrod, P and Sidgreaves, I, *SKIP: skills for new information professionals*, University of Plymouth, 1998.
24 Library and Information Commission, *Building the new library network: a report to government*, Library and Information Commission, 1998 (available at **http://www.lic.gov.uk/publications/policyreports/building/index.html**).
25 van der Wait, P W and van Brakel, P A, The Webmaster: a new player in the information centre's online team, *The Electronic Library*, **15** (6) 1997, 447-54.

Suggestions for further reading
Technology trends

Crawford, W. and Gorman, M, *Future libraries: dreams, madness and reality*, American Library Association, 1995.

Promoted as a technologically informed response to simplistic visions of the all-digital future, this compact book (c200 pp) advocates a rational human-oriented approach to technology. Twelve chapters include the madness of technolust, coping with electronic information, economics of collection and access, survival guide to the serials crisis. Chapters have useful subheadings, footnote references and end with 'points to remember'.

Biddiscombe, R (ed) *The end-user revolution: CD-ROM, Internet and the changing role of the information professional*, Library Association Publishing, 1996.

Contains 15 contributions showing how CD-ROMs and networks have transformed information service delivery for providers and users. Includes case studies from industrial, public and university libraries; chapters on database publishing; and comments on intermediary rôles in end-user training, interface development, quality control and systems support.

Klemperer, K and Chapman, S, Digital libraries: a selected resource guide, *Information Technology and Libraries*, **16** (3), 1997, 126–31 (available at http://www.lita.org/ital/1603_klemperer.htm).
Adopting a broad definition of 'digital libraries', provides an annotated listing of more than 60 websites as an introduction to and review of current issues. Separate sections cover retrospective digitization, electronic publication, metadata, archiving, copyright, etc, and the review concludes with current awareness sources, such as listservs and online journals. (The online version of this article also provides electronic links to the websites discussed.)

Calhoun, K, Koltay, Z and Weissman, E, Library gateway: project design, teams, and cycle time, *Library Resources and Technical Services*, **43** (2), 1999, 114–22.
Describes a project to develop a common entryway to networked resources and services at Cornell University Library (in 17 weeks), covering project organization and lessons learned from the process. Sets out the project milestones, costs in staff hours, service benefits, and four key ideas underpinning successful innovation and rapid product development.

Networked provision

Cox, A, Hypermedia library guides for academic libraries on the World Wide Web, *Program*, 30 (1), 1996, 39–50.
Discusses advantages and disadvantages of web guides and reviews existing examples of (mainly US) university library guides. Suggests 13 design principles, drawing on various sources, and outlines types of information and other features worth considering as content.

Bevan, S and Evans, J, Managing the library Intranet at Cranfield University, *Managing Information*, 3 (9) 1996, 38–40.
Compares intranet with groupware technologies and explains reasons for adoption at Cranfield University as an information and communications tool for library staff. Gives examples of usage, notes rôle in 'upskilling' staff and comments on problems to overcome.

Bishop, M, Laying down the law, *The Bookseller*, (20 June 1997), 24–6.
The Online Services Manager of HarperCollins offers a publishing house perspective on setting up a company website, providing ten gold-

en rules to assist newcomers to this task.

Campbell, S, Guidelines for writing children's Internet policies, *American Libraries*, **29** (1) 1998, 91-2.

Draws on the author's book on this subject and provides a practical checklist of points to consider when formulating a policy on web access, with references to relevant websites.

Harper, S, Newton, R and Dixon, D, Instant access – or filter? *Public Library Journal*, **14** (2), 1999, 46-7.

Discusses issues surrounding the use of filtering packages by public libraries offering access to Internet sites, raising questions about the legality of such practices in the UK and referring extensively to published literature on the subject covering the last three years.

IT strategy

Gallimore, A, A public library IT strategy for the millennium, *Journal of Librarianship and Information Science*, **28** (3), 1996, 149-57.

Case study of a large public library, which sets out the main elements of an IT strategy and relates it to key corporate policies, other external influences and user expectations. Includes checklist of elements for IT audit and issues for future strategy development, such as network development, public access, staff skills, management efficiency and partnerships.

Gallimore, A, *Developing an IT strategy for your library*, Library Association Publishing, 1997.

Clear and comprehensive guide (c190 pp) which explains the needs and benefits of an IT strategy and elaborates the components of the process from objectives to implementation. Covers internal audit, external context, physical infrastructure, policy issues, management aspects, strategy evaluation, implementation planning, monitoring progress and updating.

Bevan, N and Dolphin, P, Preparing an IT strategy, *SCONUL Newsletter*, **12**, 1997, 16-21.

Case study of a small academic library, which discusses the participative developmental process used to develop an IT strategy for incorporation into the library's strategic plan, involving nine groups over six months. Outlines the aspects of IT covered, the methods of research used, and the set of issues addressed in presentations and reports of each group.

Automation and migration

Brewerton, A W, Notes from a 'man recover'd of the byte' or helpful hints in choosing automated systems for small academic libraries, *Assistant Librarian*, 83 (11), 1990, 163-7.

Offers practical tips for non-specialists, covering reasons for automation, planning and objectives, setting selection criteria, selecting system type, and choosing the system. Also comments on assessing advice from colleagues and communicating with governing bodies.

Duval, B K and Main, L, *Automated library systems: a librarian's guide and teaching manual*, Meckler, 1992.

Useful guide for those new to the management of automated library systems. Separate sections include useful overviews of core system modules and good coverage of different stages in the planning process; also includes a glossary and pointers for further reading.

Pachent, G, Network '95: choosing a third generation automated information system for Suffolk Libraries & Heritage, *Program*, 30 (3) 1996, 213-28.

Explains the rationale and process for system replacement, covering technological and functional criteria, timetable for selection and installation, and evaluation of tenders. Key features included the active involvement of elected councillors, other public library users, library and record office staff, and the broad strategic style of the system specification.

Matthews, J, Moving to the next generation: Aston University's selection and implementation of Galaxy 2000, *VINE*, **101**, 1995, 42-9.

Summarizes the strategic, financial and service case for replacement, describes pre-tender and final evaluation, and comments on implementation in relation to staff training, data conversion and documentation. Includes suggestions on writing operational requirements and advocates using scenarios and end-user tests for evaluation of most critical elements.

Scott Cree, J, *Library systems migration: technical and management considerations*, LITC Report 12, Library Information Technology Centre, 1998.

In-depth examination (70 pp) of the management of systems migration projects in the libraries of ten UK government departments during the mid-1990s. Covers reasons for migration, use of consultants, specification and procurement, selection and evaluation, data conversion and testing, communication and training, with bibliography of 224 items.

Service convergence

Foster, A, The emergence of convergence, *Library Manager*, **11**, 1995, 12-13.

Provides a concise overview, explaining the reasons for convergence, functions typically covered in UK and US universities, and areas where integration offers particular benefits.

Sykes, P and Gerrard, S, Operational convergence at Roehampton Institute London and Liverpool John Moores University, *The New Review of Academic Librarianship*, 3, 1997, 67-85.

Compares experiences at two teaching-led multi-site institutions where library and IT user support (but not hardware, software and networking services) have been operationally and organizationally converged. Covers the reasons for restructuring, forms chosen, problems encountered, impact on people, success of the changes, and appropriateness as a strategy.

Field, C, Building on shifting sands: information age organisations, *Ariadne*, **17**, 1998, 6-7 (full version with references available at **http://www.ariadne.ac.uk/issue18/main/**).

Based on experience of large-scale convergence at the University of Birmingham, covering libraries, IT, computer-based learning, teaching space and language laboratories; considers environmental imperatives of new structures and prerequisites for successful change, with particular emphasis on the flexible deployment of financial, spatial and human resources.

The human element

Sykes, P, Automation and non-professional staff: the neglected majority, *Serials*, 4 (3) 1991, 33-43.

Based on published literature and personal experience at a former polytechnic library, discusses typical reactions of library assistants to the introduction of new technology and suggests ways of managing change successfully, with particular emphasis on management style, sensitive communication, sensible training and proper involvement in the process. (Originally published in *Library Management*, **12** (3) 1991.)

Curry, S and Watson, M, Staff development and training: an IMPEL2 guide, *Personnel Training and Education*, **15** (1), 1998, 9–12.

Introduces the eLib project on the IMpact on People of Electronic Libraries and reproduces the full text (with some additional comments) of the guide on staff development and training for the electronic library. Covers development needs related to IT and to changing rôles, and comments on factors within the institution and in the information service affecting the success of development and training. (The five IMPEL guides are also available at **http://ilm.unn.ac.uk/impel/**.)

Lavagnino, M B, Networking and the role of the academic systems librarian: an evolutionary perspective, *College & Research Libraries*, **58** (3) 1997, 217–31.

Relates the changing rôle of systems specialists in libraries to technological developments evolving from operational responsibility for library housekeeping systems to strategic management of the technical infrastructure, including electronic information services, networks, office applications and a systems team; outlines changes in tasks, knowledge and skills involved.

van der Wait, P W and van Brakel, P A, The Webmaster: a new player in the information centre's online team, *The Electronic Library*, **15** (6) 1997, 447–54.

Discusses the various rôles, skills and tasks of webmaster posts, and suggests six potential contributions to information services: home page design for current awareness and links to essential sources; web-based online searching; search engine selection; push technology/personalized information services; intranets and extranets; and internal database publishing.

Part 3   Managing the organization

7

People management

Introduction

Managing people, formally or informally, is often the most challenging and the most rewarding part of a professional's job. Personnel management has evolved from a largely reactive specialist function to a broader more strategic model, involving service managers in a proactive and collaborative approach to managing and developing staff in a changing environment. This chapter introduces the concept of human resource management and the processes of the staffing life cycle, in the specific context of information and library services. It also covers leadership, motivation, teamwork, disciplinary issues and changes in employment patterns, with reference to both management and library practice.

Employment changes

As with the other areas we have considered, two key themes run through any consideration of staff management in information services today - the management of change, and the need for vision.

Change affects all aspects of staff management. As we have already seen, technological change has had an effect on the day-to-day working practice of virtually all information service staff, has informed the demands and expectations of our users, and revolutionized the options available to staff for collection and service development and promotion. Economic constraint has brought a move to flatter management structures, an increase in teamwork and a pronounced change in the tasks undertaken by paraprofessional staff and library assistants. Other environmental factors mean that the 'world of work' has changed more generally. Job security has decreased and fixed-term contracts have become commonplace: the job – or even career – for life has become largely a thing of the past. 'Employability', rather than employment, has become the imperative. The numbers of smaller employers and self-employed people have risen, as has the number of women in the work-force. Trends look set to continue in this direction in the UK, with the new Labour Government removing tax/benefit barriers to employment so that Britain can become a 'high work' society.

We can therefore anticipate an increasingly flexible approach by employers to staff recruitment and deployment. The distinction between full-time and part-time work is becoming blurred, with organizations using whatever time they can buy from trained people, negotiated on an individual basis. Likewise, the boundary between retirement and paid work (already largely eroded in Japan) is being softened, as people 'retire' then go straight into some other (part-time) work. The division between full-time education and full-time work is also disappearing: already, many 'full-time' students work long hours in paid employment; and it is becoming increasingly common for people with full-time jobs to be undergoing additional programmes of training outside the workplace. Other changes are happening in the fields of voluntary work and self-employment, which are emerging as 'add-ons' to the working week. All these changes can only be successfully accommodated by organizations with a bottom-up flexible approach to management rather than a top-down command style. Altogether they make management even more challenging.

The need for flexibility and staff development programmes to facilitate the successful management of change in library and information services has already been widely recognized, notably in the Follett report which observed that 'failure to provide staff with adequate training and to deploy them effectively represents one of the single most important constraints on change and development in library and information provision.'[1] The first five sections of the SKIP report all consider IT training against a background of wider environmental change, and the *New library* report explicitly states the need for staff training to make the proposed 'people's network' a success.[2-3]

Equally important in a time of change (and potential confusion) is a clear, well communicated vision. We have already shown how the mission and objectives of the parent body should translate down into the information service's mission and *operational* objectives. Nowhere is this more important than in people management, especially at a time of change when clarity is needed to steer the individual through what can often feel like a sea of chaos. Departmental goals, targets and priorities should be reflected in the individual's job description and forward plan, which (in turn) should provide the basis of performance management and staff appraisal programmes, ensure that staff development is 'relevant' and (ideally) inform reward schemes. All of this needs to be managed as part of the wider strategic management of the organization.

Management trends

Recent years have seen a shift from the concept of personnel management to that of human resource management (HRM). **Personnel management** traditionally provides a reactive approach to the 'problem' of staff management: staff are viewed as the organization's biggest expense and merely a means to an end; and staff development is a way of solving some of these problems. **Human resource management,** in contrast, views staff as the organization's greatest asset and accordingly sees staff training and development as investment in that asset. Furthermore, it is a *strategic* approach, as explained by Michael Armstrong:

> HRM is a strategic approach to the acquisition, motivation, development and management of the organisation's human resources. It is devoted to shaping an appropriate corporate culture, and introducing programmes which reflect and support the core values of the enterprise and ensure its success. HRM is proactive rather than reactive, ie always looking forward to what needs to be done and then doing it, rather than waiting to be told what to do - about

recruiting, paying or training people or dealing with employee relations problems as they arise.[4]

In the real world, this is not the only management model in operation, and
any investigation of the literature will reveal a wide spectrum of views on
the behaviour of both managers and managed.

Managers and leaders

Much of the literature uses the terms 'management' and 'leadership' interchangeably. Allen Veaner, for example, discusses the qualities of the
leader/manager/administrator/boss without distinguishing between the
rôles.[5] Robin Middlehurst and Lewis Elton, on the other hand, offer a clear
distinction: **management** is defined in terms of policy execution, resource
deployment, procedural planning and coordination and organization of
local units; **leadership** is defined at a more institutional level in terms of
developing and directing strategy, articulating and promoting the strategic
vision, and generating confidence and cohesion. The 'leader' rôle is particularly important in the management of change.[6] From this definition it is
clear that the two rôles will often coincide in an individual, be that a senior,
unit or team manager.

Styles of management similarly spawn different views. Smith identifies
two kinds of leadership: *power* leadership and *influence* (or Socratic) leadership: **power leaders** are strong individuals around whom the organization
revolves; **influence leaders** bring change by sitting down with the person
doing the job to learn and adapt that job. The influence leader can accept
leadership from below, so leadership and delegation become joint factors.[7]
Smith's models mirror Rensis Likert's analysis of *authoritative* and *participative* management styles.[8] More generally, management styles can be
placed in three broad categories:

- **autocratic** – one person takes control and makes all the decisions
- **democratic** – decisions are made with the full involvement of the team
- **laissez-faire** – a total hands-off approach, allowing the team/individuals
  to make decisions with complete freedom.

It is important to note there are many variations within these categories, and that a democratic/participative style is more likely to mean full consultation than total democracy or majority rule.

ACTIVITY

Consider your experience of different styles of management. Which styles worked and why? How did different members of staff react to each style? What are the principal benefits/drawbacks of autocratic, democratic and laissez-faire management styles? Is a particular style more appropriate than others in some decision-making situations?

PERSONAL QUALITIES

Different managers will approach the difficult task of management with the styles which they consider most appropriate for themselves and their organizations. But what qualities make a good manager? Warren Bennis and Bert Nanus, in their 1985 study of 90 successful US corporate leaders identified four 'kernels of truth' that seemed to characterize all the leaders interviewed:

- **attention through vision** – an intense belief in the mission of the organization
- **meaning through communication** – the skill to articulate (usually the vision) and listen
- **trust through positioning** – an ability to be consistent and hence develop trust
- **positive self regard** – an undeniable (and usually non-egotistical) self-confidence.[9]

Sheldon's follow-up study (1987-90) of the library and information sector found that of the 61 senior managers interviewed, all exhibited these four essential qualities. Additional to these, though, was a 'passion for the profession', something lacking in the corporate sector.[10] Other commentators have produced more comprehensive lists of high-level skills required for successful leadership/management. For example, Middlehurst lists the following areas: communication, presentation, negotiation, committee work, judging/assessing, interpersonal, planning/objective setting, financial management, counselling, leading by example, listening, decision-making, delegating, political ability, research/scholarship, motivation, public relations, teaching/training, and holding a group together.[11]

Motivation

'Perhaps the greatest challenge for the library and information manager . . . is managing and motivating staff at a time of rapid and continual change'. Thus Beryl Morris succinctly highlights one of the key concerns facing the information service manager today.[12] Human beings are complex, and the staff manager needs to accept that he/she will always be learning! Having acknowledged that, we should think about our approach to staff management, and it is worth considering motivation and management theories in this context.

MOTIVATION IN THEORY

As management theory has turned away from the 'classical school' (which views organizations as machines and human feelings as irrelevant) to the 'human relations school', more time has been devoted to the issue of motivation, which is part of the equation for success. Successful performance requires *ability* (the technical skill to perform a task), *clarity* of objectives (an understanding of what we as individuals, a team and an organization are aiming to achieve), *resources* (the people, tools and money to complete a task) and *motivation*. No matter how able your staff, how clearly your vision is communicated, and how much money you invest in your activities, without high levels of motivation you will not get high levels of performance.

The question of how to motivate staff is not an easy one to answer, despite the quantity of literature on this subject. Early theories held human kind in low regard; for example, Frederick Winslow Taylor's 'scientific management' at the turn of this century saw greed and fear as the prime motivators for any workforce. But in the 1920s, Elton Mayo proved that taking an interest in working conditions – and hence the welfare of the staff themselves – was more effective in increasing contentment and output. (This was the birth of the 'human relations' school.) More recently, the most influential thinkers have stressed that staff are usually motivated more by job satisfaction, the feeling of being valued or by opportunities for self-fulfilment, than by mere money alone. In the 1950s, Abraham Maslow's 'hierarchy of needs' suggested that as long as our *physical* and *safety* needs are met, we cease to be motivated by money. Frederick Herzberg went even further in the 1960s, stating that money only affected morale when it was missing.

MOTIVATION IN PRACTICE

So how can we motivate our staff in practice? The first thing to recognize is that not everyone is motivated in the same way, and (most certainly) not everyone is motivated in the same way as his or her manager! Many managers, for example, subscribe to Douglas McGregor's 'Theory Y' which states that work is a natural, enjoyable activity and that people seek to direct themselves where possible; while some members of staff seem to subscribe to 'Theory X' and prefer to be told what to do. Bearing this in mind, what steps can you take to *try* to improve motivation? Few information service managers have direct control over pay and conditions of employment, but other factors can be influenced.

Maslow's **safety** need can be satisfied with adequate training, communication and feedback to make the individual feel more confident in the post. Physical safety and working conditions should also be given attention to make staff feel 'at home' in the workplace. The **social** need can be met with effective teamwork to develop a group identity and a sense of belonging for the individual. The need for **self-esteem** can be addressed by remembering to say 'thank you' (as long as it is sincere and appropriate) and providing *effective* feedback. Managers should celebrate the successes of individuals in newsletters and annual reports; for example, the Southern Methodist University Libraries in Texas has run a well-publicized 'Library Staff Recognition Awards' programme to praise and reward able and motivated staff in a time of economic constraint.[13] Christmas parties (paid for by senior managers) can both show gratitude – especially if it has been a difficult year – and foster team spirit. Finally, invest in your staff for their own **self-actualization**. Staff development programmes should allow individuals to develop transferable skills to broaden their repertoire, to improve the quality of their working life in your organization and give them scope to develop professionally. Promoting a 'fun at work' ethos can combat stress, and also satisfy both the social and (more importantly) the creative needs of team members. Some of these issues are covered in more detail later in this chapter.

REFLECTION

What motivates you? How has this changed (if at all) over recent years? From observation, are your colleagues motivated in different ways?

Teamwork

As already suggested, effective staff management today invariably equals effective team management. Teams have been used in British public libraries since the early 1970s and are now increasingly common in academic libraries, as advocated in the Fielden report commissioned as part of the Joint Funding Councils' Libraries Review.[14] The working papers on university library staffing structures published by SCONUL, show a range of diverse frameworks, most comprising subject, technical or locational teams.[15] With the move to flatter management structures, the greater utilization of paraprofessional staff and the trend towards service convergence, the need to develop teamworking skills looks set to become even more important in the future.

ACTIVITY

What is the staffing structure in your organization? Produce a representation of the structure in diagrammatic form. What (in your opinion) are its strengths/weaknesses?

So what do we really mean by 'teams'? Whereas a **group** is merely a collection of individuals with a common interest or theme, a **team** has a *common purpose* – a team works together in joint action towards a particular goal. Teams consist of *complementary individuals*, and the whole should be greater and more effective than the sum of the parts. This is an important concept to grasp, especially for the manager concerned with staff selection. Just as a football team would not flourish if it were made up of eleven strikers or eleven goalkeepers, so effective information service teams need an effective combination of rôle players. The psychologist

Meredith Belbin has identified eight rôles which he considers must be covered in every successful team, with the following *qualities*:

- **resource investigator** – extroverted, enthusiastic, curious, communicative; *willing to explore new ideas and respond well to a challenge*
- **completer-finisher** – painstaking, orderly, conscientious, anxious; *capacity for following ideas through and perfectionism*
- **teamworker** – socially orientated, rather mild and sensitive; *ability to respond to people and situations well and to promote team spirit*
- **monitor-evaluator** – sober, unemotional, prudent; *judgment, discretion and hard-headedness*
- **plant** – individualistic, serious-minded, unorthodox; *imagination, intellect and knowledge*
- **shaper** – highly strung, outgoing, dynamic; *drive and willingness to challenge inertia and resistance*
- **chair** – calm, self-confident, controlled; *capable of welcoming all ideas on their merits, with a firm vision of over-riding objectives*
- **company worker** – conservative, dutiful, predictable; *organizational ability, common sense, hard work and self-discipline.*[16]

Observation of any team should reveal most, if not all, of these rôle players. Some people will function in more than one rôle, and function in different rôles at different times. Understanding these rôles should help to make the staff manager more tolerant of different team players and more appreciative of their worth. This framework may also help the manager to understand the dysfunctional team.

REFLECTION

What are the benefits of teamwork? From your experience, what promotes or prevents teamwork? How can this be addressed?

The staffing life cycle

We can use our familiar planning cycle/life cycle approach (as illustrated in Figure 7.1) to focus on some of the practical aspects of people manage-

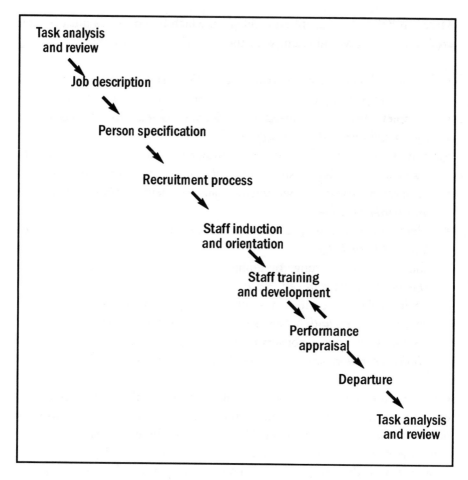

Fig. 7.1   *The staffing life cycle*

ment. The following sections concentrate on the key processes of selection, development, appraisal and departure of staff, before moving on to consider some of the difficulties that can arise in the workplace.

Staff selection

A lot of time needs to be devoted to staff selection procedures, as the effectiveness of any information service depends largely on the ability of the manager to select the right people to make up the team. When someone leaves your team, the first question to ask is 'do we need to replace that person at all?'[17] Your options include:

- **not replacing the person at all** – hardly an option in these lean days, when few services have any fat to live off
- **promoting an existing member of staff** – excellent for motivation and morale, less good for new ideas
- **transferring an existing member of staff as a 'sideways move'** – good for personal development
- **recruiting someone from outside the organization** – to bring 'new blood' into the team
- **redesigning the job** – in these days of constant change this is increasingly becoming the Number One Option
- **leaving the job the same** – and this is increasingly no option at all.

It is essential to give considerable time to thinking about the future of the post. (Effective managers think ahead and have ideas in readiness for resignations.) It is also important to bear in mind that the organizational processes of producing a job description, advertising the post, short-listing, obtaining references, interviewing, and actually getting someone (who will usually have to work out a period of notice) into post takes a *significant* amount of time. It is worth considering whether you can take on extra hours (within your staffing budget), possibly from existing part-time staff, to cover basic duties in order to reduce pressures on you and the team to make rushed decisions.

JOB DESCRIPTIONS, PERSON SPECIFICATIONS AND RECRUITMENT ADVERTISEMENTS

Once you have decided upon the direction, nature and scope of the (new) post, this needs to be documented. A **job description** must describe specific requirements of the post and reflect the objectives and priorities of the service as a whole. A typical job description includes:

- **job title/grading**
- **overall purpose** – the main aims of the post

- **reporting relationships** – who the postholder will report to, and who the postholder will line-manage or supervise
- **specific responsibilities** – the operational (functional) objectives, generally set out in a series of short paragraphs
- **general responsibilities** – including a 'catch-all clause' for any other unspecified duties that management may reasonably require
- **additional information** – such as the expected hours of service and where the post is primarily based.

The job description should be supported by a **person specification** which outlines the qualifications, expertise and other attributes required to carry out the post. Characteristics are often divided into **essential** and **desirable**, and these should be *measurable* and *non-discriminatory* – for example, instead of demanding a 'good general education' alone, qualify this with 'four GCSEs [*measurable*] or equivalent [*non-discriminatory* against older applicants, overseas applicants, etc]'.

The third stage of this process is to produce the **recruitment advertisement.**

ACTIVITY

Look at job advertisements in (1) specialist information and librarianship publications; (2) national newspaper supplements covering your wider sectoral field – for example, education, public services, health care; (3) national newspaper supplements covering other non-related fields – for example, business, the media. Which ones do you consider to be good advertisements? Which ones do you consider to be bad? Why? What can be done to improve our advertisements? Can we learn anything from employers in other fields?

Other recruitment channels used in addition to (or as an alternative to) advertising include specialist agencies, searching/head-hunting, speculative applications and word-of-mouth; advertisements in specialist journals and local/national newspapers remain the predominant method in public sector information services, but often supplemented with web advertising.

SELECTION METHODS

To find the individual who best meets your person specification you will have recourse to several means:

- **applications** – does your organization favour CVs or application forms? Which is more useful for the *selector*?
- **references** – consider what is covered . . . and what is missed out
- **tests** – consider how appropriate they are to the actual tasks the postholder will be expected to carry out
- **interviews** – what problems can you foresee regarding excessive nerves . . . or slickness?

When planning interviews, preparation is of the utmost importance. If an interview programme has several parts (such as informal interview, test, formal interview), timetable candidates to ensure that individuals do not have to wait around for long periods of time between the interview elements. In the formal part of a panel interview, the chair should welcome the candidate, introduce the panel members (and explain in what capacity each member is attending), re-affirm the purpose of the interview, and give some indication of its structure and anticipated length. The panellists should discuss what kinds of questions they intend to ask before the interview; this does not always happen! No interview can be tied to asking exactly the same questions, but a standard approach should be applied where possible to ensure fairness. A typical structure for a post combining client liaison with technical work is given in Figure 7.2.

TERMS AND CONDITIONS OF EMPLOYMENT

Managers need to be familiar with the terms and conditions of employment in their organizations. These can range from policy on smoking through disciplinary procedures to pension benefits. Policy documents (often included in a staff handbook) should be widely publicized. In the wider arena, staff managers should be familiar with equal opportunities legislation and practices, and support programmes to combat both direct and indirect discrimination in the workplace. Although libraries, as stores of great thought, may seem like liberal havens, they are not always so. **Sexual harassment** does happen in libraries, as Will Manley was surprised to discover,[18] and racism is alive and kicking, as Deborah Curry has so bleakly displayed.[19] While professional organizations can (and do) exercise leadership

```
1  Welcome — by panel chair
2  Introductions and explanations — by panel chair
3  CV-based questions, about career to date and achievements
   (to put candidate at ease and investigate any significant gaps)
4  Job-related liaison questions — from relevant panel member
5  Job-related technical questions — from relevant panel member
6  Wider professional/organizational questions, if appropriate
7  Outline of terms and conditions of employment
   — generally by personnel representative or panel chair
8  Opportunity for questions from the candidate
9  Closing formalities — chair asks if candidate is still interested
   and checks where s/he can be contacted in the immediate future
10 Close — chair thanks candidate and says goodbye
```

Fig. 7.2   *Example of an interview plan*

in this area, it is up to individual managers to ensure equality of opportunity becomes a reality.

Activity

What is the equal opportunities policy of your organization? How are equal opportunities supported in your library or information service?

Staff development

If we employed every member of staff with the right skill mix, if the world of work and technology was not constantly changing, if the needs of our customers and demands of our stakeholders remained static, and if we did not believe in HRM concepts or the human relations school's motivation theories, then we would probably not need to worry about staff development! A staff development programme is essential if we are to make effective and efficient use of staff, and to provide them with the skills to succeed in an ever-changing environment. Much has been written on this theme in the information services context over the last few years and managers are finally starting to accept that a training budget used up by a few keen individuals does not constitute a staff development policy. A service-

wide approach with support from senior management is essential if initiatives are to succeed. Funding and staff time must be set aside. Commonly
used guidelines are at least 2% of payroll and 5% of staff time (as recommended by Fielden) - but such statements do not properly acknowledge
that a large proportion of development activity takes place on or around
the job, rather than through planned formal events.

TRAINING NEEDS ANALYSIS

Training Needs Analysis (TNA) allows the organization to examine systematically who needs what training. This can be done using an individual (task
and job analysis) or service-wide (organizational analysis) approach. Task
analysis and job analysis measure the 'training gap' between the person
specification and the postholder's skills. Needs can be identified by interviews with staff, individual questionnaires, group forums, discussions with
stakeholders (managers, customers, colleagues in other departments), tests,
and observations. Organizational analysis identifies service developments
or environmental changes that will create training needs for whole or large
parts of organizations. The benefit of this approach is that training needs
can be anticipated before the change has taken place.

The TNA approach means that relevant training can be offered to all
staff regardless of level and job content. Historically, some groups of library
staff have fared far better than others when it came to opportunities for
development. New staff invariably benefit from induction and orientation
training. In the UK, candidates for chartership of the Library Association
will often have a specially constructed in-house programme. Professionally
qualified staff are generally offered an array of conferences and visits which
their employer will pay for (in terms of both expenses and staff time). But,
as Fielden recognized, some staff have been neglected in the past: senior
staff are often expected to rely on common sense and experience; while
paraprofessional staff and library assistants have had fewer opportunities
than the professionally qualified. However, many UK institutions (particularly in the public library sector, but increasingly in the academic sector)
have positively embraced National Vocational Qualifications (NVQs) as a
way of redressing the balance. Despite some misgivings about the lack of
theoretical underpinning to provide truly transferable skills, most commentators recognize that NVQs offer staff lacking formal qualifications a

valuable opportunity to receive documented proof of their abilities.

ACTIVITY

What formal options are there for staff development in your organization? How much is involvement in staff development initiatives left to the individual? What works best in your opinion, and why? How can this be managed to get the best results for both individuals and the organization? Consider these questions with reference to the following headings and examples.

LIBRARY TRAINING EVENTS
- induction programmes
- orientation programmes
- lectures/talks
- seminars/workshops
- weekly training hour
- visits to other departments.

ON-THE-JOB DEVELOPMENT
- job rotation
- shadowing
- project work
- meetings
- quality circles
- coaching
- delegation
- mentorship networks.

PROFESSIONAL ACTIVITIES
- conferences
- exhibitions
- evening meetings.

SELF-PACED LEARNING
- guided reading
- interactive media
- distance learning
- formal qualifications (eg ALA, MBA, NVQs).

VISITS
- attending
- hosting.

Staff appraisal

'Staff appraisal, like the hydrogen bomb, was an American invention that emerged at the time of the Second World War.'[20] As Andrew Green's comment suggests, staff appraisal is not always highly regarded by information professionals. Such schemes often provoke hostile reactions (in the same manner as quality audits) as they invariably raise fears of punishment rather than praise. More specifically, opposition can arise because of a lack of clear purpose and the fact that seemingly time-consuming and cumbersome official procedures loom once a year with no evident link to day-to-day activities. In these circumstances, appraisal is at best seen as a time-wasting paper exercise; at worst, it is something that might one day be held against you! Effective staff appraisal and review should not function like this. Much of the apprehension about appraisal comes from misconceptions about it. So what is appraisal, what is it for, and how can we use it?

APPRAISAL IN THEORY

Formal staff appraisal should be part of a wider programme of staff review, offering positive and constructive feedback, and stimulating professional and personal development. Staff appraisal fits into this wider framework, but is at the same time separate. It is significant in that it provides a *formal* and *documented* system to allow for the *periodic* review of an individual's *performance*. It should be developmental in its aims, rather than punitive. It should provide benefits to the *individual* (primarily, in the shape of rôle, task and priorities clarification, target-setting and feedback), to the *line manager* (for example, in developing teamwork and problem-solving to increase the efficiency of the team) and to the *organization* as a whole (providing a forum for clarifying the vision and current priorities of the service) and this must all take place within the strategic and operational framework of the organization. As Verrill has so rightly stated:

Appraisal ought to be an essential and fully integrated part of academic library management. The library employee is entitled to know what the organisation's goals are, what role she or he is expected to play, how effectively she or he may contribute to those goals and what the employee should do to make future contributions even better.[21]

As with any element of management, effective appraisals can only come from effective planning. There are several general questions that we need to answer: who should carry out appraisal? How often should it be done? What outcome do we want? Do we employ scales or grading? It is generally agreed that appraisal should be a function of line management. (If you are appraising too many people, then you are line-managing too many people.) Frequency will probably be dictated by the procedures of your organization, but as a manager you need to consider how organizational appraisals fit into your own schemes of performance review. Methods and outcomes will be dictated in part by your organization, but mostly by the objectives of the process.

Appraisal in practice

So what do we need to make appraisals work? The primary requirement is clear objectives – this is the key to success. Gerry Randell has highlighted three main types of review: *performance review*, mainly used for improving performance through staff development; *potential review*, which concentrates on future rôles; and *reward review*, used as the basis of performance-related pay schemes.[22] It is vital that everyone is absolutely clear about the **purpose** to avoid confusion and disenchantment. Other success factors include:

- sufficient **time** for preparation, discussion and follow-up
- a **system** that is easily understood and easy to operate
- informed, involved and committed **appraisees**
- skilled and committed **appraisers**
- the right **atmosphere** with regard to environment and philosophy
- follow-up **action** – the appraisal discussion should be the beginning, rather than the end of the process

- maintenance and **review** of the appraisal system – as always, we need to monitor, review and reform systems, employing a planning cycle approach.

Appraisal discussions – this term is preferred to 'interviews', with their rather negative connotations – should be tailored to meet the needs of the individual, but they will often have a similar format. Good *preparation* is vital. Both appraiser and appraisee need a clear timetable to plan for the discussion. The appraiser should also plan the environment to ensure the discussion can take place in a neutral location, with suitable seating arrangements and no disturbances. It is essential that the appraiser (acting as 'chair' of the meeting) should signify when the discussion formally starts and ends. Building an agenda will allow for the clarification (and, if necessary, grouping) of items for discussion. This can also help focus action points at the end. The appraisee should be encouraged to talk with open questions, and the appraiser must resist the temptation to jump in with 'helpful' suggestions if answers are not swiftly forthcoming. Effective feedback is essential: any criticism should be constructive; all praise must be specific, not just the 'You've all done very well!' approach.[23] Objectives for agreed future action must also be specific, measurable, realistic and given a timescale for achievement. After the meeting, a record should be written up and given to the appraisee to agree, with the opportunity to add his or her own comments.

REFLECTION

What is the purpose of staff appraisal in your organization? Considering theoretical and practical implications, what are the benefits/drawbacks of reward review appraisals?

Staff departure

As we have seen, the departure of a member of staff allows us to review posts, and hence the make-up and structure of the team. Two practical issues need further consideration:

- **Exit interviews.** Do you automatically hold interviews or offer them to the willing departee?

- **Farewell parties.** Often overlooked, this should be a prime concern for the manager of staff.

Leaving parties allow you to say a final 'thank you' and allow all the team (and other colleagues) to say 'goodbye'. They also have the additional function of reinforcing social cohesion at a time of upheaval and stress.

REFLECTION

What are the benefits of exit interviews? Are there any drawbacks?

People problems

Dealing with 'the difficult member of staff' is one of the most challenging tasks for a manager - especially for the individual new to management, who may be much younger than those he/she is supervising. Staff 'problems' are as many and complex as the number and variety of human beings, but there are common manifestations of trouble: poor or variable performance, in terms of both quality and quantity; lateness and absenteeism; rudeness to colleagues and customers; irrational judgments and erratic work patterns. Teams - and team members - have always faced difficulties from time to time, but today's environmental pressures have made this problem more acute. Rapid technological and structural changes in organizations have raised stress levels. Lack of job security, the effects of the (mis)management of change and a general feeling of uncertainty about the future mean that the already stretched manager will have even more staffing issues with which to deal. The workplace is becoming more 'emotional' for all of us.

The 'solution' is both simple and complex: **communicate.** The individual new to management may feel he/she ends up 'wasting' a lot of time talking with his/her staff, but this reaches the essence of why we are employed. Dysfunctional behaviour is the manifestation of personal unhappiness. As managers we must:

- resolve to take action - we all hate conflict and most of us will find any reason to put off confronting the problem, but procrastination is rarely the best policy here

- recognize symptoms, before they become aggravated
- consider causes, before we take action – are there motivational problems? a mismatch between the individual and the task? conflict with other team members? management, environmental or health-related issues? personal problems?
- carry out a counselling interview, to understand the problem and provide (where possible) an agreed strategy to overcome difficulties
- monitor success in an allotted time.

The 'mechanistic' school would argue that a manager should counsel his/her staff purely in terms of work-centred problems (considering the definition of rôles, abilities and skills, training needs, the use of appraisal schemes, and so on) and discussions about underlying causes should not be encouraged. However, some observers feel that we need to go much further than this: the 'organic' school advocates a more person-centred approach to understand problems fully, arguing that as tensions rise in teams we need to take on the rôle of a counsellor – or even a therapist, 'managers must acknowledge their therapeutic rôle and be prepared to apply a variety of interpersonal skills regardless of their genuineness, and to create institutional structures that will promote the personal self-fulfilment of staff as a primary goal of the organization.'[24] Librarians are thus becoming increasingly aware of the need for stress management, and workshops on this theme are becoming more commonplace.[25-6]

ACTIVITY

Workplace stress can arise for a number of reasons. Consider the following list of common stress factors. What experience do you have of any of these in your team or personally? How could such difficulties be tackled? What problems can you envisage in dealing with them?

- overwork
- inadequate resources
- unrealistic expectations and demands
- interpersonal relationships (with colleagues, managers, customers)
- conflict of rôles
- change/management of change

- feelings of (job) insecurity
- working conditions
- working hours
- lack of job satisfaction.

Managing absence

As previously mentioned, one common manifestation of stress or unhappiness is extended staff absence. Managers in general – and library managers in particular – do not like acting on issues relating to staff absenteeism. We naturally feel that the manager who tackles absence – no matter how liberal and caring that person might be – will be considered Draconian, and any staff who are tackled in this respect are in effect being called liars and malingerers. But managing absence is an essential part of a line manager's function, along with staff selection, training and development, and other elements of HRM. Not tackling absenteeism can be costly. The UK Confederation of British Industry recently estimated the average cost of absence per employee at £553 per year in the public sector.[27] On top of this are the hidden costs of stress amongst the remaining staff, reduced morale across the team and increased staff turnover. If absenteeism is tackled properly, team members can spend less time covering for colleagues, and managers can devote less time to 'fire-fighting' and more to planning and developing services.

ACTIVITY

The return to work interview has been described as the cornerstone of successful absence management.[28] What procedures are in force in your organization? How could absenteeism be more effectively managed? What barriers do you envisage to any proposed policy?

Disciplinary procedures

Sometimes managers will have to discipline a member of staff formally. No-one likes to embark on this path and such steps should be taken only as a last resort. Fortunately, if the manager addresses the situation at an early stage, tackles the problem rather than the person, talks and (most importantly) listens, most potential disciplinary problems can be successfully dealt with before recourse to formal procedures is needed. If such procedures are judged necessary, it is essential to work closely with colleagues in personnel/human resource departments and adhere strictly to institutional and legal guidelines.

References

1 Joint Funding Councils' Libraries Review Group, *Report*, The Councils, 1993 (Chairman: Professor Sir Brian Follett).
2 Garrod, P and Sidgreaves, I, *SKIP: skills for new information professionals*, University of Plymouth, 1998.
3 Library and Information Commission, *New library: the people's network*, Library and Information Commission, 1997 (available at http://www.ukoln.ac.uk/services/lic/newlibrary/).
4 Armstrong, M, *A handbook of human resource management*, Kogan Page, 1988.
5 Veaner, A, *Academic librarianship in a transformational age: program, politics and personnel*, G K Hall & Co, 1990.
6 Middlehurst, R and Elton, L, Leadership and management in higher education, *Studies in Higher Education*, **17** (3), 1992, 251-64.
7 Smith, J, Living in interesting times: the management of change. In White, A G D and Taylor, A F (eds) *Peebles '82: proceedings of the 68th annual conference of the Scottish Library Association, 3-6 May 1982*, Scottish Library Association, 1982, 57-64.
8 Likert, R, *New patterns of management*, McGraw-Hill, 1960.
9 Bennis, W and Nanus, B, *Leaders: the strategies for taking charge*, Harper & Row, 1985.
10 Sheldon, B, Library leaders: attributes compared to corporate leaders, *Library Trends*, **40** (3), 1992, 391-401.
11 Middlehurst, R, Management and leadership development in universities: what's happening and where are we going? In Eggins, H (ed) *Restructuring higher education: proceedings of the annual conference, 1987*, Society for Research in Higher Education and Open University Press, 1988, 137-50.

12 Morris, B, *First steps in management*, Library Association Publishing, 1996, 10.

13 Pastine, M and Searles, J, Library staff recognition awards, *The Bottom Line*, 7 (2), 1993, 12-14.

14 John Fielden Consultancy, *Supporting expansion: a report on human resource management in academic libraries, for the Joint Funding Councils' Libraries Review Group*, The Councils, 1993.

15 Priestley, J (ed) *Staffing structures*, SCONUL Working Papers, Standing Conference of National and University Libraries, 1996.

16 Belbin, M, *Management teams*, Heinemann, 1981.

17 Jago, A, Selecting your team: how to find the right people, *Librarian Career Development*, 4 (3), 1996, 27-31.

18 Manley, W, Librarians and sex, *Wilson Library Bulletin*, 66 (10), 1992, 66; No laughing matter this month: sexual harassment by library patrons, *American Libraries*, 24 (1), 1993, 68; Sexual harassment by patrons: part two, *American Libraries*, 24 (7), 1993, 652; Sexual harassment by patrons: part three, *American Libraries*, 24 (8), 1993, 756.

19 Curry, D A, Your worries ain't like mine: African American librarians and the pervasiveness of racism, prejudice and discrimination in academe, *Reference Librarian*, 45/46, 1994, 299-311.

20 Green, A, Staff appraisal in university libraries, *Library and Information Research News*, 18 (60), 1994, 34-8.

21 Verrill, P E, Performance appraisal for the 1990s: managerial threat or professional right? *British Journal of Academic Librarianship*, 8 (2), 1993, 98-112.

22 Randell, G, Packard, P and Slater, J, *Staff appraisal: a first step to effective leadership*, 3rd edn, Institute of Personnel Management, 1984.

23 Fowler, A, How to: provide effective feedback, *People Management*, 11 July 1996, 44-5.

24 Birdsall, W F, The library manager as therapist, *Journal of Academic Librarianship*, 16 (4), 1990, 209-12.

25 Ollendorff, M, How much do librarians know about stress management? *Behavioral and Social Sciences Librarian*, 8 (1/2), 1989, 67-98.

26 For example, 'Managing workplace stress' run by the Burrington Partnership (e-mail: partners@burrington.prestel.co.uk).

27 Confederation of British Industry, *Managing absence*, Confederation of British Industry, 1997.

28 Brewerton, A, In sickness and in health?: managing absence, *SCONUL Newsletter*, **15**, 1998, 30-2.

Suggestions for further reading

Armstrong, M, *Human resource management: strategy and action*, Kogan Page, 1992.

Compact text (c230 pp) defines HRM and considers its scope, philosophy and how it differs from personnel management. Discusses contribution of HRM at the corporate level, and strategic and operational issues, such as change management, organizational commitment, performance management, reward strategies and the rôle of HR/personnel specialists.

British Journal of Academic Librarianship, **9** (3), 1994, 145-242.

Special issue devoted to the Fielden report and HRM, which contains eight articles providing critical comment on issues raised by the report and related topics, including an article by John Fielden. Subjects covered include HRM, NVQs, management development, team management, and the rôle of the library staff development and training manager.

Jordan, P with Jones, N, *Staff management in library and information work*, 3rd edn, Gower, 1995.

Comprehensive book (c265 pp) which covers general areas such as 'the working environment' and background themes (including an extensive chapter on motivation theory and job satisfaction) in addition to the practicalities of day-to-day people management. Includes useful checklists covering staff development and supervision/interpersonal skills.

Johnson, P, Managing changing roles: professional and paraprofessional staff in libraries, *Journal of Library Administration*, **22** (2/3), 1996, 79-99.

Defines the differences between professionals and paraprofessionals (a high-level subset of support staff) and discusses their changing rôles, responsibilities and relationships. Considers the causes and consequences of these changes and suggests ways to manage them effectively, with reference to published literature based on practical experience.

Motivation

Herzberg, F, One more time: how do you motivate employees, *Harvard Business Review*, 87 (5), 1987, 109-20.

Classic article and best-selling reprint (1.2 million copies) originally published in 1968. Reviews nine personnel practices developed to instil motivation (but ultimately ineffective) and then explains the difference between 'hygiene' and 'motivator' factors and suggests seven principles and ten practical steps towards achieving motivation via job enrichment.

Teamwork

Bluck, R, *Team management*, Library Training Guides, Library Association Publishing, 1996.

Concise practical guide (c50 pp) which explains the concept and potential benefits of a team structure before considering the training needed for effective implementation. Covers awareness and skills training for team members and leaders, team-building, and team development (including a short section on how teams can survive in a converged structure).

Shaughnessy, T W, The library director as change agent, *Journal of Library Administration*, 22 (2/3), 1996, 43-56.

Reviews the recent past in the library and information services sector, outlines some of the difficulties involved in developing teams and offers some strategies for overcoming them.

Staff selection

Birdsall, D G, Recruiting academic librarians: how to find and hire the best candidates, *Journal of Academic Librarianship*, 17 (5), November 1991, 276-83.

Written from an academic perspective, but contains messages and tips relevant to all information services; covers all stages of recruitment, emphasizing the marketing aspect.

Parry, J, *Recruitment*, Library Training Guides, Library Association Publishing, 1994.

A short but comprehensive guide (c60 pp), providing a practical introduction for managers which takes the reader through all stages of

recruitment from job analysis, job descriptions and person specifications to recruitment, selection processes, decision-making and follow-
up, and concludes with 20 pages of real-world examples of library
recruitment documentation.

Staff development

Noon, P, Starting from scratch: developing a staff training and development
programme in an academic library, *Personnel Training and Education*,
9 (3), 1992, 65-71.
Provides tips on how to develop a successful programme, emphasizing
the need for a clear vision and sound objectives if training is to be relevant and integral to the library's activities, rather than viewed as a 'bolt
on' by staff.

Oldroyd, M (ed) *Staff development in academic libraries: present practice
and future challenges*, Library Association Publishing, 1996.
Collection of essays, partly responding to the Fielden report.
Background sections include Patricia Partington's overview of changes
in higher education, Nik Pollard's review of learning models and Julie
Parry's concise 'Who?/What?/Why?' of continuing professional development. Other chapters focus specifically on the development of
library assistants (by Phil Sykes), subject librarians (by Robert Bluck)
and chief librarians (by Pat Noon).

Whetherly, J, *Management of training and staff development*, Library
Training Guides, Library Association Publishing, 1997.
Provides a compact overview of factors relevant to planning and
organizing training and development programmes, including practical
guidance on formulating policy, identifying needs, selecting methods,
assessing outcomes and clarifying responsibilities. Appendix reproduces
actual examples of library and information service policies and programmes.

Paterson, K and Munro, J, The training hour at Reading University Library,
SCONUL Newsletter, 14, 1998, 32-9.
Describes the practicalities of planning and organizing a weekly train-
ing hour programme for more than 100 staff at a university library.
Reproduces a sample timetable and example of publicity material and
reports with candour some of the challenges encountered.

NVQs

Stott, H, A quick guide to achieving information and library services NVQs, *Managing Information*, 3 (3), 1996, 36-8.

Defines competence in the context of NVQs, explains how these awards are structured and the type of evidence required for assessment, and lists ten benefits of following this route.

Lewis, N, Level 4 NVQs: an alternative route to professional status?, *Library Association Record*, **101** (2), 1999, 94-6.

Compares and contrasts knowledge and skills requirements of Level 4 Information and Library Services NVQs with competencies acquired through initial professional education courses; identifies limitations and argues the need to extend or supplement these awards if they are to be recognized as equivalent to an undergraduate or postgraduate qualification.

Mentoring

Fisher, B, *Mentoring*, Library Training Guides, Library Association Publishing, 1994.

Covers the rôles, purposes and benefits of mentoring and being mentored; skills and qualities for mentors; formal systems and other arrangements. Appendices include details of mentoring organizations and examples of documentation used in training programmes.

Nankivell, C and Shoolbred, M, *Mentoring in library and information services: an approach to staff support*, British Library Research and Innovation Report 20, British Library Research and Innovation Centre, 1996.

Describes findings of questionnaire and interview survey indicating striking differences between the eight sectors covered and considerable demand for mentoring among LIS staff. Provides extensive bibliography, examples of good practice, and guidelines for formal and informal mentoring, covering objectives, skills, structure, problems and evaluation.

Berry, C, Mentoring: putting theory into practice, *Personnel Training and Education*, **15** (2), 1998, 3-9.

Award-winning article, based on a Human Resource Management Diploma project undertaken by an assistant librarian in an academic library, who moved on to customer support with a systems supplier. Discusses the benefits of mentoring and its different forms, referring to library examples and exploration of mentoring at Birkbeck College.

Staff appraisal

Verrill, P E, Performance appraisal for the 1990s: managerial threat or professional right? *British Journal of Academic Librarianship*, 8 (2), 1993, 98-112.
Thought-provoking article exploring the nature and benefits of appraisal, its relationship to motivation, methods of appraisal, and the managerial issues involved in its implementation.

People problems

Birdsall, W F, The library manager as therapist, *Journal of Academic Librarianship*, 16 (4), 1990, 209-12.
Argues that library managers must balance the needs of the individual staff member for self-fulfilment with the objectives of the organization; suggests that to be successful in this process managers should adopt a therapeutic rôle, acknowledging the difficulties involved.

Fowler, A, How to cut absenteeism, *People Management*, 8 January 1998, 44-5.
Offers a useful general introduction to the issues, written from a business perspective. Considers definitions and (weighted) measurements of absenteeism, and then discusses various ways of combating the problem, promoting the return-to-work interview as the most effective way of reducing absence.

8

Financial management

This chapter covers:

- sources of funding
- budget types and methods
- the planning and budgeting cycle
- purposes of costing
- classification of costs
- costing methods and techniques
- types and methods of accounting.

Introduction

The combination of static or reduced budgets, spiralling costs of printed materials and the volatile state of electronic resources has made financial management a critical issue for information professionals in the 1990s. Moves towards participative management, devolved responsibility and charging for services (externally or internally) mean that staff at all levels need to understand the financial context of their service operations and to be aware of the cost implications. This chapter introduces key concepts and models for budgeting, costing and accounting. It also covers the sources of funding for information services in the context of recent organizational trends and developments.

Funding

The two main sources of funds for a company are its shareholders (or owners) and its creditors. Few libraries or information services are independent trading organizations having to raise or generate all the income required to

resource their activities, the commonest examples being freelance information brokers/consultants and library and information cooperatives, but
changes over the past decade have moved many services closer to this
model. Most information services are dependent on a parent organization,
and their main source of income has traditionally been a *grant* (allocation,
subsidy or 'vote') with some additional funds coming from *income-generating* or *revenue-earning* activities. Various economic and political factors
have combined to change this situation so that library and information services are increasingly characterized by multiple sourcing – often reflecting
diversification of 'income streams' flowing into the parent organization –
and a shift in the balance between grants and earnings or other supplements to their income.

In both universities and companies, the trend towards *devolved budgeting* has created *internal markets* which have changed the way funds are
allocated and managed internally, through business units, cost centres and
other arrangements, sometimes leaving the information service entirely
dependent – at least on paper – on payment for services rendered. General
cutbacks in public expenditure have also prompted library directors to put
more effort into *fund-raising*, in the hope of supplementing their basic
grant with donations, sponsorship or grants from other sources (notably
charitable foundations) – although this type of income is normally not
intended for general operating expenditure. The range of revenue-earning
services offered has also expanded and diversified; for example, the British
Library has expanded its income generating activities so that in 1997–8 30%
(£36.2 million) of its total expenditure came from that source, compared
with 11% (£1.5 million) in 1974–5, its first full year of operation.[1] In addition, some academic and special libraries have extended their clientele
beyond their primary constituency – by selling their services to other
libraries, other organizations and individuals, and also through 'franchising'
and other contractual arrangements – and thus begun to operate in more
competitive mode. A novel example of income supplementation is the affin-
ity card (a credit card issued to an organization's supporters) introduced by
the University of New Mexico (UNM) Libraries as a joint venture with
UNM Athletics.[2]

Current sources of **funds** for library and information services can be
summarized thus:

- **basic annual grants** or other forms of allocations from the parent organization
- **'one-off' (capital) grants** from the parent body, for special purposes – for example, purchase of a new computer system, refurbishment or remodelling of facilities
- **loans** (from the parent body) for similar purposes to those given above
- **annual interest** from investments/endowments (from charitable trusts etc) for general or specific purposes, such as purchase of particular types of materials/collections
- **grants from other bodies** (typically government agencies or charitable foundations) to develop/improve collections, facilities or services
- **donations and sponsorship** from private benefactors, institutions or companies
- **fees for services**, organized on one or more of the following systems:
  - *charging back* involves charging individuals, projects or departments for the costs of library support, normally as a paper transaction via the organization's finance/accounting department, which debits the budget of the relevant unit
  - *charging out* is similar to the above, but involves billing external clients for the costs of work contributed by the library to jobs or assignments carried out for them (irrespective of whether the clients have explicitly purchased information services)
  - *charging fees* direct to the recipients of services or users or facilities, either on a pay-per-transaction/reaction basis (charge per loan, copy, search, etc, or per overdue, damaged or lost item) or on an annual membership or subscription model
- **profits from retailing/merchandising**, typically from sales of greetings cards, souvenir items, etc
- **rent and/or percentage of profit** from independent businesses accommodated on library premises, for example bookshops and cafeterias
- **royalties or shared profits** from joint ventures, such as publications.

REFLECTION

What are the main sources of income for your information service as a whole? Has the funding pattern changed significantly over the last five years? How do you expect your service to be funded over the next five years?

This shift from grant to earnings has several implications. It represents a significant change in the predictability of income, and it puts more pressure on services to attend to the needs of multiple constituencies – both funders and users – to ensure an adequate resource base. With internal charging systems, even if the sums available for library and information services are in theory unchanged, the introduction of *transfer pricing* – sometimes known as *shadow pricing* – creates a different psychological climate which makes service consumers/customers more sensitive to costs and value, and more likely to consider alternative sources of supply – or indeed alternative resources (other than information) that could be purchased. There will also almost certainly be an additional cost to the unit in terms of the staff time required to administer any form of priced service.

Devolved models often make it harder for service managers to obtain funding for strategic initiatives or developments planned to benefit the whole community, as customers frequently focus on their own shorter-term needs. Other problems encountered include difficulties in funding multi-disciplinary information resources and general reference works. New financial management models often require not only a review of individual rôles and responsibilities (within the service and the client department) but also new channels of communication, committees or working groups to handle liaison, negotiation and decisions on purchasing and investment.

Budgeting

Budgeting involves the allocation of scarce resources among competing activities, programmes or services. This implies a knowledge of the *costs* of the activities and an understanding of the *objectives* of the organization. Ideally, the budgeting process is integrated with a planning process, which determines objectives and priorities for various timespans, and supported by data collection and analysis to inform decision-making. Thus five-year service strategies will be accompanied by five-year financial projections, and the annual budget submission will be considered in this context, as part of a review or 'rolling forward' of longer-term plans.

The budget is a **financial plan** or statement of organizational intent expressed in financial/monetary terms – a series of conscious or implied goals with price tags. A budget is both a plan for the distribution of resources and a tool for the prediction of costs. It is also a control mechanism and **evaluation tool**, and it can assist with communication and coordination. Budgets cover defined periods, are approved in advance, and can be either directive or participatory in nature. Budgeting requires both technical and behavioural skills; it is a social process, which can be approached reactively or proactively, and it also has motivational and political aspects.

Budgets – like plans – can be defined in terms of their timescale, scope and focus. The main types of budget are:

- **capital budgets**, which are usually multi-year budgets, to fund things of enduring worth that are not consumed quickly (typically high-cost investments, such as a new building or a computer network)
- **revenue or operating budgets**, which are year-by-year budgets, generally drawn up on an annual basis, for the organization as a whole and for its constituent parts, to fund current operations
- **special budgets**, which have varying time periods and may include both capital and operating funds, for smaller projects (typically single-purpose grants from government agencies or charitable foundations).

Traditionally different arrangements have applied to recurrent, operating income and expenditure and large 'one-off' capital expenditures, but a five-year financial plan may bring these two types of expenditure together (and sometimes these large purchases have to be *depreciated* year-by-year during their useful life). Moreover, with budget reductions and diversity of income streams, the traditional division of budgets into capital and recurring, pay and non-pay, is disappearing. Many service managers are now expected to find the funds for major purchases such as library management systems or CD-ROM networks from their operating budgets by achieving savings in salaries or other areas of the budget, either making *provisions* over several years or taking out a loan (with interest) from the parent organization.

The different methods of preparing and presenting budgets vary in complexity and level of detail. The main approaches used are the following:

- **line-item budgeting** – the simplest, most common form, where each category of expenditure is represented by a line. Lists components of expenditure and amounts projected for each (for example, salaries, equipment, supplies, library materials, which might be further subdivided into categories of staff, types of materials, etc). Usually based

on past year's budget with amounts adjusted marginally to reflect inflation.

- **functional or programme budgeting** – the next stage, more prevalent
  now, especially with the development of devolved responsibility and
  service level agreements. Designs budget around service areas, typically
  reflecting organizational structure (for example, bibliographic services,
  lending services or services for particular client or geographically based
  groups).
- **bottom-up or zero-base budgeting** – the most complex and least used
  method, it requires full justification of all programmes at all levels, and
  is a decentralized method which requires departments to identify component programmes or 'decision units' and then build up a budget representing different levels of activity, from the minimal (zero cost) to
  ideal funding situation.[3]
- **formula-based budgeting** – generally associated with publicly funded
  services, and most commonly used in academic libraries. Factors such
  as the size of population served and levels of usage are used to determine either all or part of the allocation to the library, and/or the
  percentage share of the library budget to be allocated to each sub-
  division or client group.
- **one-line or lump-sum budgets** – where a service gets a budget (usually
  based on the previous year's allocation) that is not broken down into
  specific expenditure categories and has no explicit link to a plan,
  although a plan is generally required.

The common *incremental* approach to budgeting, which takes the previous
year as the starting point and adds – or subtracts – a percentage amount, is
a method typically favoured by organizations which do not plan strategically or holistically, and tends also to be associated with unsophisticated
evaluation of financial performance. We need to shift our thinking from
'How shall we spend our money?' to 'What will it cost to achieve our goals?'
and 'How will we fund it?'

Within organizations there are many different systems and devices for
managing budgets and distributing responsibilities between top management and other organizational units:

- **Cost centre** is a term used in various ways in different organizations/sectors, but basically denotes any organizational unit, process or activity to which it is felt useful to ascribe costs – a way of structuring the budget in order to ascertain, collect or group costs for the purposes of cost control. Cost centres often reflect organizational structures, but they can represent functions, services and people, as well as departments. The term can be used more specifically to differentiate 'non-productive' or non-earning units from those with revenue/income targets. Other terms with various meanings in different contexts include *budget centre, responsibility centre, revenue centre* and *profit centre*.

- **Devolved budgeting** is a system of decentralized or delegated budgetary management, which extends responsibility and accountability for financial management from the centre of an organization to its divisions and business units/departments. In some models, central support services (such as libraries) are dependent on the purchase decisions of consumer departments for most or all of their funding, in an **internal market** where goods and services are 'traded' within a framework of *service level agreements* and/or transfer prices. This concept originated with divisionalized corporations in the private sector but is now common in the public/not-for-profit sector, and it requires accurate calculation of costs. In some cases purchasing departments must buy from the internal provider, in others they can choose to use external suppliers if they can show this will provide better value for money.

- **Virement** is the power to transfer funds from one budget heading to another – it allows managers to reallocate funds between categories of expenditure and helps them to deal with changing situations. It is often restricted: for example, virement between staffing and non-staffing heads is what most managers want, but is rarely sanctioned at operational level.

REFLECTION

Who determines (a) the overall and (b) the detailed level of funding for your service? What are the main factors and processes that influence these decisions?

Budget cycles

Planning and budgeting are iterative and interactive processes that should take place as a systematic and cyclical activity. The financial or fiscal year varies from sector to sector and country to country. In addition to the calendar year (January to December), common variants include April to March (UK central and local government) and August to July (UK higher education). During any one year there will be tasks associated with the budget for the current year, the previous year and forthcoming year(s) and the outturn for one year is never finalized until several months into the following year. Figure 8.1 summarizes the key stages and steps in creating, executing and documenting the budget.

This is a simplified representation, based on a budget process for a medium-sized information unit. These steps then have to be related to the planning and budgeting cycle of the parent organization, as there will be further iterations 'up the line'. For larger service units, the internal process may similarly have several iterations as section heads invite bids from team leaders, etc.

Data gathered for **budget estimates** can come from a variety of internal and external sources, such as management information systems, advice from suppliers and published indices, or may have to be calculated or estimated specifically for the bidding exercise. Formal budget submissions should include some background information on the service and its plans for the period, showing how these relate to the parent body's goals, with comments on significant changes from the previous year and any special factors (for example, impact of inflation or currency fluctuations) indicating phasing of expenditure if appropriate. In practice, annual budget submissions are quite often treated just as number-crunching exercises with minimal commentary, largely confined to explanation of tactics to achieve savings targets ('efficiency gains') and/or changes from previous allocations.

Regular **budget reports** need to be accurate, timely, clear, auditable, tailored to management requirements – bearing in mind that senior management and operational managers require different levels of detail – and consistent in their content and format to enable comparisons. Such reports are typically set up to include the budget allocation for each item for the year, the expenditure to date (sometimes also expressed as a percentage) and the amount remaining. Budgetary control and expenditure analysis can be improved by setting month-by-month targets; in some cases managers

Key stages in the annual budget cycle

PREPARE AND ESTIMATE	**Plan**	Strategic objectives reviewed and confirmed by senior management/strategy group. Operational plans drafted by middle managers/team leaders.
	Collate	External data gathered from colleagues, publications, suppliers, etc. Internal cost data collected from colleagues/management information system.
	Moderate	Institutional guidelines notified (eg inflation allowance, savings target). Financial planning assumptions confirmed by senior management.
SUBMIT AND APPROVE	**Propose**	Bids invited from service managers/budget holders (supported by operational plans, commenting on changes and items related to strategic initiatives).
	Decide	Options appraised, priorities assigned and draft budget agreed by resource coordinator and senior management (and communicated to colleagues).
	Inform	Provisional allocations confirmed or revised, and notified to budget holders and other service staff, local accounts team and organization's finance office.
CONTROL AND MANAGE	**Monitor**	Monthly system reports from accounts team to budget holders (showing spend to date against benchmark targets) with summary reports to senior managers.
	Analyse	Monthly/quarterly management reports from budget holders to senior managers (commenting on variances and indicating whether corrective action is required).
	Review	Quarterly and year-end evaluations by resource coordinator and senior management, leading to corrective actions and/or prospective decisions.

Fig. 8.1   *The planning and budgeting cycle*

will expect an even pattern of expenditure throughout the year (8.3% per month) but in many cases there will be predictable seasonal variations, which should be reflected in the benchmarks used.

How do you personally contribute to the planning and budgeting cycle?

Costing

The ability to cost activities has become more important with diminishing resources, increased accountability, more choice in methods of delivery, and continuing interest in benchmarking, charging and outsourcing. An inherent problem for information service managers is that information work is *labour-intensive*, with staff costs typically accounting for 35%–55% of the department's costs (depending on whether accommodation costs are charged to the service). This reduces the scope for short-term budget adjustment – unless many staff are employed on fixed-term contracts – and puts a premium on accounting for staff time, which runs counter to tradition (especially in public-sector organizations). Various methods of data collection can be used, including work sampling and selective or continuous time-logging/diary-keeping, but there are real dangers here of introducing systems which are themselves labour-intensive, demotivating and ultimately counter-productive; attempts to control staff time too rigidly may inhibit initiative, reduce responsiveness, and damage service quality and customer relations. A further problem for information service staff is the amount of time likely to be required for professional updating and skills refreshment, which may be difficult to attribute to specific services.

Costing is also complicated by the range of different elements that must be included to arrive at the total cost of a product or service, which has been exacerbated by information technology developments (bringing in the challenge of apportioning the capital and recurrent costs of, for example, hardware, software, technical support and user documentation). Confusion often arises over the identification of *fixed* and *variable* costs, the difference between *average* and *marginal* costs, definition of *direct* and *indirect* costs, treatment of organizational *overheads* (including utilities and other accommodation-related costs) and policy for *depreciation* of capital purchases, such as workstations and furniture. As always, internal consistency and institutional compliance are important considerations.

Reluctance to get to grips with costing concepts and techniques often stems from an association of cost data with budget cuts, but there are many other **purposes** for which cost data can be used. The following list provides examples:

- to decide between alternative methods of service delivery
- to investigate the costs of new or improved service provision
- to explore the scope for cost-recovery and inform pricing decisions
- to isolate costs of providing specific services and/or serving particular customers
- to prepare more accurate budget estimates and support funding bids
- to demonstrate financial competence and improve credibility
- to compare performance with peers or competitors
- to measure efficiency and effectiveness
- to satisfy internal and external audit
- to prove value for money.

Cost concepts

Costs can be classed in two main categories:

- **Direct costs**, those which can be directly identified with a particular job, product or process (for example, productive labour, or materials which form part of a product – such as the binding of a publication). Direct costs are also known as **prime** costs.
- **Indirect costs**, those costs of the business which cannot be identified with specific outputs (for example, executive staff, or services/utilities which support production – such as heating and lighting). Indirect costs are also known as **overhead** costs.

There is another fundamental categorization:

- **Variable costs**, those which vary *directly* with changes in the level of an activity (for example, materials consumed in delivering a service – such as paper in photocopying – but not necessarily the associated labour costs, see below).
- **Fixed costs**, those costs which are not directly affected by changes in volume but are incurred irrespective of activity level – at least in the short term (for example, salaried operators, rent and rates). Fixed costs

all become variable costs in the long term.

Costs do not conform neatly to this pattern:

- **Mixed costs** are those where there is a fixed amount of cost and also an element which varies with output (for example, for a telephone, the line rental is a fixed amount but the call charges are variable). Mixed costs are alternatively known as **semi-fixed** or **semi-variable** costs.
- **Stepped costs** are a category of fixed costs which vary with the level of output, but in large steps or jumps, rather than gradually and proportionately to output (for example, when demand for photocopying requires an additional machine, but machine costs then stay fixed until demand grows significantly again).

ACTIVITY

Choose a service with which you are sufficiently familiar to identify the operations and resources involved. List all the cost components (eg equipment, materials, frontline and managerial staff). Classify these cost elements according to the categorization given above (direct/indirect, fixed/variable, etc).

In addition to these basic categories, there are many other terms used to explain the behaviour/functions of different types of cost data. The following are common concepts:

- **Full costs** are figures representing a combination of the allocated direct costs and apportioned indirect costs of a product, service, task or other unit (or alternatively a combination of all the variable costs and an appropriate share or proportion of the fixed costs). Full costs are also known as **total** costs.
- **Life-cycle costs** are the total costs associated with an asset over its entire life, covering not only its initial acquisition – from development and decision to purchase and installation, including training and promotion – but also the annual operating and maintenance costs (such as consumables, operators and utilities).
- **Marginal costs** are increases or decreases in total costs that result when

output is varied by one unit – ie the additional cost of the next unit of output, based on the costs of variable inputs employed to produce it. Marginal costs are also known as **incremental** costs.

- **Opportunity costs** represent the highest value of the alternative opportunities foregone by consuming a good or service, based on not only the money spent purchasing a good, but also the value of the time spent and opportunities lost when the good or service was consumed. (This is an *economic*, rather than an accounting term.)
- **Standard costs** are notional costs in the form of predetermined figures representing what it should cost to produce a unit of a given product or service, based either on a detailed analysis or an informed estimate. They are used as criteria or benchmarks for measuring performance.
- **Unit costs** represent the amount of resources used to produce one unit of a specified product or service, based on the total cost divided by the total output over a given period of time (and usually including the costs of fixed inputs or overheads). These are also known as **average** costs.

Costing methods and techniques

There are various approaches to costing related to the above concepts which can be used to establish the costs of products and services, and your choice of method will depend on your purpose (such as budget preparation, internal/external comparisons, or pricing decisions):

- **Cost-benefit analysis** is used to determine the *economic* feasibility of a proposal, by identifying both the monetary/financial and opportunity/social costs and benefits – to decide whether an activity, product or service is worth the 'price'. This type of analysis aims to evaluate both monetary and non-monetary/intangible costs and benefits, and can thus be distinguished from **cost-effectiveness studies**, which aim to maximize performance output in relation to input costs; and **cost-efficiency** studies, which aim to minimize input costs.[4]
- **Life-cycle costing**, acknowledges that similar assets may have proportionately different purchase and operating/maintenance costs and aims to identify total ownership costs. It is used in investment decisions, and is especially useful for estimating and comparing the costs of IT-based systems, and for raising awareness of the longer-term costs of library

acquisitions – the hidden 'downstream' costs of binding, repair, storage, etc – as demonstrated by pioneering work at the British Library in the context of its Review of Acquisition and Retention Policies in the 1980s.[5]

- **Marginal costing** and **break-even analysis** are used to analyse relationships between cost and volume, and to determine the point at which a priced product or service covers its costs. Such techniques are often used for setting prices/charges, especially in not-for-profit organizations.

ACTIVITY

Using the service previously selected, identify and list the key stakeholders (such as the service users and service staff). List the costs and benefits for each stakeholder group: include direct and indirect service costs, and also opportunity costs, as well as potential benefits. Consider how you could verify your assumptions, and how you would measure or otherwise assess the value of each cost and benefit. Construct a matrix showing how the costs and benefits relate to each group, indicating whether quantitative data or qualitative comment should be sought.

There are several different techniques that can be used in costing exercises. You need to be aware of the range of different methods that can be employed and to become involved in discussions on costing methodology within your organization. This is particularly crucial in the context of devolved budgeting and charging arrangements. Apportionment of indirect costs or overheads to departments or services is usually carried out to encourage optimal use of organizational resources and to build understanding of the 'true' costs of activities, but there are several different ways of doing this, which do not all produce sensible results. Traditional bases for distribution include labour and machine hours, but more recently organizations have used techniques such as **activity-based costing**, which acknowledges that many indirect costs are variable and tries to identify the *cost drivers* – the factors that drive or cause consumption of particular costs – and then assign overheads on that basis.

The main steps typically involved in costing are shown in Figure 8.2. Further details of methods and techniques can be found in many management accounting textbooks (see suggestions for further reading).

Main steps involved in costing

1   Decide the focus and level of the costing exercise – the product, service, process or system which will be the subject of study or *cost objective*.
2   Determine a sensible activity or period base – unit measures of output, or time units (such as an hour, day, week, month, year).
3   Identify all the relevant cost components, gather available data, and plan how to collect data not readily available (such as staff time spent on various tasks).
4   Classify the costs according to their type – direct/indirect, fixed/variable – and establish behaviour patterns of variable and any stepped costs.
5   Calculate (via measurement or estimation) and allocate the *direct* costs.
6   Group or aggregate the indirect costs, on the basis of their homogeneity or similar causal relationships with the cost objective, to form *cost pools*.
7   Identify *cost drivers* as basis for relating costs to objectives, select method for (re)distributing overheads and apportion the indirect costs.
8   Consolidate the data and choose a suitable form of presentation.

Fig. 8.2   *A basic model for costing*

Accounting

In general terms, accounting covers the processes involved in categorizing, recording and summarizing the monetary flows associated with an organization's activities, and its subsequent communication and interpretation. Accounting is the technical aspect of **financial reporting** and uses standardized methods, which enable comparisons of performance over time and among organizations. There are three main types of accounting:

- **Financial accounting** is the public reporting and disclosure of financial information according to various professional and legal practices and standards, exemplified in the UK by the accounts deposited by companies at Companies House or the accounts published by universities with their annual reports. Such statements are at a global level, referring either to the whole organization or semi-autonomous units within it, and intended for use by shareholders, government and other outside parties.

- **Cost accounting** is the operational recording and reporting of the cost in monetary terms of an activity, product or service, based on the identification and calculation of the resources associated with it, using techniques which originated in manufacturing industry but are now commonplace. Such accounts are at a much more detailed level of analysis, usually relating to sub-units, departments, cost centres, products, services or activities, and are intended for use internally by managers and other staff.
- **Management accounting** is the preparation and presentation of financial/accounting information to assist management with policy-making and decision-taking, tailored to need in the detail, format and timing of reports – rather than conforming to any prescribed or standard practice. The term is often used interchangeably with cost accounting, but management or managerial accounting tends to operate at a higher level of generality, and in effect embraces both financial and cost accounts.

Accounting methods and techniques

Within this overall framework, all organizations thus have some formal requirements (both externally driven and internally determined) but they also adopt different methods for recording and reporting financial transactions. Managers need to be aware of the conventions followed in their own organization as practices vary between and within sectors, and failure to understand what figures actually represent can result in misinterpretation and lead to ill-informed decisions. At a fundamental level, people need to know at what point an item of expenditure is recorded in the accounts – when the order is placed? when the item is received or used? when the bill is paid? The three main methods used are as follows:

- The **cash accounting** method records a transaction in the accounting system when cash flows in or out of the organization; this method is useful where there are strict rules about not carrying forward unspent funds from one year to the next.
- The **commitment accounting** method records a transaction when a pur-

chase order is raised, or a client is billed for a service; this enables managers to track activity against plans, irrespective of the vagaries of cash flows. A commitment can also be referred to as an *encumbrance* in this context.

- The **accrual accounting** method records expenses when they are incurred in providing services, regardless of when they are paid (or ordered) and similarly records revenue when it is earned, rather than when payments are received. An *expense* here (something actually used) is distinguished from an *expenditure* (which might include items purchased for use in subsequent years).

Other issues that you need to consider in the preparation and presentation of accounts include the fact that buildings, equipment and other assets wear out and thus reduce in value or *depreciate* over time, and this situation will be exacerbated if prices rise or *inflate* at a significant rate so that the purchasing power of currency is reduced. There are special techniques for **depreciation accounting** and **inflation accounting** that can be used to adjust figures to provide more accurate statements.

Underpinning the recording and reporting of financial information, you will normally find some form of **coding system**. A good coding system enables expenditure and income to be tracked, reported and analysed at various levels of detail and with different perspectives for the organization as a whole or for individual departments, cost centres, etc. A fundamental requirement is that everyone in the organization uses the same code for *primary expenses* (defined as a type of expenditure that cannot be divided further into two or more distinct types of expenditure) so that, for example, expenditure on wages and salaries, or on books and periodicals, can be aggregated across the whole organization, as well as being reported for each department or other accounting unit involved. Coding systems in practice vary considerably in the level of detail provided. Many systems are designed around a minimum (mandatory) requirement of two coding elements to denote the expense category and the cost centre, with scope for further levels of analysis through the use of additional codes to identify more specific cost units or other perspectives on activities. Departments/business units often have the freedom to decide their own levels of coding within an agreed overall organizational framework.

References

1   British Library, *Strategic review: consultation paper*, British Library, 1998, 2.
2   Trojahn, L and Lewis, L K, Of banks, books and balls: the Lobo Library credit card, *College & Research Libraries News*, 58 (1), 1997, 10-11.
3   Foskett, D J and Brindley, L, Zero-base budgeting: the Aston experience, *Library Management*, 12 (4), 1991, 25-33.
4   Kingma, B R and Irving, S, The economics of access versus ownership: the costs and benefits of access to scholarly articles via interlibrary loans and journal subscriptions, *Journal of Interlibrary Loan, Document Delivery & Information Supply*, 6 (3), 1996, 1-76.
5   Stephens, A, The application of life cycle costing in libraries, *British Journal of Academic Librarianship*, 3 (2), 1988, 82-8.

Suggestions for further reading

Roberts, S A, *Financial and cost management for libraries and information services*, 2nd edn, Bowker Saur, 1998.
  Comprehensive textbook (c400 pp) which places detailed treatment of cost measurement in its strategic context. Discusses management information needs, explains accounting concepts and technical terminology, and provides checklists to determine costing methods. Also includes glossary, extensive lists of references and examples of data recording forms.

Fund-raising

Kemmis, B, Changing trends in library fund raising, *Library Administration & Management*, 12 (4), 1998, 195-8
  Argues that new trends in philanthropy and changing demands on libraries present an opportunity to rethink and retool library development and programming; surveys strategies and options, such as friends groups, endowments, grants, corporate sponsorship, individual philanthropy, and the use of information technology in fund-raising activities.

Budgeting and accounting

McKay, D, *Effective financial planning for library and information ser-*

vices, Aslib Know How Guide Series, Aslib, 1995.

Concise practical guide (c50 pp) covering different methods of budgeting, costing and reporting/accounting. Includes chapter on software packages, examples showing use of spreadsheets for LIS budgeting, sample budget submission (for a special library) and concludes with lists of accountancy organizations and recommended reading material.

Prentice, A E, *Financial planning for libraries*, 2nd edn, Scarecrow Press, 1996.

Wide-ranging text (c195 pp) with US and public-sector bias, but useful coverage of strategic issues and extensive bibliography. Covers the environmental context, the links between budgeting and planning, and special factors affecting information services. Describes data gathering, budgeting and accounting methods, and the use of reports as evaluative tools.

Coates, J, Rickwood, C and Stacey, R, *Management accounting for strategic and operational control*, Butterworth-Heinemann, 1996.

Comprehensive and extensively referenced textbook (c330 pp) which includes separate chapters on strategic and budgetary planning, standard costing, activity based costing, management accounting in service industries, and budgeting and performance measurement in the public sector, as well as various aspects of control and performance assessment.

Jones, B M, *Financial management in the public sector*, McGraw-Hill, 1996.

Clear user-friendly guide (c250 pp) for both students and managers, organized in four quite different sections: discursive introduction to the political and governmental context; encyclopedia-style articles on key concepts; articles on numerical techniques with worked examples; exercises and case studies. Also includes a glossary and annotated reading list.

Diedrichs, C P, Off to see the wizard: demystifying your financial relationships, *Library Administration & Management*, 10 (2), 1996, 105-109.

Written from the perspective of an acquisitions librarian, identifies eight different functions/offices involved in financial activities within the library and its parent organization. Explains the benefits of establishing contacts, improving mutual understanding and building effective working relationships with the relevant individuals.

Formula-based budgets

Budd, J M, Allocation formulas in the literature: a review, *Library Acquisitions: Practice & Theory*, **15** (1), 1991, 95–107.

Based on examination of more than 50 published articles and unpublished dissertations; discusses collection growth, the concept of allocation, the variable factors used in formulae, the specific means of formulation, and the political dimension, concluding that good decisions require a mix of exhaustive understanding, objective data and judgment.

Durckheim-Montmartin, M E G E von et al, Library materials fund allocation: a case study, *Journal of Academic Librarianship*, **21** (1), 1995, 39–42.

Describes background, principles and components of formula introduced at the University of Stellenbosch in 1991. Discusses weightings, 'balancing' and procedural issues, and concludes that the outcome represents a significant improvement on the previous situation.

Costing

Lancaster, F W, *If you want to evaluate your library* . . . , 2nd edn, Library Association Publishing, 1993.

Comprehensive guide (c350 pp) to methods for evaluating library and information services, with examples of questionnaires and forms used in US libraries. Considers evaluation of collections, database searching, answering reference questions and bibliographic instruction; covers cost-effectiveness, cost-benefit and quality control.

Snyder, H and Davenport, E, *Costing and pricing in the digital age: a practical guide for information services*, Library Association Publishing, 1997.

Introductory text (166 pp) which explains concepts and techniques of accounting and costing in relation to operational decisions, investment appraisal, service pricing and internal control. Includes c50 worked examples, ten exercises, references to accounting and library literature, and a glossary of technical terms. (Displays some bias towards US terminology.)

Broady, J E, Costing of bibliographic services, *Journal of Librarianship and Information Science*, **29** (2), 1997, 89–94.

Introduces basic costing concepts and gives library-related examples of direct, indirect, fixed and variable costs. Uses the costs of book acquisition and processing to illustrate the difference between marginal and total absorption costing for budgetary control, and concludes with another example showing the calculation of unit costs for the same process.

Cost-benefit analysis

Kingma, B R, *The economics of information: a guide to economic and cost-benefit analysis for information professionals*, Libraries Unlimited, 1996.

Clearly presented and fully documented textbook (200 pp) which introduces the basic economic concepts of demand, supply, benefits and costs, with examples and exercises taken from the information marketplace. Discusses resource-sharing, user fees, and the value of information, and explains the key steps and pitfalls of cost-benefit analysis.

Hawbaker, A C and Wagner, C K, Periodical ownership versus fulltext online access: a cost-benefit analysis, *Journal of Academic Librarianship*, 22 (2), 1996, 105-9.

Compares the costs of providing access to business periodicals via subscriptions to print products with the costs of access via a fulltext database (*Business ASAP*) and then identifies other factors influencing purchase decisions – such as user preferences, operating costs, multiple access, vendor reliability, equipment requirements and browsing capability.

Harris, G and Marshall, J G, Building a model business case: current awareness service in a special library, *Special Libraries*, 87 (3), 1996, 181-94.

Describes the techniques used by a Canadian government library to assess value for money of in-house current awareness bulletin, which included a questionnaire survey, focus groups, and cost-benefit analysis comparing existing service with outsourcing or withdrawal. Refers to other published studies and reproduces the survey instrument in full.

White, G W and Crawford, G A, Cost-benefit analysis of electronic information: a case study, *College & Research Libraries*, 59 (6) 1998, 503-10

Discusses the nature of cost-benefit analysis with reference to published library studies. Describes a project at Penn State University to compare the costs and benefits of *Business Periodicals Ondisc* with traditional interlibrary loans and also comments on benefits not examined in the study; argues that cost-benefit analysis can be used as a marketing tool for new products and services.

9

Space management

This chapter covers:

- the service as a place
- future learning environments
- space planning and design
- space management responsibilities
- furniture, fittings and facilities
- security and safety
- disaster management.

Introduction

The operational facilities and physical setting of information and library services have a significant effect on the quality of service delivery, and they also represent an important part of the resource management responsibilities of all information professionals. Irrespective of the scope for a new building or extension, all managers need to consider remodelling, adapting or otherwise improving their existing accommodation to match changing demands. This chapter is concerned with the physical environment of service provision. It covers forward planning, day-to-day management and emergency situations, and includes assumptions about future needs, advice on planning and design, and examples drawn from operational practice.

The service as a 'place'

In order to inform either long-term or short-term decisions on space matters, as an information professional you need to form a view of the library (or information centre) as a physical place. There has been much discussion about the 'virtual library', the 'logical library', the 'electronic library' and the 'library without walls' in recent decades, and different opinions expressed on how library services will be affected by **information technology** and whether libraries will continue to exist as physical entities in anything resembling their current form. In his seminal article published in 1986, John Sack offered a radical view,

> the library might disappear simply because it blended so successfully into the background of a scholar's activity that the scholar never needed to regard it explicitly as a place to go . . . Thus, libraries disappear because they become invisible and because their location is wherever you are: 'without walls' . . . More than a physical location, the library becomes a medium or ubiquitous utility, a service always ready at hand.[1]

Professional debate and speculation have continued during the intervening period, with some consensus emerging that at least for the foreseeable future 'the library will have walls'. Indeed, in the academic sector, where many leading-edge electronic library developments are taking place, the last five years have been a time of phenomenal physical growth, with around 100 building projects in the UK higher education sector (largely as a result of the Follett report) and comparable activity in the USA (without national pump-priming funds). The term **'hybrid library'** is gaining currency as a way of conveying the message that new modes of service delivery will co-exist with traditional print-based collections, and communicating the notion that services are in a transitional phase, which will continue for some time.

Many professionals believe library buildings will be just as important in the electronic environment, with continuing and expanded functions as a place for instruction and interaction, reflection and refreshment. The Standing Conference of National and University Libraries (SCONUL) representing 135 library and information services in higher education institutions, national libraries and museums in the UK and Ireland, endorses this view in its published vision of the academic library in the year 2002:

> Many resources and services will be available electronically via the network, but students will choose to use the library as a place to work, both for quiet private study and for group project work. They will see the library as one of the places where they can get help with using IT, as well as information and

advice on the availability and use of learning materials.[2]

REFLECTION

How do you think IT will affect the use of physical library facilities in the future? Do you see the areas devoted to storage, services and staff changing? What will be the most important function of the building?

Learning environments

Assumptions that are being made about libraries in the academic sector are increasingly applicable to both public and special libraries with the current convergence of interests around the theme of community learning, whether expressed in terms of lifelong learning for individuals or organizational learning for companies. Many corporate information centres and industrial library services are being reinvented as *learning centres* or *knowledge centres* (often with bigger budgets) as organizations introduce formal skills development and knowledge management programmes. The rôle of public libraries in supporting part-time, independent and distance learners is set to expand and develop over the next decade with growth in access to networked resources and provision of electronic content as learning materials. Common to all sectors is the trend towards combining libraries with other specialist and more general facilities, for example, media services, print units, seminar rooms, training suites, vending machines (see Figure 9.1).

Service managers also need to consider general trends in working practices and office design, such as the development of 'virtual offices' and 'anytime, anywhere' work environments. In *virtual offices*, staff are not based at a fixed work location, but work in any place where they can get work done – which might include working at home, on trains, or with clients (for example, an information specialist based in a client department). In order to optimize use of space and equipment, some organizations have introduced 'non-territorial offices' and 'hot desking', so that staff do not have their own permanent desks but move around available accommodation to occupy vacant cubicles or workstations. (Special telephone technology allows them to take their telephone extensions to any available desk.) This practice originated with IT companies and consultancy firms, but is now

Planning assumptions	Design implications
Learning is more collaborative	Need for 'collaboratories' – group study tables/carrels/rooms with shared access to technology and presentation facilities
Learners have different preferences	Need variety and 'zoning' – quiet private areas and busy social areas, with low-level seating/tables and refreshment facilities
Technology is developing rapidly	Need facilities for continual training and retraining of users and staff – in large classes, small groups and as individuals
Access to network resources is universal	Need cable management for wired-up study places (workstations and plug-in points) with adjustable seating
Demand for multimedia resources is high	Need equipment to enable images to be incorporated into text documents – colour copiers, printers, scanners, etc
Self-service issue / return predominates	Central service counters are smaller, supplemented by multiple service points distributed throughout the building
Inter-disciplinary studies are the norm	Less use for separate departmental/ subject-based collections, but more demand for department-based inform- ation specialists

Fig. 9.1   *Common assumptions about libraries as future learning environments*

gaining in popularity. Advocates claim that mixing people up in this way fosters creativity, but others are concerned about the reductions in social interaction and the impact on job satisfaction. Managers need to balance potential gains in space utilization against personal preferences to have a fixed physical base for individuals and teams, but some types of informa-tion work are less place-dependent (for example, abstracting and indexing).

Service managers also need to bear in mind that provision of 'quiet space' is another key factor for service staff, as well as for service users.

In the past, the main motive for building or extending libraries was to provide more accommodation for print-based collections. While shortage of space for stock is still an important issue for many library managers, a current concern for most is the appropriateness and adequacy of accommodation to meet present and future needs. Buildings designed 30 years ago have often proved difficult to adapt to meet changing demands. Inadequate wiring is a common problem, but older buildings are also frequently under-provided with meeting/interview rooms, staff offices and training facilities (for staff or users). However, with current pressures on budgets, shortage of capital funds and competing demands for resources, service managers face a hard task in convincing purse-holders of the need to invest in building, extending or remodelling accommodation: the self-service virtual library with scaled-down stock, skeleton staffing and a minimal physical presence is a model which is very attractive to paymasters.

Planning and design

Space planning is similar to other types of planning in many respects, but has some special features: it combines strategic planning and *project planning*, it requires *close liaison* with another set of professionals, and it works with *multiple timeframes*. Planning horizons will vary for different aspects of a building project; for example planners might work to a 50-year time-span for the building structure, 15 years for utilities, and seven years for fixtures and fittings.

The use of **strategic visioning** in planning new facilities is becoming more widespread as a means of helping decision-makers and other stakeholders to form a clearer view of the kind of library envisaged and the rôle it will fulfil in the future. Scenario writing is a variant of this approach, which involves developing alternative visions of the future, and is thus a useful technique for illustrating the difference a new building could make to the local learning environment. This technique was used at Reading University Library in 1997 to make the case for a new building, where it proved to be a highly effective communication device. Each scenario was around 900 words in length, opening with a scene-setting paragraph summarizing the key points, and headed by a carefully chosen title and sub-title. Scenario 1, '*the research* *library and learning centre: integration with specialisation'*, was the 'preferred future' based on a four-storey extension to the existing main library building. Scenario 2, *'the all-purpose library: consolidation and dissipation'*, represented a genuine attempt to remodel current accommodation to meet future needs. The second scenario was not intended to be a 'doomsday' vision, although it was obviously a less attractive picture than the first one, and showed resources spiralling downwards as a knock-on effect of space constraints.[3] The scenarios were published in the University Bulletin and helped to raise awareness of the implications of not investing in a new building and to stimulate debate around the campus.[4]

In the following year, a more structured approach to scenario development was used at the University of Reading's Bulmershe Library serving the Faculty of Education and Community Studies, in an exercise involving a wide range of stakeholders. This event surpassed the expectations of library staff in terms of both the level of engagement of the participants and the radical vision of reconfigurated accommodation for collaborative service provision which emerged as the 'core' scenario.[5-6]

There are three widely accepted **principles** of planning and designing library buildings:

- fitness for purpose
- ease of use
- economy in operation.

Beyond these fundamental principles there are several **qualities** that have been identified as important for library buildings. The list in Figure 9.2 dates

---

A library should be . . .

• flexible	• organized
• compact	• comfortable
• accessible	• constant in environment
• extendible	• secure
• varied	• economic

Fig. 9.2   *Faulkner-Brown's ten commandments*

from the 1960s and is attributed to Harry Faulkner-Brown, a British architect who designed many award-winning library buildings around the world.

While these concepts are still relevant today, changes in the way these terms are used, together with changes in the wider service environment (including the use of information technology) indicate the need for revision. Andrew McDonald has provided a revised list, suggesting that academic library space should be:

- **adaptable** - for example, floor loading sufficient for book stacks throughout the building (expensive) and wiring provision for connecting all reader places to networks
- **inviting and accessible** - including compliance with requirements for disabled access, and consideration of 24-hour access to meet user demand and reduce overcrowding
- **varied** - to fulfil a range of library and related functions (including training and teaching) and to satisfy the different needs and preferences of individuals and groups
- **interactive and well-organized** - to optimize use of space and to promote interaction
- **conducive** - facilitating access to information and reflective work over long periods
- **suitable in environmental conditions** - acoustics, lighting, temperature and humidity for the comfort of readers, efficient operation of computers and preservation of materials
- **safe and secure** - paying particular attention to requirements for non-standard working hours, noting that security often conflicts with convenience, aesthetics and safety
- **efficient and environmentally appropriate** - minimizing running and maintenance costs, delivering value-for-money, and conforming to environmental policies and standards
- **suitable for information technology** - with cabling specified to accommodate future requirements, taking advice from computer specialists and networking experts.[7]

These qualities are equally relevant to any space planning project, large or small - for a new building, extension, refurbishment, adaptation, or just making better use of existing space.

Experience shows that the design process is characterized by tensions and trade-offs, including differences in priorities of the various professionals involved in the project. For example, librarians are particularly concerned with function and *use*, and they prefer to draw inspiration from successful buildings elsewhere; whereas architects are interested in form and *look*, and they like fresh innovative interpretations. Librarians generally accept the need for flexibility, compromise and diplomacy, but architects often want to make a personal statement and see any form of compromise as a threat to their singular vision. Organizations have to consider trade-offs between capital and recurrent costs, which will depend on their financial circumstances. At a more practical level, people have to take decisions about issues such as whether to optimize or maximize the number of computer places, in consequence perhaps making the learning environment less attractive and less conducive to study.

Kate Ragsdale (Planning Officer at the University of Alabama Libraries, Tuscaloosa) has identified some **fundamental issues** which apply to many – if not all – library construction projects, and she offers ten practical tips to assist librarians planning a new building or a major renovation:

1 Hire an interior designer.
2 Remember the library signs.
3 Include the book detection system in the building contract.
4 Pay careful attention to the accessibility of the building.
5 Take lots of photos throughout the project.
6 Be prepared to compromise on items that are not vital to library service and to stand firm on the ones that are.
7 Join the architect on weekly site inspections as soon as the finishes begin.
8 Be generous in estimating the amount of time you will spend on the project, and plan to accommodate your other responsibilities.
9 As much as possible, follow up informal communication in writing.
10 Keep complete files on each building project.[8]

In a briefing paper prepared on behalf of SCONUL's Advisory Committee on Buildings, Jean Sykes provides guidelines on choosing/specifying/designing furniture for libraries and learning resource centres, covering issues such as size, layout, safety, finishes and colour. She also includes some general advice on **choosing furniture**, summarized below.

1   Always start work on this as soon as possible – don't listen to architects and your own administrators who will tell you there's plenty of time.

2   It helps to go and visit other recent buildings to get ideas of what you like/dislike and what works/doesn't work. Take photographs of both good and bad features to show to your architects, or take your architects with you.

3   As soon as the general plan of your building is nearing its final stage on the drawings, start to model your furniture in all the rooms/areas – using a CAD system if you can – just to ensure that the spaces will work.

4   Watch for health and safety features and talk to your health and safety officer.

5   At least nine months before your building is due to be handed over to you, start the tendering process. Make sure that delivery/installation are included.

6   When you have chosen your preferred supplier(s), give them at least four months from firm order to delivery.

7   The order in which you should get things done is:
   a   Power/data/telephones should be in before building handover, together with kitchens, bathrooms, all plumbing, decoration and carpets
   b   fixed furniture – before building handover
   c   shelving as soon as building is handed over
   d   then free-standing furniture
   e   then chairs.[9]

While projects vary significantly in their scale and complexity, some common factors emerge as **crucial aspects** of the planning process which are likely to influence its ultimate success:

- ability to articulate concerns, and willingness to challenge assumptions
- paying attention to detail, and keeping full records of discussions
- awareness of costs, and a realistic view of economic issues
- effective partnerships with architects and other professionals
- involvement of stakeholders, with a determined focus on user needs

Underpinning these issues, *communication* is the key to successful collaborative planning.

Managing space

Space management is a relatively neglected area of professional education, and is almost exclusively discussed in the context of the planning and design of library buildings. It is also frequently neglected in the operational situation, with rôles and responsibilities in relation to space matters often not properly assigned – either not made explicit or not covering all the necessary areas and tasks. This is somewhat at odds with the perceived importance of 'the library as a place' and represents a significant shortcoming in resource management, as noted by McDonald: 'Space is a precious and expensive resource that should be planned and managed within a strategic framework for the development of the service as a whole, but it has sometimes received less professional attention than the other resources the librarian manages.'[7]

Operational management responsibilities for safety and security, portering, cleaning, etc, are the most likely areas to be formally assigned. Strategic management responsibilities for space are often assumed to rest with the service head, but some services – usually larger libraries – have explicitly assigned this rôle to a member of the senior management team, on the basis that this will help to focus attention, establish a continuing interest and encourage a proactive approach. Every space-related decision should be seen as an opportunity to adapt to new conditions and to create a better environment, thus representing short-term incremental steps towards longer-term change.

ACTIVITY

List the management responsibilities and tasks associated with the total space occupied by your service. Try to put staff names or job titles against all the items listed. Are there any gaps?

In many libraries, space management is largely a reactive process, characterized by solving problems – rather than anticipating them – and putting things right only when a customer comments or complains. Regular tours of inspection tend to be associated with health and safety obligations, taking place at best every three or four months. In order to create and manage a customer-oriented environment, all staff - from shelvers to senior management - need to accept a continuing responsibility for maintaining and improving the physical environment.

REFLECTION

What contribution do you personally make to this area? What could you do to improve the physical environment?

One way of doing this is to use regular 'customer care tours of inspection' to identify and report faults. This approach was introduced at Aston University Library & Information Services (LIS) in 1993, as part of a TQM programme, which identified 'an open and inviting physical environment' as a critical success factor. One staff member offered to coordinate the initiative and drew up a set of guidelines for the tours; these were then used by staff volunteers, who carried out the inspections in pairs and reported findings to the coordinator for subsequent action. The guidelines took the form of a simple checklist, as shown in Figure 9.3.

Security and safety

For many library and information service managers, security is a major preoccupation. Most libraries are spending a lot more money now on security measures than they were ten years ago, and for some this has become sufficiently large to justify a separate budget line. Library concerns about security reflect more general concerns in society at large, evidenced by increasing investment in security devices in both the business and domestic environment. The continuing expansion of IT facilities in libraries, in parallel with the growth in the market for personal computers, has also made libraries much more vulnerable to the organized theft of computers (or chips and other parts of computers). The other main risks perceived by library managers are damage or theft of collections, violence to staff or users, and damage of fabric or facilities.

GUIDELINES FOR CUSTOMER CARE TOURS OF INSPECTION

Common problems to look out for:

1 **Ceilings**
Slats missing/dirty, lights not working.

2 **Floors**
Carpets stained or not stuck down properly, litter on floor.

3 **Shelves**
Are they safe? Shelf guiding missing or inaccurate, books overflowing or very untidy. Are there enough kick stools?

4 **Notices/Noticeboards**
Notices untidy/not in appropriate house style. 'Unofficial' notices should be in coffee lounge (vetted by Customer Care Coordinator first). Check for out of date information.

5 **Furniture**
Damaged items or missing screws/bolts, graffiti, inappropriate use of furniture by LIS (ie have we got the right chairs and tables for that particular area?).

6 **Library Handouts**
Are the stands well stocked? Are they sited in the right place?

7 **Clocks**
Showing the right time?

8 **Terminals (IS and LIS)**
Are they clean? Already checked daily by IS and LIS to make sure they are working?

9 **Signs and Guiding**
Are they in the right place, do they stand out?

10 **Toilets and Back Stairwell**
Do the hand driers work? Are the doors/washbasins etc damaged? Look out for graffiti. Is there any litter on the stairs?

11 **Litter**
Are there enough bins, and are they in the right place? Watch out for signs of eating and drinking.

Fig. 9.3 *Aston University LIS guidelines for customer care tours*

There are also several features particularly associated with public and academic libraries which make them more susceptible to crime:

- open-access policies, enabling anyone to enter at will
- long service hours, including late evenings and weekends
- separate/self-contained accommodation, often physically isolated
- multistorey buildings with remote areas, difficult to monitor
- staff inexperienced and/or untrained in crime prevention
- security personnel with unrealistically large spans of control.

REFLECTION

Are there any obvious safety or security hazards in your library/information unit?

While people often look for technical solutions to security problems, security has to be seen as a management issue (rather than a technical matter). Security involves balancing risks, costs and access: the level of security provided will depend on an assessment of the risks, and of the costs and benefits of the measures proposed, including the implications for access. Availability of resources and feasibility of implementation are also critical factors. Information managers have a responsibility to protect the assets of their organizations, and to provide a safe environment for both staff and users, but they may also have a specific responsibility to promote access to their collections and facilities which might be undermined by certain security measures (such as card-entry systems and closed storage areas). Security management is also about creating perceptions of safety: it is impossible to provide absolute protection for a public building such as a library, but there are things that can be done to make people feel safer.

Security planning requires coordination of three particular aspects of security provision:

- **physical security**, including building/accommodation design and mechanical devices
- **operating procedures**, covering both day-to-day routines and emergency arrangements
- **security personnel** - specialist staff, and also those with designated security rôles.

When planning or reviewing provision, it makes sense to take advice from local crime prevention officers and specialists within the organization, and also to look at what other libraries and similar services are doing. For new security equipment, it is essential to investigate ongoing maintenance and upgrading costs, in addition to initial purchase and installation costs.

Examples of security measures commonly used in libraries include:

- closed-access protected storage arrangements for fragile, rare and valuable items
- cameras that scan customers as they exit and/or record movements around the building
- triggers inserted in books and other materials to prevent unauthorized removal of stock
- sensors linked with alarm systems to detect intruders when the library is closed
- limpets, wobblers and various other devices fitted to computers and other equipment
- uniformed personnel patrolling the building and/or posted at the entrance/exit point
- card-entry systems, restricting access to registered or approved users
- panic buttons at service counters reassuring for staff on duty late at night
- escorts for staff taking money to the bank, or working late into the evening
- regular awareness and training sessions, for example an annual safety seminar.

For both service managers and staff, **safety** is a formal responsibility, regulated by legislation (for example, in the UK, the Health and Safety at Work Act, 1974). Organizations as employers are required to protect, as far as is practicable, the health and safety of all workers, and all employees in turn have an obligation to take reasonable care to avoid injury to themselves and to others by their work activities. Within this framework, managers assume particular responsibilities determined by the organizational context in which they operate. At the most basic level, this includes duties in connection with accidents and emergencies (for example, first aid provision, fire evacuation procedures) as well as more general issues relating to premises management, plant and equipment. In addition to general awareness of health and safety matters, you need to be familiar with regulations covering display screen equipment and manual handling operations: a great deal of lifting and carrying takes place in libraries and information units, but all too often people are not given adequate training on simple things, such as the correct way to grip and hold books and boxes.

Disaster management

Disaster planning is a convenient term used to describe a set of activities or measures intended to enable organizations to cope with unforeseen disasters. Other terms often used for this concept include *disaster preparedness* and *disaster control planning*. Some commentators prefer the terms *emergency* planning, *contingency* planning or *business continuity* planning as less negative and emotive expressions, while others argue that disaster *management* suggests a broader interpretation and underlines its importance as a management issue. Disaster preparedness has been acknowledged as a management concern in libraries ever since the damage caused in Florence by the flooding of the River Arno in 1966. Over the last two decades, the British Library has sponsored various initiatives in this area, including publication of an outline disaster control plan in 1987.[10] In the UK, recent widely publicized disasters – the IRA bomb which hit the Commercial Union Library in the City of London,[11] the fire at Norwich Central Library,[12] and the flood at the Fawcett Library of London Guildhall University[13] – have raised professional awareness of the risks.

John McIntyre has pointed out that statistics suggest that over a ten-year period, every library should expect to experience a disaster of some sort.[14] However, despite the publicity given to disasters in the library world in recent years, and the efforts of the National Preservation Office and others to raise awareness and promote good practice, many libraries are still inadequately prepared. The most common examples of disasters in the library and information services context are floods and fires, but the term covers a range of natural and man-made phenomena, including storms, earthquakes, pests, explosions, asbestos, bombs, thefts and civil disorder. People tend to think of disasters as events of catastrophic proportions, but small incidents (such as a burst pipe, a leaking window, missing tiles or poor wiring) can cause large amounts of damage, especially if they happen at the 'wrong' time. Certain types of disaster which act over a long period of time – for example, the chemical deterioration of paper caused by acidity – are sometimes referred to as 'slow disasters' or 'quiet disasters' and are generally excluded from disaster management discussions.

Library dependence on computer-based systems for record-keeping and service delivery has complicated matters: electronic systems may be easier to back-up than manual files, but managers often have to rely on others (for example, IT departments, system suppliers) for system/software back-ups.

REFLECTION

Do you feel competent to deal with accidents and other emergencies? What measures could be taken to improve preparedness in your library/information service?

Disaster management is generally seen as covering four main areas of activity:

- prevention
- preparedness
- reaction
- recovery.

These areas are described in Figure 9.4.

Emergency supplies is used here as a general heading to cover a range of equipment, materials, facilities and services required to deal with an emergency. In addition to supplies such as buckets and sponges, this includes protective clothing and record-keeping items. Some libraries keep a basic kit on mobile trolleys (or in 'wheelie bins') for immediate use, with further supplies in central storage. *Potential external resources* include cold storage and freeze drying facilities, equipment hire and transport services. Many of the published guides to disaster planning include detailed advice on identifying and assembling resources for emergency use; Susan George lists useful items (with quantities) for both a small basic 'disaster kit' and a larger central 'disaster closet'.[15]

Staff training is a critical component of disaster planning and can take a variety of forms including awareness talks, briefing sessions, hands-on prac-

The four key components of disaster management

1   The focus of **prevention** is on reducing the likelihood of a disaster occurring, and this is generally pursued through a programme of risk assessment, remedial action and regular inspection, drawing on expert advice from within and outside the organization. Effective prevention requires continuing attention to operating procedures and constant vigilance by service staff; proper systems for reporting problems and recording actions taken are vital.

2   The purpose of **preparation** is to enable an effective response when a disaster occurs, and this is typically achieved through a combination of documented plans, emergency supplies and staff training, supported by internal and external contact arrangements. Plans need to be simple and flexible, using checklists and flowcharts for ease of use; names and addresses of contacts must be kept up-to-date, and similarly with refresher training for staff.

3   The management of **reaction** to a disaster includes raising the alarm, evacuating the building and organizing initial and immediate actions to protect undamaged materials, to salvage damaged materials and to stabilize the environment. As well as contacting emergency services and staff 'on call' this may involve contacting advisers and insurers (for damage assessment) and communicating with service users, other stakeholders and the local media.

4   The process of **recovery** from a disaster includes resuming service provision, restoring damaged resources and reviewing management procedures, and this can extend over a long period if a major programme of conservation and/or refurbishment is required. Maintaining service continuity can be particularly challenging (especially if this has to be done from an alternative operating site) and can add to the physical and mental stress for service staff.

Fig. 9.4   *The four key components of disaster management*

tice, simulation exercises and video presentations. Information service managers often involve local fire officers and other experts to reinforce and supplement input from service staff with designated responsibilities for emergencies. Joint training events with neighbouring library and information services on a one-off or annual basis can be a useful means of sharing expertise and a lead-in to pooling resources and considering back-up arrangements. *Post-disaster counselling* is also recommended by those who have experienced a major disaster, and therefore needs to be incorporated into management thinking and plans.

References

1 Sack, J R, Open systems for open minds: building the library without walls, *College & Research Libraries*, 47 (6), 1986, 535.

2 *The SCONUL vision: the academic library in the year 2002 prepared by . . . a task force convened by SCONUL's Advisory Committee for Information Systems and Services*, SCONUL Briefing Paper, Standing Conference of National and University Libraries, 1998, 2 (also available at http://www.sconul.ac.uk/vision.htm).

3 Corrall, S, Scenario planning: a strategic management tool for the future, *Managing Information*, 5 (9), 1998, 34-7.

4 Corrall, S, University library: visions of the future, *The University of Reading Bulletin*, 313, 1997, 6-7 (available at http://www.rdg.ac.uk/libweb/Lib/Report/scenarios.html).

5 Brewerton, A, First, find some visionaries, *Library Association Record*, 101 (6), 1999, 354-6.

6 Brewerton, A, *Bulmershe 2002: learning support services in the year 2002: visions of the future*, 1998 (also available at http://www.rdg.ac.uk/libweb/Lib/Report/bulm2002.html).

7 McDonald, A, Space planning and management. In Baker, D (ed) *Resource management in academic libraries*, Library Association Publishing, 1997, 189-206.

8 Ragsdale, K W, Planning library buildings: ten practical considerations, *College & Research Libraries News*, 54 (6), 1993, 318-21.

9 Sykes, J, *Choosing library furniture*, SCONUL Briefing Paper, Standing Conference of National and University Libraries, 1998.

10 Tregarthen Jenkin, I, *Disaster planning and preparedness: an outline disaster control plan*, British Library Information Guide 5, British Library, 1987.

11 Saunders, M, How a library picked up the pieces after IRA blast, *Library Association Record*, 95 (2), 1993, 100-1.

12 Fire rekindles debate, *Library Association Record*, 96 (9), 1994, 69.

13 Wise, C, The flood and afterwards: a new beginning for the Fawcett Library, *Library Conservation News*, 48, 1995, 1-2.

14 McIntyre, J, Disaster control planning, *Serials*, 1 (2), 1988, 42-6.

15 George, S C, Library disasters: are you prepared? *College & Research Libraries News*, 56 (2), 1995, 80-4.

Suggestions for further reading
Planning and design

Blagden, J, Building for the future: Cranfield's new library, *New Library World*, 95 (111), 1994, 15-24.

Describes the planning, design and construction of the award-winning library (designed by Sir Norman Foster and Partners), covering the case for a new building, the feasibility study and user survey, and criteria for selecting architects. Key features include the visibility of library staff, and the focus on information access rather than book delivery.

Michalak, S, Planning academic library facilities: the library will have walls, *Journal of Library Administration*, 20 (2), 1994, 93-113.

Identifies environmental and service trends affecting building layout and space utilization; anticipates shorter change cycles in future, suggests different approaches to reallocating space, and argues for preparation of a long-range facilities master plan and consideration of wider campus changes to inform strategic short-term moves in library facilities planning.

Woodward, J, The tale of the terribly high-tech library building, *American Libraries*, 26 (4), 1995, 308-10.

Presents a cautionary tale about the running costs and maintenance problems of state-of-the-art computer-controlled heating, cooling and lighting systems. Argues the need for library directors to view the design and upkeep of environmental facilities as part of their job and suggests ways of gathering information and retaining control of such systems.

Sannwald, W W, *Checklist of library building design considerations*, 3rd edn, American Library Association, 1997.

Provides a series of checklists with more than 1000 questions to assist librarians, architects and others involved in planning or evaluating library space. Arranged in 12 sections, ranging from site selection to dedication ceremonies, with extensive lists on interior organization, disabled access and communications equipment.

Hurt, C, Building libraries in the virtual age, *College & Research Libraries News*, 58 (2), 1997, 75-6, 91.

Outlines some assumptions about the academic environment and the role of libraries in the 21st century and considers their implications for building design. Concludes with six reasons why the library will continue to be an important place in an academic community.

Curry, A and Henriquez, Z, Planning public libraries: the views of architects and librarians, *Library Administration & Management*, **12** (2), 1998, 80-90.

Based on interviews with librarians and architects involved in the design and planning of three new libraries in Canada. Compares and contrasts expectations and experiences of the principal professionals in these projects, highlighting significant differences in attitudes.

Security and safety

Chadley, O A, Campus crime and personal safety, *College & Research Libraries*, **57** (4), 1996, 385-90.

Drawing on an extensive interdisciplinary literature review (citing 65 references) provides examples of violent crime in American academic libraries, identifies six factors associated with higher incidence of crime, and suggests a multifaceted approach to library security.

Atlas, R L, Designing crime-free environments: making our buildings safer, *Library Administration & Management*, **11** (2), 1997, 88-93.

Stresses the need to plan security into building design, outlines steps towards a security master plan, and considers strategies for crime prevention through environmental design using mechanical devices, organizational methods and natural features. (Contribution to two-part section on 'Violence in the library: protecting staff and patrons'.)

Clark, J H, Making our buildings safer: security management and equipment issues, *Library Administration & Management*, **11** (3), 1997, 157-61.

Offers practical advice on security planning and risk management, and discusses the use of various standard and less common security devices for large and small libraries, emphasizing importance of operational coordination, public relations and staff education. (Contribution to two-part section on 'Violence in the library: protecting staff and patrons'.)

Disaster management

Ashman, J, *Disaster planning for library and information services*, Aslib Know How Series, Aslib, 1995.

Concise guide, written by a conservation specialist, arranged in four main sections covering disaster prevention, disaster preparedness, salvaging water-damaged materials, and conservation. Includes diagrams showing options for salvaging books and non-book media, an example of a damage list form and an annotated list of suggested further reading.

Matthews, G and Eden, P, *Disaster management in British libraries: project report with guidelines for library managers*, Library and Information Research Report 109, British Library, 1996.

Based on a comprehensive study of disaster management experience and practice in British libraries, archives and museum services, which drew on published literature, on-site interviews and management documents. Reports findings and provides detailed guidelines, supported by a list of emergency supplies and a bibliography arranged by topic.

10
Service marketing

Introduction

Marketing underpins all areas of information services management, from strategy and planning to the sharp end of everyday service delivery. It is often neglected or rejected by information professionals, who misinterpret its function and purpose, or mistakenly equate it with selling. This chapter defines marketing and explains its relevance to contemporary information service provision. It introduces the key concepts and tools, and shows how they relate to the design, development and delivery of information services, with extensive reference to published literature. It also provides examples of revenue-earning products and services and pricing practices evident in the information services sector.

Marketing defiled and defined

Librarians and information workers often resist the idea of marketing themselves or their services. Colleagues come up with lots of 'good' reasons why they cannot waste their valuable time on such frivolous activities. Typically they say that they are too busy already; their jobs 'don't lend themselves' to advertising; they haven't got money to waste on 'expensive PR campaigns', and anyway librarians shouldn't worry about 'image' – they should leave that to the 'glamorous professions', for example:

> I found the idea of a campaign to improve our image rather silly . . . our read-
> ers need us to be competent, polite, patient and reliable rather than 'forth-
> right and adventurous'. Perhaps those who want glamorous colleagues should
> go into a different profession. Personally I am grateful to be judged by the
> profession on my work rather than my appearance, and to be allowed to get
> away with the fact that I have no dress sense and have not been to a hair-
> dresser since 1974.[1]

It is true that as resources for information diminish and sources of information explode, the information professional is finding it increasingly
difficult to 'keep up', without taking on additional work. But this view suggests that marketing is an optional extra rather than a core activity.
Likewise, although we must be accountable (and certainly do not have the
advertising budget of Coca-Cola or Virgin) concerns about money betray a
lack of belief in *investing* in Public Relations (PR). Other arguments reveal
a lack of imagination. Many academic librarians, for example, believe
marketing is easier for public librarians and point to staff dressing up as
characters from children's fiction and holding storytimes in community
locations. This suggests impoverished thinking about publicizing their services. The notion that marketing should be left to 'glamorous professions'
is generally based on a misunderstanding of the opportunities available to
information professionals, and also on a misplaced view of our changing
priorities. Marketing intangible services may be less straightforward than
marketing 'product', but the same principles apply, even for non-profit organizations.

Definitive statements

There is also a more fundamental problem, which relates to the definition
of marketing. For many people, 'marketing' is a 'dirty word'. Marketers are
viewed by the public at large as being only slightly more trustworthy than
politicans, journalists and estate agents. This is because marketing is gener-

ally misunderstood: people mistakenly equate it with advertising, PR and invariably the 'hard sell' of second-hand car dealers and double-glazing companies. There are many definitions of marketing, and they can be traced back to Adam Smith, who stated in 1776, 'Consumption is the sole end and purpose of all production; and the interest of the producer ought to be attended to, only so far as it may be necessary for promoting that of the consumer.'[2]

The importance of Smith's definition lies in the **customer focus**, and indeed this is the key distinction between *marketing* and *selling*, as explained by the author of one of the classic articles on the subject, Theodore Levitt:

> The difference between marketing and selling is more than semantic. Selling focuses on the needs of the seller, marketing on the needs of the buyer. Selling is preoccupied with the seller's need to convert his product into cash; marketing with the idea of *satisfying the needs of the customer* by means of the product and the whole cluster of things associated with creating, delivering, and finally consuming it.[3]

American marketing guru Philip Kotler has provided many definitions throughout his career, exemplified by the following:

> Marketing is the analysis, planning, implementation, and control of carefully formulated programmes designed to bring about *voluntary exchanges of values* with target markets for the purpose of achieving organizational objectives. It relies heavily on designing the organization's offering in terms of the target markets' needs and desires, and on using effective pricing, communication, and distribution to inform, motivate, and service markets.[4]

Another widely quoted definition is attributed to the UK-based Chartered Institute of Marketing (CIM): 'Marketing is the *management process* that identifies, anticipates and supplies customer requirements efficiently and profitably.' The CIM also stresses the difference between sales, which 'is about *influencing customers to purchase* what a company provides' and marketing, which ' is about putting the needs of the customer first and then *providing what they want* to buy'.[5]

These definitions are obviously relevant to information professionals. We are all concerned with identifying, anticipating and satisfying user needs, and doing so efficiently. Many colleagues have difficulty with the word 'profitably' here, although others simply interpret it as 'productively' or 'beneficially'. Tim Hannagan argues that for non-profit organizations, *accountability* replaces profitability as the 'bottom line', and he describes marketing in this context as 'that function of an organisation in the public and non-profit sector that can keep in constant touch with the organisation's consumers, assess their needs, develop services and products that meet these needs, and build a programme of communications to express the organisation's purpose'.[6] No-one could dispute the relevance or value of marketing, when expressed in those terms.

Finally, Michael Baker argues that marketing is both a *management orientation* and a *business function*. A marketing orientation *starts with the customer*, rather than seeing the customer as the finishing point of the supply chain. Baker suggests three other essential features, namely taking a *long-term perspective*, making full use of *organization-wide resources*, and *innovation*. The marketing function is concerned with managing the 'marketing mix' (see below) but does not necessarily require a specialist marketing unit.[7]

Image matters

There is another reason why information professionals need to embrace marketing. In addition to the general management case, there is a particular argument in respect of information services: we need to combat the potentially damaging effects of our public image. With very few exceptions, the media presentation of library staff is almost universally negative: literature and films are full of unattractive librarians behaving badly.[8-9] Factual accounts in careers guides offer more accurate pictures of our work than fictional portrayals, but we cannot afford to ignore negative perceptions of our profession which may colour the views of our customers and paymasters – and also affect our ability to recruit staff of the right calibre into the profession.

A negative image means that we need to devote more effort to *promoting* our services, and especially to *public relations*. Further evidence that this is a serious issue comes from Carl Clayton, in his bluntly titled article, 'Lack of status due to image problem', where he describes how college principals and representatives from UK educational bodies met with The Library Association to discuss concerns. Professionals in all sectors should reflect on his comments and conclusions:

> Librarians, it was stated, were not meeting the needs of the colleges. They were too fixed in their ways, not flexible enough and not open to new ideas. Librarians insisting on silence in libraries was given as an example of this. Librarians did not market themselves or their services to principals. They did not sell the benefits of the library or explain how the service contributed to the goals of the college. They tended to present everything in terms of problems rather than solutions. They sometimes lacked IT skills. They often lacked management skills, especially strategic planning, problem solving and human resource management. Above all they were accused of lacking political nous. This was defined as recognition that they were part of an organisation and the ability to influence the right people . . . These views are based on broad generalisations, stereotypes and even myths about librarians. However, they need to be taken seriously. They do seem to represent the commonly held opinions of college principals. We may well believe that they are unjustified but we cannot ignore them.[10]

One of the most disturbing images of libraries and librarians to appear in recent years is the customer-hostile 'nightmare library' portrayed in M & C Saatchi's advertising campaign for the computer giant Packard Bell, which is contrasted with an idyllic cottage where information is being accessed via the Internet, using the slogan 'Wouldn't you rather be at home?'[11] While the image is far-fetched, it is based on stereotypical views of libraries and highlights the need for us to *reposition* our services for the Internet age, and show how we can help people to access information effectively even if they wish to do this at home. Proper attention to market research and judicious use of the 'marketing mix' (see below) can help us to deal with such issues.

The marketing toolkit

Moving on from theoretical definitions, we need to consider how marketing helps us in practice. As indicated above, marketing is largely about shifting from a *product* and *service* orientation (the offering) to a *customer* and *need* orientation (the benefit). The discipline of marketing provides us with several concepts and tools that assist us in our task of designing, developing and delivering our services, and many of these are already widely used by information professionals. Among the key concepts are *segmentation* and *positioning*, the *product life cycle* and the *marketing mix*. Popular tools include *SWOT analysis*, *portfolio analysis* and various techniques under the collective heading of *market research*. It is beyond our scope to deal with these topics in depth, and there are many textbooks offering guidance in this area (see the suggestions for further reading at the end of this chapter). We shall therefore provide only brief coverage of some areas and select a few themes to show how marketing is an essential part of our management repertoire.

SWOT analysis

SWOT analysis and the portfolio strategy matrix were introduced in Chapter 2 as useful techniques for environmental appraisal and strategy development. SWOT is essentially a *marketing* planning tool, but it is the most widely used of practical analytical tools in *strategic* planning, indicating how market analysis is a central part of all service planning processes. It involves identifying the organization's Strengths and Weaknesses in relation to the marketplace, and the Opportunities and Threats presented by anticipated environmental trends.

The SWOT is a deceptively simple tool, but is often used in a sloppy and ineffectual manner through lack of thought and focus. There is frequently little evidence of *analysis*, with the exercise failing to move beyond description in the most general terms. SWOTs often involve comparing and combining the work of different groups, and if not properly managed can result in overlong unstructured lists, with no prioritization or weighting of factors, unclear and ambiguous words and phrases, and apparently conflicting statements (for example, the same point listed as a Strength and a Weakness). You can improve the quality of your analysis by following these guidelines:

- Test each alleged strength and weakness by asking whether there is any evidence that *customers* see these features as strengths and weaknesses in the same way as staff

- Deal with statements about things alleged to be both a strength *and* a weakness by asking what *particular aspects* of these characteristics are a strength or a weakness
- Assess each opportunity and threat by considering both the potential *impact* on your service and the *probability* of it happening, and concentrate on items with high ratings.

Market research

Effective customer focus requires a determined effort to find out whether people have been satisfied with our service in the past and what they want in the future as stated by Morgan and Noble: 'A true marketing orientation exists when the major task of marketing within the organisation is directed towards determining the perceptions, needs and wants of targeted customers. Once known, these are satisfied through the design, communication, 'pricing' and delivery of appropriate and competitively viable offerings.'[12]

In the 1970s and 1980s, libraries primarily collected quantified service data. By the 1990s, financial stringency and the need to demonstrate 'value for money' for an increasingly empowered customer base meant subjective concepts like 'customer satisfaction' had become more important. The result was an upsurge in user satisfaction surveys, often targeted to assess service provision for narrowly defined groups of information service customers. Some have argued that this is a 'dangerous' trend, and that too much attention is paid to customer demands, disputing whether our customers can make responsible, informed judgments. Can students, for example, be trusted to determine their own learning requirements, or will they merely give higher priority to having 24-hour access to the Internet to e-mail their friends? Will local public library users embrace the web or just want more paperback fiction because that is what is familiar to them? In short, is the customer always right?

The view that the customer is *not* always right is prevalent in many non-profit organizations, where (by faith or training) it is often felt that the service provider 'knows best'. Such a view is the antithesis of the customer focus that is the essence of marketing and renders market research, the 'marketing mix' and marketing planning obsolete. In a world where information units in all sectors are under pressure to justify their existence and fight off the competition of commercial Internet providers, this view seems at best naïve, and at worst arrogant and self-defeating.

The importance of understanding customer needs and embracing them as a foundation of our marketing philosophy cannot be over-estimated. History is littered with entrepreneurs who have ignored market research and believed (mistakenly) that products could be developed and then a market created for them. As Levitt stressed in his seminal article on 'marketing myopia', it is essential that we focus on **customer benefits**, not products. In the USA, the railroad companies went into decline when the environment changed, because they defined themselves too narrowly as being in the *railroad* business rather than in the *transport* business.[13] Others have learned from this lesson, and today bookshops and record retailers are not confined to selling their traditional media. Many library managers have been keen to follow this approach, and see themselves in the *information* and *knowledge* business, not the book business.

Market research can provide us with valuable guidance in the delivery of 'appropriate offerings'. It has several related purposes, namely to:

- understand existing customers
- identify potential customers
- validate producer/supplier assumptions
- test product/service ideas
- monitor performance and progress.

There are many different ways of carrying out such research and assessing customer satisfaction, formally and informally. These range from the informal one-to-one conversation over the service counter to the more wide-arching and administratively time-consuming 'user survey'. Irrespective of the methods chosen, it is essential that we obtain information from as wide a customer base as possible within the existing constraints of time and money: suggestion forms and committee meetings might provide 'quick and dirty' feedback, but how representative are they? As we become more experienced in obtaining data, targeting of identifiable groups (and hence concerns) is managerially useful and politically sensible. Market research programmes must be ongoing, to take account of the ever-changing environment and the corresponding effect on customer expectations, but we must guard against survey fatigue for our customers (and staff). Finally, the publicity of findings – and action resulting from surveys, in the short, medium and long term – should be an integral part of the whole process.

So what are the market research tools on offer to the already busy information professional? The options available include:

- customer questionnaires
- formal customer interviews, including 'critical incident' studies
- focus group discussions, general and targeted
- informal discussions or conversations with users/non-users
- analysis of usage statistics
- post-transaction surveys or checks ('trailer calls')
- unobtrusive testing ('mystery shopping')
- complaints solicitation/analysis
- feedback from library or other committees or panels
- suggestion books, boxes, forms, etc
- staff observation of customer behaviour
- experimenting with new services ('trial and error')
- interviewing new staff (before they 'accept' practices as the norm)
- investigating experiences elsewhere/learning from the mistakes of others.

REFLECTION

Consider these methods of measuring customer satisfaction. What are the benefits and drawbacks of each approach? Have you encountered any other methods? Which do you feel could be used most successfully in your organization?

Segmentation

Segmentation, also referred to as *target marketing*, is based on the assumption that markets contain within them distinct groups of customers with quite different detailed needs and wants, which each represent a different *segment*, with different purchasing/usage characteristics. Many information service managers already practise segmentation and offer different services to particular user groups (for example, children in public libraries; distance learners in university libraries). Common bases for segmentation include:

- **geographic** – where people live, work or study
- **demographic** – variables such as age, gender and nationality
- **socio-economic** – factors such as education, income or occupation
- **psychographic** – 'life-style', attitudes, values, etc
- **behavioural** – dimensions such as usage patterns, resistance to service changes or take-up of new offerings, and benefits sought.

A segment needs to be *managerially viable,* and the key criteria here are:

- **relevance** – large enough to matter, justify attention and be *actionable*
- **distinctiveness** – characteristics that are separately *identifiable* and *measurable*
- **homogeneity** – relatively *conformable* in behaviour, and reasonably *stable* over time
- **access** – easily *reachable* as a group, in a manner that is *practicable*.

Positioning

Positioning is closely related to segmentation and the processes often overlap, but it is conceptually distinct, and is normally considered at the end of the segmentation process. Whereas segmentation applies to the market itself and the customers within it, positioning applies to the product or service, and is about what the supplier can do with these offerings to best 'position' them in relation to identified segments. This involves deciding where to place your product or service in terms of dimensions such as grade/level and price/value. The concept can also be applied at a strategic level to the service as a whole, for example some corporate libraries have successfully *repositioned* themselves as knowledge centres.

Product life cycle

The *product* life cycle is based on an analogy between the *biological* life cycle and the pattern of sales growth exhibited by most products. It assumes four (or five) stages: introduction or birth, growth, maturity and saturation, decline. (Saturation is sometimes represented as a separate stage.) Its principal value is in reminding us of the inevitability of change and the need to relate our marketing activities to the current competitive environment, rather than presuming that if a service has performed well in the past it – or something similar – will continue to flourish in the future. The Product Life Cycle (PLC) model assumes slow take-up of a new offering at the introduction stage, requiring much effort in promotion, followed by periods of increasing and then steady demand, until a point when it falls off. The challenge here is to anticipate and prevent decline by *rebadging* or otherwise *relaunching* the service, but sometimes the producer has to acknowledge that a product is no longer relevant and accept its 'death' (notably, with offerings based on 'old' technologies).

The PLC is often depicted in graphical form, but some commentators argue that this is misleading as it suggests a *predictive* rather than a *descriptive* model. The duration or durability of a product can be affected by environmental forces, inherent characteristics and by management action, and the basic message here is for regular reviews of your service and product portfolio to ensure continuing vitality and viability.

REFLECTION

Select a service offered by your organization, and consider this in the light of the Product Life Cycle theory. What stage has it reached? How was initial demand generated? Can steps be taken to avoid the 'decline' stage?

The marketing mix

The marketing mix describes those aspects of a product or service over which the organization has control and which need to be individually or collectively managed to achieve marketing objectives. It is in effect a framework for considering the things we can do to influence usage of our services, by asking questions such as:

• What range of services, products and facilities should we offer?
• How should we distribute our offerings through service points etc?
• What charges (or other costs) should we impose on our customers?
• How should we communicate our offerings to potential beneficiaries?

Although several models exist, the most common is the '4Ps' – Product, Place, Price and Promotion – originally proposed by Jerome McCarthy.[14] In an effort to update this model, Kotler has suggested that McCarthy's *seller's* paradigm' of 4Ps should become a *'buyer's* paradigm' of '4Cs' to reflect true customer focus, substituting Customer value, Convenience, Cost to the customer and Communication.[15] We have retained McCarthy's marketing mix here, but reflected Kotler's concerns in our explanations:

- **Product** includes tangible goods (such as publications) as well as all our intangible services and facilities, and their design, features, packaging, etc, which should be related to *customer needs*, identified by carrying out *market research*
- **Place** covers both the physical distribution and accessibility of our services (represented by location of service points and transport facilities) and their *convenience* and availability (in terms of opening hours, remote access, etc)
- **Price** includes not only direct charges levied (for priced products and services, lost or damaged material, overdue loans, etc) but also *hidden costs* to customers, such as time spent waiting for service or the effort required to find items
- **Promotion** covers overt techniques (such as advertising and selling) and less direct methods, including branding (via logos, house style, etc) and *public relations* activities (such as exhibitions, newsletters, open days, and relations with media). It is worth noting that surveys of information service users and suggestions for improvement often reveal a lack of awareness of services available, indicating a need for much better *communication* with our customers.

Service marketing gurus have suggested further elaboration of the model and provided an expanded marketing mix to take account of the special features of services, such as their *impermanence, intangibility* and the *inseparability* of their production and consumption. Valarie Zeithaml and Mary Jo Bitner list '7Ps' for marketing services, adding another three dimensions:

- **People** includes not only contact people, but all the human actors involved in service delivery who influence customer perceptions, notably service staff, service managers and other customers in the service environment – for many professional relationship-based services (such as consultancy and teaching) the provider *is* the service

- **Physical evidence** covers both the environment where the organization and customer interact and any tangible components that facilitate performance or communication (for example, brochures, business cards, letterheads, signage and other issues mentioned in the previous chapter, such as the accuracy/currency of clocks and notices, cleanliness and tidiness of equipment, fixtures and furniture)
- **Process** covers operating systems and procedures – the flow of activities, number of steps and level of involvement of staff and customers, raising questions about *simplicity* and *flexibility* (for example, whether staff are empowered to provide non-standard services customized to meet individual needs).[16]

Marketing your service

Drawing on Kotler's work, Zeithaml and Bitner conceptualize service marketing as a three-way process, involving the organization (management), its service providers (contact people) and customers (beneficiaries). They identify **three dimensions** of service marketing:

- **external** marketing, or *setting the promise*, which covers anything that communicates from the organization to the customer *before* service delivery
- **interactive** or **real-time** marketing, or *delivering the promise*, which covers actual service delivery by employees interacting directly with the customers
- **internal marketing**, or *enabling the promise*, which covers the training, motivating and rewarding of employees to ensure their ability and willingness to deliver the promise.[17]

This reinforces Baker's point about using *all* the organization's resources. We need to see our marketing efforts in the wider organizational context and to work with other operational units and services as our **marketing partners**. We also need to view the recipients of our services as *beneficiaries* or *customers*. The following sections cover the **key players** in service marketing.

Service staff

The most critical element in any service's marketing strategy is its staff. The voice on the end of the telephone and the face behind the desk are far more important than any expensive advertising campaign. The most effective marketing device is also the cheapest – the smile. Friendly staff can often make up for shortcomings elsewhere in the service. Staff are also the most potentially *damaging* part of the marketing equation. Customers do not always notice good service, but they invariably notice *and remember* poor service, which is often a consequence of limited interpersonal skills. While training can make a difference here, many service problems can be traced back to recruitment and a failure to appreciate the importance of selecting staff who want to help people, rather than those who want to handle books. (It is generally easier to develop technical skills than people skills.)

Customers

As already indicated, the essence of marketing is a customer focus. The term 'customer' is used here after much consideration. Even librarians who are happy with the idea of marketing often balk at the term 'customer'. Personally, we prefer this term over others: as ex-audiovisual librarians, we are uneasy about 'reader', and 'user' seems a cold, impersonal term. 'Client' is a possible alternative, and may be preferred in some settings, though it also has its limitations – and unsavoury connotations.[18] The term 'customer' reminds us that the people we serve are paying (directly or indirectly, with their time and effort) for our services. It also fits with current concerns with customer care, customer charters, etc, and with the philosophy of quality management and the concept of an 'internal customer' – the notion that everyone in the organization has 'customers' (as explained in Chapter 2).

ACTIVITY

Traditionally, when the term 'customer' is used we tend to think of 'front of house' users, and customer care has been left to staff who work at enquiry and issue points. Increasingly, the notion that 'everyone is our customer' is being promoted. Consider your rôle in your organization, and list the people you regard as your 'customers'.

PR partnerships

Fruitful partnerships also extend beyond our own service and our own organization to include other partners. Information service marketing and PR partners typically include the following groups:

- **Internal partners.** Your parent body (college, council, firm, hospital, etc) will probably have an information office/marketing department, whose staff may be able to provide advice on campaigns and also help publicize your successes.
- **Professional associations.** Professional bodies can often provide advice and tangible support. The (UK) Library Association, for example, produced free publicity materials for National Libraries Week '97, as well as a 'toolkit' and a regular newsletter filled with tips and suggestions for those wishing to get involved in the celebrations. The LA also has a Publicity and Public Relations Group with its own publications, events programme and annual public relations and publicity awards.[19]
- **The media.** Journalists are looking for stories, and we are looking for publicity, so by working together we can form a mutually beneficial partnership.
- **Sponsors.** Sponsors are looking for publicity, and we are looking for financial support for our projects: we need to assess and sell the benefits of sponsoring our activities in a professional manner.
- **Other marketers.** We are all used to getting ideas from the publicity efforts of colleagues in other information services, but we can also learn from other marketers.

ACTIVITY

Consider the marketing of service providers outside the information sector. What can we learn from their approaches, and what techniques could be adopted in your organization?

Marketing in practice

It is clear that true marketing touches every element of day-to-day service provision. This can range from the formal (for example, how the library is represented at committees) to the informal (for example, how staff interact with customers, including chance encounters). Some activities will be explicitly related to the marketing process, such as the conduct of customer surveys, the publication of survey findings and resultant changes in service provision. Other elements of marketing will be implicit, such as customer care training programmes for all staff. Some marketing is almost subliminal: everyday aspects of our organization are so familiar to us that we hardly see them, but we must strive to view our services through the eyes of a stranger, and consider what they see. We need to ask what impression is conveyed by our building, our publications, and our staff – how do they appear and react to customers? How can we create a professional corporate image?

REFLECTION

Consider the following quotation from Christine Olson in relation to your own service:

> A library's image is composed of everything in and about the library that a client encounters. This includes all the paper and products your library generates: fax cover sheets, routing slips, and overdue notices, as well as research findings, current awareness lists, and database reports. Everything from the library newsletter to the notepaper you use to communicate to clients – all of it projects an image and represents your library, and its services and staff to the client.[20]

Do you have guidelines on house style? If so, how could they be improved? If not, what do you think they should include?

PR INITIATIVES

As well as *ongoing* marketing strategies, we should also consider *one-off* PR initiatives. These are often the most newsworthy, and if we use a national programme or event as a 'hanger' for our activities, we can take advantage of any general publicity and maybe also get help with local efforts. So what types of activities should we pursue? Although there is a place for stunts (most libraries seem to have at least one member of staff who is willing to abseil down buildings!), we should – remembering the 4Ps – concentrate on our *product* and its *value* to the *customer*.

The introduction of new services or facilities, such as the migration to a new computer system or the opening of a new building, will be the result of a lot of hard work (often involving both staff and customers) and this should be the cause for celebration, well worth a few bottles of wine and some accompaniments. You should also think about *branding* your product: does your system or building have a name that will be meaningful to your customers, with its own PR potential? You could run a competition to name it. You may also want to consider a *logo*. All these elements help to promote new services to customers (and staff) and offer scope for further publicity. If you make your new building different and exciting, it might appear in the professional or national press – or even on a record cover![21]

ACTIVITY

Consider the design of a logo for a new service initiative of your choice, or for your information service as a whole. List the qualities you feel a logo should possess.

Some one-off initiatives will evolve into more permanent marketing programmes. Many library 'Friends' groups have grown out of successful campaigns to save local branch libraries and then helped to deflect future cuts, as well as fulfilling a more proactive rôle in extending the branch's support base. A more vibrant library is a less vulnerable library. Even more frivolous events can have serious results: at Reading University Library monitoring of usage patterns for the headline-grabbing 'all nighter' for National Libraries Week in November 1997 informed policy for late-night opening during the examination period of the following summer term. Indeed, everything we do has a marketing dimension, and every service we provide has PR potential. We all need to be alert to such opportunities and to exploit them imaginatively and professionally.

PUBLICITY

If a job is worth doing, it is worth telling others about it. Publicity is a vital area of practical marketing. For PR programmes in particular, publicity must be fully utilized before *and* after events. Publicity can often be simple, but it must always be targeted. We should consider all the options available and tailor our approach accordingly.

News items or features in in-house newsletters or magazines will show that the library/information unit is an active part of the organization. Local newspapers always include news of new bank managers – why not library managers? If your staff win awards or prizes, offer the press a 'local librarian makes good' story. Look at the information press and sectoral titles. Is your news of local or national interest? Should it be directed at a general or specialist audience? Consider whether your successes can best be conveyed by a news 'soundbite', a picture or a full-blown article. Most important of all, make it easy for your news to get published. Look at the style of your target newspaper or periodical. Talk to the editor about your ideas, and find out about the preferred submission medium (eg disk, e-mail, hard copy) and copy dates. If you can write the story yourself, you will get the information across in the way that you want, and the hard-pressed journalist will have one less job to do.

ACTIVITY

Consider the marketing of your information service, and list initiatives taken as:

- on-going programmes to market the service as a whole and specific offerings
- one-off PR events.

What components have proved the most successful? What problems have been encountered? How could any elements be improved in the future? What additional programmes or events should be adopted? How have achievements been publicized? How would you improve this?

Devise a strategy for improved marketing of your service over the next 12 months.

TIMING

Having considered some aspects of the 'why', 'who', 'what' and 'how' of marketing, it is worth briefly pondering some of the practicalities of *when*. Generally speaking, *all the time* is marketing time: no-one in a service industry should have 'off' days, especially not in front of their customers (whoever their customers are). However, there are some specific practical issues to consider in the context of planning events, and it makes sense to do this in relation to our PR partnerships:

- **Staff.** It is vital to consider other staff commitments (such as holidays, major projects, recurring annual activities) which will affect your colleagues, and remember that PR activities may not a high priority for everyone! Plan backwards from launch dates and – most important of all – give your team a long lead-in period.
- **Customers.** You also need to think about what time of year is best for your customers (for example, the examination season is unlikely to be a good time to target students) and also what time of day (perhaps lunch time or early evening to attract local business people).
- **Other partners.** Don't forget to check on the availability of other key players (such as the senior manager you hope will open the event and a photographer to record the occasion) and to find out about other practicalities (for example copy dates, if media coverage soon after the event is important).

Priced products and services

We noted in Chapter 8 that economic and political pressures had prompted some library and information services to consider fund-raising and/or revenue-earning services as a means of dealing with the challenge of 'doing more with less'. While the principles of marketing priced services are the same as for those that are free to users, there are benefits and pitfalls to note, and special issues to consider – notably your rationale for charging and your policy on pricing.

Information services have always operated in a 'mixed economy', but the 1980s represented a watershed in the UK, with various government initiatives strongly encouraging a more entrepreneurial approach. The ITAP report promoted the notion of information as a tradeable commodity,[22] the PUPLIS report suggested joint ventures in publishing and information services involving the public and private sectors,[23] the British Library sponsored studies of income-generating activities,[24] and a Green Paper raised questions about charging for public library services hitherto provided free at the point of use.[25]

Pros and cons

Many priced research services for business users were launched by academic, public and national libraries during this period, but not many have proved viable in the long term.[26] Managers often underestimate the *administrative effort* and *start-up costs* involved, and the *competence* and *confidence* required to market commercial-style services effectively, not to mention resistance among long-standing staff and customers. You also need to consider whether the proposed services have *compatibility* with your existing operations, strategy and culture.[27]

Nevertheless, if carefully planned and managed, charging can actually help in *service promotion* and increase *customer valuation* of offerings; it can enable better services to be offered, make the library or information service appear more professional and businesslike, and improve its efficiency and credibility. There can also be real 'bottom line' gains both through *increased income* and 'invisible earnings', such as a higher profile and *improved status* for the service, and significant development of *staff knowledge and skills*. Bill Simpson, whose Library at Trinity College Dublin regularly earns more than £1 million per year by charging tourists and visitors to the Old Library and Book of Kells, acknowledges that few research libraries have the capacity to generate income of that magnitude, but argues that 'all libraries can make some contribution to their own funding' and cites evidence of those that have done so successfully.[28] Some common examples of priced information products and services are shown in Figure 10.1.

Compensation for reduced funding is only one of several reasons why managers might decide to introduce charges for services. It is essential to be clear about objectives when considering pricing strategies, and also to communicate the rationale for charging to both staff and customers. Other **reasons** commonly given for introducing charges include the following:

- to control or constrain demand
- to ensure that services provided meet real needs
- to differentiate core/basic and marginal/optional/value-added services
- to enable new or improved services to be offered
- to generate income to support core activities.

Pricing and payment methods also vary. Some services (including library memberships and locker hire) are generally offered as annual subscriptions,

Priced information products and services

- photocopying, printing and specialist reprography
- interlibrary loans and reservations
- current awareness/SDI services
- publications, post cards, etc
- enquiry and (re)search services
- hire of lockers, carrels and meeting rooms
- stationery and computer disks
- membership schemes – library facilities for 'outside' users
- special exhibitions of rare books/heritage items
- binding and conservation work
- filming and reproduction rights
- training courses and consultancy work

Fig. 10.1   *Examples of income-generating activities*

but most are charged as individual transactions, with a few examples of upfront/bulk purchase options (such as photocopying cards and research services). The main approaches to **pricing** evident from information service literature are as follows:

- **nominal sum** or **token contribution** – typically used to control demand and/or ensure that the service is really needed (for example, charging 20% of the cost of an interlibrary loan; setting an annual membership fee at a level that has no relationship to the costs incurred)
- **cost-related** – often used to differentiate 'core' and 'non-core' services, sometimes conceptualized as different categories of services for which the cost-recovery policy varies depending on where the service category is placed on the core-periphery spectrum
- **buyer-related** or **demand-related** – based on perceived *value* to the customer ('what the market will bear') and used to discriminate among different market segments, including charging different amounts to different customer groups for the same service
- **competitor-related** – based on assessment of the competition, which can include charging the same amount ('the going rate') as well as

undercutting/discounting to increase market share, or differentiating the service in some way in order to charge a higher price.

ACTIVITY

List opportunities for income generation in your organization. Could they – and should they – be expanded? What management implications can you foresee for any planned initiatives in this field?

References

1 Letter, *Assistant Librarian*, 86 (5), 1993, 68.
2 Smith, A, *An inquiry into the nature and causes of the wealth of nations*, Book 4, Oxford University Press, 1976, 660.
3 Levitt, T, Marketing myopia, *Harvard Business Review*, 38 (4), 1960, 50.
4 Kotler, P and Bloom, P N, *Marketing professional services*, Prentice-Hall, 1984, 4.
5 What is the difference between sales and marketing? Chartered Institute of Marketing (available at **http://www.cim.co.uk/cardev/career/carfaq/365c2ee842.htp**).
6 Hannagan, T, *Marketing for the non-profit sector*, Macmillan, 1992, 30.
7 Baker, M J, 'One more time – what is marketing?' In Baker, M J (ed) *The marketing book*, 4th edn, Butterworth-Heinemann, 1999, 3–15.
8 Taylor, A, *Long overdue*, Mainstream, 1993.
9 Raish, M, Librarians in the movies: an annotated filmography (available at **http://www.lib.byu.edu/dept/libsci/films/introduction.html**).
10 Clayton, C, Lack of status due to image problem, *Library Association Record*, 98 (1), 1996, 20.
11 Saatchis' ad shows nightmare library, *Library Association Record*, 98 (12), 1996, 605.
12 Morgan, P and Noble, S, Marketing library and information services in the '90s, *Australian Library Journal*, 41 (4), 283–92, 285.
13 Levitt, T, Marketing myopia, *Harvard Business Review*, 38 (4), 1960, 45–56.

14 McCarthy, E J, *Basic marketing: a managerial approach*, 6th edn, Richard D. Irwin, 1978.

15 Mazur, L, Silent satisfaction, *Marketing Business* (December-January, 1991-92), 24-7.

16 Zeithaml, V A and Bitner, M J, *Services marketing*, McGraw-Hill, 1996, 23-7.

17 ibid, 22-3.

18 El Nasr, M A, The term 'client' in the social work profession, *International Social Work*, 32, 1989, 311-18.

19 See http://www.la-hq.org.uk/directory/about/pprg.html.

20 Olson, C A, Test your library's marketing IQ, *Medical Reference Services Quarterly*, **12** (3), 1993, 75.

21 See the sleeve of Catatonia's 'Road rage' (1998) which features the pyramid-topped headquarters building of Cardiff County Libraries.

22 Cabinet Office, Information Technology Advisory Panel, *Making a business of information: a survey of new opportunities*, HMSO, 1983.

23 Office of Arts and Libraries, *Joint enterprise: the roles and relationships of the public and private sectors in the provision of library and information services*, Library and Information Series 16, HMSO, 1987.

24 For example White, B, *Striking a balance: external services in academic libraries*, British Library Research Paper No 30, Brenda White Associates, 1987.

25 Office of Arts and Libraries, *Financing our public library services: four subjects for debate*, Cm 324, HMSO, 1988.

26 Webber, S A E, Priced business information services from the public sector: will they succeed? *IFLA Journal*, **16** (2), 1990, 220-30.

27 Nicholson, H, Uncomfortable bedfellows: enterprise and academic libraries, *Journal of Librarianship and Information Science*, **24** (1), 1992, 9-13.

28 Simpson, B, Can academic libraries fund themselves? *Perspectives: Policy and Practice in Higher Education*, **1** (4), 1997, 128-31.

Suggestions for further reading

Levitt, T, Marketing myopia, *Harvard Business Review*, 38 (4), 1960, 45-56.

Seminal article with a simple message, which is still widely cited and well worth reading (particularly if you need to be convinced about the true value of marketing). Uses impressive examples to show the difference between (unsuccessful) organizations that are product-led and (successful) ones that are motivated by providing benefits to customers.

Hannagan, T, *Marketing for the non-profit sector*, Macmillan, 1992.

Clear well-structured guide (190 pp) to marketing concepts and techniques, which explains the similarities and differences between commercial and non-profit organizations. Provides good coverage of marketing research methods and five chapters on the 'marketing mix', with many useful diagrams and case studies (including some references to libraries).

Mercer, D, *New marketing practice: rules for success in a changing world*, Penguin, 1997.

Unconventional presentation of marketing ideas as a series of practical 'rules of thumb' for marketing strategy, tactics and operations, and some general rules of management. There are 15 chapters (285 pp) covering standard topics, such as segmentation and positioning, the customer, marketing research, public relations, new products, pricing and marketing planning.

Adcock, D, Bradfield, R, Halborg, A and Ross, C, *Marketing: principles and practice*, 3rd edn, Financial Times Pitman Publishing, 1998.

Substantial textbook (480 pp) offering an accessible introduction to the subject, moving from definitions to environmental factors and then to customer behaviour. Covers the marketing mix and the management of the marketing function in depth, with many familiar real-world examples and case studies to bring theory to life, as well as useful questions for reflection.

Baker, M J (ed) *The marketing book*, 4th edn, Butterworth-Heinemann, 1999.

Comprehensive overview (c700 pp) of contemporary thinking which contains 30 self-contained contributions by mainly UK-based authors of definitive texts on core topics. Includes numerous figures, tables, references and further readings, with new chapters for this edition on small-to-medium enterprises, the Internet, social marketing and retailing.

Information services marketing

Morgan, P and Noble, S, Marketing library and information services in the '90s, *Australian Library Journal*, **41** (4), 1992, 283-92.

Outlines practical steps to help information professionals apply commercial marketing principles to their services, from situation analysis and objective-setting to evaluation and control procedures; emphasizes segmentation and positioning, arguing that the needs of information service users are too diverse for them to be regarded as a single group.

de Saez, E E, *Marketing concepts for libraries and information services*, Library Association Publishing, 1993.

Concise text (145 pp) which introduces marketing concepts and theories, and discusses their application to information services. Separate chapters cover mission statements, the marketing mix, segmentation and targeting, marketing research, identity and image, and marketing plans. Includes extensive bibliography and references to literature on marketing.

Olson, C A, Test your library's marketing IQ, *Medical Reference Services Quarterly*, **12** (3), 1993, 75-83.

Written in an informal style, and relevant to information professionals in all sectors, despite being published in a specialist journal. Provides numerous hints and tips about image, mission statements, political skills and product branding, and argues strongly and convincingly that there are opportunities for marketing everywhere that should be grasped.

Hart, K, *Putting marketing ideas into action*, The Successful LIS Professional, Library Association Publishing, 1999.

Practical guide (c110 pp) which assumes no prior understanding of the subject and demonstrates the applicability of marketing concepts and techniques to LIS through four ongoing case studies covering public, medical, industrial/business and academic services; includes exercises to aid local application and chapter on evaluation of marketing activities.

Market research

Andrews, J, The use of critical incident technique in an academic library, *Library and Information Research News*, **14** (50), 1991, 22-7.

Describes the use of Critical Incident Technique in interviews with library users to discover problems encountered at Manchester Polytechnic Library, and discusses its limitations and viability as a research method, drawing on practical experience and published literature.

Doyle, C, The perceptions of library service questionnaire (PLSQ): the development of a reliable instrument to measure student perceptions of and satisfaction with quality of service in an academic environment, *The New Review of Academic Librarianship*, **1**, 1995, 139–59.

Discusses approaches to library evaluation and describes the multi-faceted method used at Trinity and All Saints College, Leeds, involving factual and attitudinal questionnaires, observational studies and interviews (covering help desks and online catalogue). Includes questions and results from the attitude survey, and the 16-item instrument finally produced.

Harvey, L, Student satisfaction, *The New Review of Academic Librarianship*, **1**, 1995, 161–73.

Describes methods used to obtain student feedback at the University of Central England, including an annual institution-wide survey for all aspects of educational provision. Covers types of questions, identification of topics, analysis of data, content of reports, response to findings and feedback to students. Discusses library-related issues, reproducing questions on library services and table of composite ratings.

Russell, A and Shoolbred, M, Developing an effective questionnaire, *Library and Information Research News*, **19** (63), 1995, 28–33.

Describes the successful development of a survey instrument to investigate public library use by students with literacy problems. Discusses the design aims, language, pre-testing, special features and reciprocity, and provides references to relevant articles and books.

Line, M B, What do people need of libraries, and how can we find out? *Australian Academic and Research Libraries*, **27** (2), 1996, 77–86.

Distinguishes 'needs' from 'wants', 'demands' and 'uses', and discusses the strengths and weaknesses of both common and less conventional methods of market research. Also comments on what is already known about people's likes and dislikes in relation to library services and facilities, and suggests some fundamental rethinking is required for the future.

Horrocks, A, What do students want? Using 'Priority Search' surveys to determine user satisfaction with library services, *SCONUL Newsletter*, **15**, 1998, 21-4.

Outlines features of the Priority Search methodology used by more than 65 academic and commercial libraries in the UK (such as focus groups, paired comparisons and satisfaction scales) and considers advantages and disadvantages. Also comments on some common findings from recent surveys, based on experience of academic and government libraries.

Promotion and public relations

Fuller, J, Library promotion? It's all dots and dashes! *Link Up*, 1996, 3-6.

Provides numerous tips for an ongoing cost-effective promotional programme: advocates collecting service 'anecdotes' (from satisfied customers) as the basis for PR initiatives, discourages 'stunts', and stresses importance of building political skills and media links.

Henderson, P W and Cote, J A, Guidelines for selecting or modifying logos, *Journal of Marketing*, **62** (2), 1998, 14-30.

In-depth and thought-provoking report, which reviews a research project to monitor logo recognition and offers guidelines to assist managers in the development of logos as a means to achieve corporate image goals. Assesses logos for their naturalness, elaborateness and harmony, providing illustrative examples throughout and also an extensive bibliography.

Rock, F, To raise your profile, raise the roof, *Library Association Record*, **100** (4), 1998, 188-9.

Candid assessment of the programme and planning process for National Libraries Week '97 in Birmingham's public libraries, offering practical guidance to others similarly motivated. Covers formation of the NLW Team, setting project objectives, developing an events programme, the search for sponsorship, evaluation of the week and lessons learned.

Coult, G, Raising the profile: promoting information services, *Managing Information*, **6** (2), 1999, 29-35.

Contains an introduction with 13-point checklist for developing promotional activity, followed by mini case studies from both public and private sectors, including the use of a heritage exhibition to promote a community IT service, the relaunch of an advertising agency information unit as a knowledge centre, and an open house event at a property firm.

Resources on image and librarians (available at **http://www.wam. umd.edu/~staciemm/project/resources.htm**).

A convenient starting-point for bibliographic research in this area: contains sections on the history of librarians, stereotypical images, professional status and image, and changing technology; indexes books, articles and websites, and provides hypertext links to Martin Raish's extensive site, *Librarians in the movies* and the (infamous) *Lipstick librarian*.

Priced products and services

Brindley, L J, Information service and information product pricing, *Aslib Proceedings*, **45** (11/12), 1993, 297–305.

Discusses principles and practices of pricing and charging for tradeable information, covering library-related services, the electronic information industry and government policy, with comments on adding value, service levels and suggested further reading.

Tilson, Y, Income generation and pricing in libraries, *Library Management*, **15** (2), 1994, 5–17.

Based on a questionnaire and interview survey of academic, public and special libraries in London; discusses pricing techniques identified, attitudes towards cost recovery, and policies determining which services were provided free, regulated by charges, or priced to generate income, and also refers extensively to previous published material on this subject.

Mendelsohn, S, Making money – forget it! *Library Manager*, **1**, 1994, 6–8.

Draws on interviews with university librarians in the UK, revealing different views on potential money-earners, ranging from the 'old faithfuls' such as fines and photocopying to consultancy, publishing and selling (eg withdrawn books and back issues of periodicals).

Kay, K, Making cash for libraries, *The Bookseller* (1 May 1998), 25.

A short report on the establishment of a sales point for merchandise at Liverpool Central Library, which has turned out a success (despite initial fears) with the library exploiting its high profile to attract passing trade and enthusiastic staff adding new skills to their CVs.

Part 4 The information professional

11

Personal development

This chapter covers:

- continuing professional development
- professional competencies
- learning and development opportunities
- development rôles and responsibilities
- personal profiles
- personal development plans
- learning logs.

Introduction

Developing your personal capacity to perform effectively at work and in other areas of your life is vital if you wish to survive and thrive in a rapidly changing and highly competitive environment. This chapter defines personal development and related terms and explains their significance. It covers competencies required of modern information professionals and the opportunities available for their development. It also considers rôles and responsibilities in the development process, and introduces models and tools to assist with identifying learning opportunities and organizing your own development, with checklists and examples drawn from both librarianship and management literature.

Personal and professional development

In one of the few books specifically devoted to personal development for information professionals, Sylvia Webb emphasizes that while *training* plays an important part in **personal development**, the latter is a broader process, concerned with motivation, attitudes and personal qualities, as well as job-related skills:

> it is a constant process in which the individual seeks to enhance his or her abilities, skills and knowledge, and/or develop new ones; a process of continuous self-building and realisation of his or her full potential. It takes place by linking abilities with preferences to achieve personal goals, and applies to all aspects of the individual's life.[1]

Continuing professional development (CPD) is closely related to the above, but with a more specific focus on work-related development. There are two widely quoted definitions of CPD in the documentation produced by the (UK) Library Association to accompany its Framework for Continuing Professional Development. The first statement was produced by a group of librarians in 1992; the second is a definition widely used by other occupational groups.

> CPD is an ongoing process aimed at monitoring and upgrading the skills and competences of individual workers in the profession. For those working as team members or on their own, CPD enhances their efficiency and effectiveness. It develops a marketable worth and promotes recognised (or recognisable) good practice throughout the profession.

> The systematic maintenance, improvement and broadening of knowledge and skills and the development of personal qualities necessary for the execution of professional and technical duties throughout the practitioner's working life.

The Library Association (LA) introduced a formal framework for CPD in 1992 as a response to the accelerating pace of change in the operating environment and to demonstrate to the outside world that the library and information profession was one 'which demands for its effective practice a high degree of skill and competence needing rigorous continuing development'. Use of the framework is voluntary – not mandatory – and the LA has not laid down any formal guidance on the amount of time members are expected to spend on CPD (unlike, for example, the Institute of Personnel and Development, which expects a member to spend the equivalent of 35 hours per year on CPD activities).

The introduction to the framework states that the 'average life' of qualifications (academic, vocational and technical) is estimated to be only five years, but this is rather misleading as you might think that you don't need to do anything for the first five years after qualification! The reality is that CPD needs to start in earnest as soon as you finish your initial professional education and to go on for ever, a point emphasized by Maurice Line, who suggests a minimum requirement of 70 hours per year: 'What is needed after that is a continuing combination of practice and learning. The need for lifelong learning applies perhaps more to the library professional than to any other. All practising librarians should spend at least two weeks every year updating their knowledge.'[2] The link between CPD and **lifelong learning** is evident from the definition of the latter taken from *The Learning Age*: 'Lifelong learning means the continuous development of the skills, knowledge and understanding that are essential for employability and fulfilment.'[3]

Initial professional education lays the foundation for subsequent training and development, and practical experience in employment provides the real-life context for the 'embryonic professional' to bring together theory and application. New professionals face the challenge of trying simultaneously to update and consolidate what they already know, and to acquire new knowledge and skills related to their job and place of work, as well as developing a professional identity and career path, which may include working towards Chartered membership of the LA with all that entails. Although the latter might seem an added burden in such circumstances – especially the prospect of producing an evaluative Professional Development Report – following this course should ensure that you have a 'helping agent' or **mentor** (in the form of a Chartership supervisor) which research has shown is a significant factor in determining the success of CPD. The adoption of a systematic approach is another critical factor – hence the relevance of the LA framework.

The world of work is being transformed, and likewise the capabilities and responsibilities expected of individuals. There is an emerging consensus that organizations in the future will replace the security and stability of employment once offered with **employability**, and employer and employee will share responsibility for maintaining (and enhancing) the individual's employability, inside and outside the organization. Individuals are thus being encouraged to market themselves, to identify their unique selling points – in effect to view themselves 'as a business'. Employers are moving beyond short lists of key skills to articulate the capabilities or **competencies** – knowledge, skills, understanding and behaviour – expected of their workforce.

Professional competence

One of the difficulties with the term 'competence' (and 'competency') is that it takes on different meanings in different contexts, and is sometimes rather narrowly interpreted. A useful definition is that offered by Alan Aspey, who emphasizes that competence involves more than possessing necessary *skills* and *knowledge*; it also includes *understanding* one's rôle and having the *motivation* to fulfil it. Aspey defines a 'competent person' as 'someone who has a thorough understanding of the responsibilities of the job and has the motivation, skills and knowledge to consistently carry out those responsibilities to the required standard'.[4]

In 1996, the (US) Special Libraries Association produced a document aimed at educators, students, practitioners and employers setting out competencies for the 21st century. It distinguishes two main types of competencies:

- **professional competencies** relate to the librarian's knowledge in the areas of information resources, technology, management and research, and the ability to use these areas of knowledge as a basis for providing library and information services
- **personal competencies** represent a set of skills, attitudes and values that enable librarians to work efficiently, be good communicators, focus on continuing learning throughout their careers, demonstrate the value-added nature of their contributions, and survive in the new world of work.

Although developed with the special librarian in mind the competencies have general applicability to information professionals. In addition to the competency descriptions set out in Figure 11.1, the document provides four to six practical examples under each of the 24 competency areas showing the variety of tasks and rôles performed by librarians. It also includes comments on the changing environment and the value of the special librarian, as well as a supporting bibliography.[5]

PROFESSIONAL COMPETENCIES
The Special Librarian . . .

- has expert knowledge of the content of information resources, including the ability to critically evaluate and filter them
- has specialized subject knowledge appropriate to the business of the organization or client
- develops and manages convenient, accessible and cost-effective information services that are aligned with the strategic directions of the organization
- provides instructions and support for library and information service users
- assesses information needs and designs and markets value-added information services and products to meet identified needs
- understands and uses appropriate information technology to acquire, organize and disseminate information
- understands and uses appropriate business and management approaches to communicate the importance of information services to senior management
- develops specialized information products for use inside or outside the organization or by individual clients
- evaluates the outcomes of information use and conducts research related to the solution of information management problems
- continually improves information services in response to changing needs
- is an effective member of the senior management team and a consultant to the organization on information issues.

PERSONAL COMPETENCIES
The Special Librarian . . .

- is committed to service excellence
- seeks out challenges and sees new opportunities both inside and outside the library
- sees the big picture
- looks for partnerships and alliances
- creates an environment of mutual respect and trust
- has effective communication skills
- works well with others in a team
- provides leadership
- plans, prioritizes and focuses on what is critical
- is committed to lifelong learning and personal career planning
- has personal business skills and creates new opportunities
- recognizes the value of professional networking and solidarity
- is flexible and positive in a time of continuing change.

Fig. 11.1 *Competencies for special librarians of the 21st century*

Competency statements of this type help to define professional rôles and responsibilities at a general level. Other publications offer guidance on new and emerging rôles, particularly those associated with technological advances. Nick Moore outlines skills and rôles for three complementary groups of 'new information professionals':

- **creators**, who design and develop products and services, exemplified by web authors
- **communicators**, who identify and interpret information, illustrated by subject specialists
- **consolidators**, who select and synthesize information, typified by management researchers.[6]

The (UK) Library and Information Commission suggests other potential rôles for public library staff in the new networked environment – *net navigator, IT gatekeeper, information consultant, information manager* and *educator* – and identifies information and communication technology tasks and skills related to each rôle for both managers and frontline workers.[7] Many people have predicted new rôles for information professionals as **knowledge management specialists**, highlighting their potential contribution in the ongoing management of content, where specialist skills in indexing systems, thesaurus construction and user profiling are needed to structure and codify information, to provide a common language and to manage customized alerting.

As indicated previously, the impact of technological (and educational) developments means that IT-related skills previously regarded as specialist are increasingly required by all information workers – such as the ability to use standard software (word-processing, spreadsheets, etc), the ability to search electronic information sources (CD-ROMs and the Internet) and to trouble-shoot hardware problems (for example, printers and scanners). In addition, the shift from mediated to self-service searching and other facilities means that all frontline staff need to be skilled in advising, instructing and supporting service users. Also, increased stress on liaison with customers and suppliers and the growth in team-based and project-based working requires good communication, interpersonal and negotiating skills. The cumulative effect of these developments, coupled with more general management and business trends, means that as an information professional today you need to develop a wider skillset than ever before. The type and level of IT skills required will depend on particular job requirements, but all information professionals will need to maintain awareness of IT developments and to consider their implications for information services management.

REFLECTION

What do you consider to be the most urgent priority areas where you need to develop your skills, knowledge and understanding? Do you think there are any significant gaps in your competence in relation to your current job? What are the important areas to work on for future career development?

Various commentators have produced checklists of the skills now expected of information professionals and also of graduates more generally (often described as 'generic', 'personal' or 'transferable' skills). A summary of more than 40 commonly identified general and specialist skills and behaviours is appended as a starting point for assessing personal development needs. A key point to note is that information-related skills are necessary – indeed essential, as the core competence for information professionals – but they are not sufficient for effectiveness, and need to be complemented by personal qualities and abilities, as well as business acumen and commercial awareness. The attributes listed in Figure 11.2 are tipped as those critical for success.

Communication increasingly means electronic communication, and in particular electronic mail (e-mail). The competence required here is not just about using the technology, but understanding *how* and *when* to use it – e-mail has acquired a bad reputation lately, and has been widely cited as a waste of time and a source of stress, particularly when used to transmit the sort of messages that are more properly dealt with face-to-face or by telephone. If used sensibly and thoughtfully, e-mail can save time and improve effectiveness. It can be really useful as a means of communicating the same message to a large number of people, and also for quick informal exchanges with people whom you cannot contact by telephone, but remember to think before you press the send button.

To move beyond the information profession into the emerging **knowledge profession**, we need to strengthen and extend our skills. On the one hand, we need to embrace *internally generated* as well as *externally pub-*

The new professional – critical attributes

- Communication
- Facilitating and helping
- Negotiation, especially financial
- IT understanding
- Presentation of information
- Problem-solving methodologies
- Project and programme management
- Self-management

Fig. 11.2   *Critical attributes for information professionals of the future*

lished information, and to progress beyond the information *container* towards *analysis* and *interpretation* of its *contents*. On the other hand, we must become *value-oriented* as well as *service-oriented*, and demonstrate our *business focus* by relating our work more overtly to specific organizational objectives. Information specialists are competing with other professionals to become major players in the knowledge economy. To be successful as a knowledge management specialist, you will need to be a multifaceted professional, who is seen as a capable and credible performer in a variety of organizational rôles, namely:

- **business professional** – well-informed about the core processes of the organization and the sector in which it operates
- **technology manager** – familiar with current and emerging information and communication technologies and a confident user of generic and specialist tools (such as databases, intranets and groupware)
- **content organizer** – expert in selecting, sourcing, structuring and synthesizing data, information and knowledge (requiring skills in user profiling, thesaurus construction, metadata management, etc)
- **communicator** – effective in capturing and articulating information and ideas, verbally and graphically
- **change agent** – able to make a substantial contribution to organizational development as coach, facilitator, negotiator and project manager
- **entrepreneur** – flexible and innovative in exploiting opportunities to use information and knowledge creatively for organizational benefit

- **team player** – active in building multidisciplinary communities and promoting cross-functional working.

Learning options

Opportunities for learning and development arise both on-the-job and off-the-job, and can be formal or informal, planned or *ad hoc*, at work or somewhere completely different. Many people equate development activities with one-to-one instruction and group training sessions (internal or external) and overlook the many other learning opportunities which typically occur on a day-to-day basis.

Opportunities on the job

Observing colleagues at work, either formally as part of a job *shadowing* process or informally, and following this through with questioning and listening, can help you learn from examples of good practice – or poor performance! Job *rotation* or *exchanges* (with other organizations) offer the chance for more in-depth sampling of different activities without permanently changing your job. Job *enlargement* or job *enrichment* involves stretching the boundaries of your existing job, and can be initiated by individuals as well as their managers.

One of the most common methods of developing on the job at present is through involvement in quality improvement or service development *projects* or *task forces*. Larger-scale undertakings of this type include externally-funded research projects, where temporary *secondment* of existing staff from their regular jobs is often an attractive option for senior managers, as it avoids the risk of employing new unknown staff on a high-profile development project. Smaller-scale examples include everyday trouble-shooting and *problem-solving* – often not seen as a development opportunity, with the result that when the problem recurs, the 'expert' has to be brought in again as the opportunity was not taken to *share learning* and involve others in problem resolution.

Participation in *committees* or *working groups* within and outside the information service (including involvement in either the parent organization or the wider professional community) is a way of developing both skills and contacts, and gaining valuable experience in cross-functional or cross-sectoral working: *representation* duties are often not properly recognized as an important responsibility – acting as the public face of your service – as well as a valuable chance to gain new perspectives and insights. Attendance at *conferences* and *exhibitions* is another example of multipurpose activity, often combining representation, professional networking, personal learning and information-gathering, on behalf of yourself, your colleagues and your organization. Other development opportunities arising from involvement in **professional activities** (such as event organization, public speaking and writing for publication) are explored in the next chapter.

Study options

Despite the shift away from 'classroom-based' learning, there is still a buoyant market for programmes leading to **qualifications**. With the continuing focus on management and business-related skills, information professionals are tending to opt for MBA programmes, rather than the more traditional vocationally oriented MLib. Such programmes have the added benefit of exposure to perspectives and experiences beyond the LIS sector, while usually providing opportunities through practical assignments for participants to apply general management theories and techniques to their own work situation. These programmes vary considerably in content, duration and mode of delivery, with full-time and part-time options, residential and distance learning, etc. A current trend is towards more specialized Masters-level programmes, exemplified by MSc programmes in Human Resource Development, in Electronic Information Management, in Information Systems and – most recently – in Information and Knowledge Management (at the University of North London).

Further study can of course be pursued less formally, notably through open/flexible learning programmes, often using technology-assisted learning methods, including web-based delivery via the Internet. At the most informal end of the spectrum, *electronic discussion lists* can be used as a professional development tool, both to supplement traditional professional reading, and as a vehicle for conducting small-scale investigations, or just obtaining information/getting help with everyday problem-solving.[8] They are a particularly valuable resource in this respect for people working on their own: both the LA and the Special Libraries Association offer discussion lists for 'solos'.[9-10]

Mentors

Mentoring is another approach to development which has grown in popularity recently, and has been covered in several publications in the library and information services sector (see the suggestions for further reading in Chapter 7). Mentoring can be casual or formal, for general or specific purposes, and initiated by the individual or the organization. Its distinctive feature is a focus on a *one-to-one relationship* between mentor and learner, which ensures individual attention and support for the learner. Examples of specific purposes include: *induction*, to help a new employee get to know the organization – often known as *buddying*, when the mentor is an experienced employee at a similar level; support for staff undertaking programmes leading to *qualifications* – for example, supervisors of people working towards LA Chartership; and mentoring arrangements deliberately aimed at developing technical skills, professional knowledge or organizational understanding.

While mentors are often *senior managers* in the same organization, they can also come from outside, and they can also be *peers*, which sometimes develops as a *co-mentoring* relationship. A key point to note here is that a mentoring relationship has significant development potential for both the mentor *and* the learner, and managers often gain insights into personal and organizational behaviour from less experienced colleagues as a result of mentoring. **Learning** sets, which are a particular form of self-development group, fulfil some of the functions of mentoring in a group environment: they are distinct from the usual discussion group, because at any one time the focus of attention is on one member of the group, and his or her learning needs. (Such sets are normally facilitated by *set advisers* who have had some special training for this rôle.)

REFLECTION

Recall some examples of past development/learning experiences. Analyse how effective these different experiences were. What does this tell you about your learning preferences? Which methods of learning and development will you choose in future?

Whose responsibility?

Many people have potential rôles to play in your personal and professional development. In the organizational environment, staff development and training has traditionally been seen as a **shared responsibility** between three key players – the employee, the employer and the line manager. However, the changing nature of employment, including the growth in fixed-term contracts and decline in single-organization careers, has shifted the balance in this triangular relationship, so that individuals at all levels are now having to take more responsibility for their own development, as indicated recently by Sir Geoffrey Holland, President of the Institute of Personnel and Development, 'Qualifications and service in an organisation no longer guarantee permanent employment for individuals. They have to ensure their own development to become [employable] or retain their own employability.'[11]

While this shift of emphasis may represent a significant change for some categories of workers, it should not be seen as such by information professionals! The maintenance and development of professional competence has long been regarded as one of the defining characteristics of a profession and its members, and this principle is often stated explicitly in codes of ethics or 'professional conduct'. Professional bodies in the library and information services sector have followed the general trend in this respect, and most of those with published codes place a **formal obligation** on their members to keep up-to-date with new developments in their field. Thus the LA states in its 1983 Code of Professional Conduct:

> 2c Members must be competent in their professional activities including the requirement
>
> i to keep abreast of developments in librarianship in those branches of professional practice in which qualifications and experience entitle them to engage;
> ii in respect of those members of the Association responsible for supervising the training or duties of another librarian, to ensure that those whom they supervise are trained to carry out their duties in a competent manner.[12]

Similarly, the American Library Association code states: 'We strive for excellence in the profession by maintaining and enhancing our own knowledge and skills, by encouraging the professional development of co-workers, and by fostering the aspirations of potential members of the profession.'[13] The (UK) Institute of Information Scientists developed its (draft) guidelines for professional ethics for information professionals more recently and impos-es a larger responsibility on its members, which relates professional com-petence to the employing organization:

3.3 Competence

> An information professional should attempt to ensure that he or she is com-petent to undertake all his or her professional duties. This includes a respon-sibility for his or her own continuing professional development. It also involves developing ongoing knowledge of the purpose and function of the organisation in which he or she works.[14]

Assuming responsibility for your own development also makes sense for another reason, namely that in practice the only person with a real long-term guaranteed interest in your competence and employability is yourself. But there are lots of other people, at work and elsewhere – bosses, col-leagues, friends and relations – who will need and/or want to become involved in your professional and personal development at different times and in various ways. The following sections look at the responsibilities of the main players in the traditional training and development triangle and then suggest other possible sources of help and support.

The tripartite partnership

- The **employer** or **organization** has prime responsibility for formulating policies and plans, and allocating resources and time, to ensure that all employees are properly trained to carry out their assigned tasks. This responsibility is normally discharged through departmental or service heads, and in larger organizations is usually delegated to a senior per-son acting as the staff development or training officer for the business unit. The responsibility also extends to ensuring opportunities for pro-fessional development, providing information and advice to those involved, and giving support and guidance to line managers.
- The **line manager** or **supervisor** has particular responsibility for identi-

fying, acting on and monitoring the training and development needs of his or her team, both as individuals and as a group. This includes finding opportunities for both training and practice, offering encouragement and help, and giving clear and timely feedback (for example, not leaving this until an annual appraisal discussion). Where people are involved in a range of activities supervised by different managers, some of these responsibilities will have to be shared, but the line manager should assume a coordinating rôle.

- The **individual** as an **employee** has personal responsibility for being an active (rather than a passive) participant in this process and for approaching his or her own development in a collaborative spirit. This includes assessing and communicating his or her needs, making good use of opportunities offered, evaluating events and activities, applying learning to day-to-day tasks, and sharing experience with colleagues. The individual may also have formal responsibilities for others as described above, as none of the rôles set out here are mutually exclusive.

Personal support systems

As already indicated, there are many rôles that other people can play in supporting your development. Most people don't think of these many and varied relationships as a 'system' but this concept can help us to appreciate some basic principles underpinning good use of such support. A 'support system' can be defined here as a *resource pool* drawn on *selectively* to help you move towards your goals – which might include acquiring some information, achieving specific objectives, developing your skills, deepening your understanding, gaining fresh perspectives, or obtaining a new job. Important principles in using support systems include:

- **maintenance** – keep in touch with people, so that when you need to draw on them (for example, as a referee) they are reasonably well informed about your situation
- **parsimony** – keep the system to a manageable size, so that you don't have to expend a lot of energy on maintaining it
- **equity** – seek arrangements than seem fair (for example, in terms of reciprocal help, or a feeling of shared achievement) to avoid build-up of guilt from a sense of debts that cannot be repaid

- **back-up** – try to have several places where you can turn for particular kinds of support, to reduce dependency and vulnerability to unavailability
- **feedback** – check how others involved (and you yourself) feel about the process of giving or receiving assistance.

Your support system – potential helpers – will probably include people closely associated with your job (for example, your boss, peers, team) and also people less directly involved (such as a partner, friends, trainers, contacts, former bosses). Some may play a variety of rôles, others will provide a specific type of support (for example, specialist knowledge, expert advice). Having a network of professional and personal supporters can be particularly helpful in coping with the stress commonly associated with *transitions* in rôles and relationships, jobs or careers. As well as emotional and practical support, your network will provide a welcome sense of continuity when other things in your environment are changing. The list below shows some of the typical categories of and functions fulfilled by such supporters, which are again not mutually exclusive:

- **rôle models** – people who can help you to define personal goals in terms of the positions or accomplishments you aspire to, by demonstrating what is possible and explaining what is involved
- **referral agents** – people who can put you in touch with required resources and/or facilitate access to individuals or organizations, through their personal knowledge, experience, insights and influence
- **sounding boards** – people who will listen to your ideas, question you and offer feedback in a constructive manner, thus enabling you to experiment and test your thinking in a supportive environment
- **interest groups** – people who share common interests or concerns (either within your own organization or in the wider professional community) can help to maintain motivation, as well as being sources of information and ideas
- **appointed persons** – people who have a formal responsibility to help you in a particular way (for example, for those working towards LA chartership, their supervisor and the local registration liaison officer).

Development tools

The case for CPD and a *systematic* approach to its organization and management is clear. However, it is crucial to get the balance right: a system that is too prescriptive or too complicated will probably be counterproductive. Some people feel that the LA CPD framework documentation falls into this category; others – including some overseas associations – have taken it up with enthusiasm. All professionals need to conduct a regular self-audit, set their personal objectives and goals, form plans to meet identified development needs, review their position and then recycle through the process. You should also document this process to some extent, and keep records of relevant activities and achievements. Tools which can be useful here include some form of **personal profile** and a **development agreement** or **action plan**, supported by a **learning log**. The following sections set out suggested minimum requirements for documentation.

Personal profile

One of the valuable features of the LA framework is that it encourages you to record and to keep up-to-date all the basic information generally needed for a *curriculum vitae* or job application, which most people – despite the best of intentions – end up frantically trying to put together from a variety of sources only when they see an attractive position advertised. This really is worth doing properly on a *regular* basis (at least quarterly) as it will save you a lot of time, and will then allow you to focus your attention on the *presentation* of the information in the context of the opportunity on offer. Seven headings are suggested here. It is advisable to compile a comprehensive record covering all the details indicated in Figure 11.3 to serve as a *master file*, even though you will almost certainly wish to omit some information – even entire sections – for some purposes.

Profile tips

- In job details, include budgetary and staff management responsibilities, and focus on *achievements* not activities.
- Use a box file to collect copies of significant documents you have authored, including internal reports and promotional material, as a tangible reminder of your achievements.

Personal profile

Education
[Secondary and tertiary institutions attended, with dates, examinations passed and grades – if you omit details, people will make assumptions]

Qualifications
[Degrees and chartered or corporate memberships of professional bodies, and any other certificates, diplomas, etc, with dates]

Employment
[Employers, job titles and final salaries (with dates) and your main responsibilities and key achievements – record three to five points for each]

Training
[Professional/technical and management courses attended, with dates, duration and names of training providers]

Committees
[Offices held and memberships of committees/working groups of professional and other external bodies, with dates]

Publications
[Books, reports, pamphlets, periodical articles, conference papers, book/product reviews, etc, listed in chronological order]

Presentations
[Details of externally presented papers, talks, seminars, workshops, demonstrations, etc, in chronological order]

Fig. 11.3   *Recommended contents for personal profiles*

- Note all external training courses attended, and selected internal/on-site events (particularly management topics and technical specialisms).

Personal development plan

The process of identifying and documenting development needs and proposed actions can be approached in a variety of ways. In many organizations an annual staff appraisal/training needs analysis process will cover much of the required ground, but these schemes do not always take the sort of *holistic* approach needed to ensure that your professional and personal objectives are sensibly aligned and full account is taken of other things in your private life. The LA framework has a special section devoted to *personal priorities*, which encourages you to list and prioritize your work-related and other interests and to set objectives for both – rather than just muddling along and assuming you can give 100% to your career, family and friends at the same time! Diagnostic instruments such as questionnaires which give feedback on management style, team rôles, etc, can be useful here and are often available via organizations' staff development officers.

Another tried and tested method of conducting such an analysis and assessment is to work through a series of questions, perhaps assisted by a colleague or friend. Many career development publications include such checklists: a simple version is shown in Figure 11.4, and a more extensive and far-reaching checklist of career questions is appended.

The results of this conversation (with yourself or with a colleague) should be documented in some form before moving on to the next stage, which is to finalize and formalize your action plan for personal develop-ment. A simple format is recommended for this, so that it can be easily

---

Personal development plan checklist

- What have I achieved in my previous jobs?
- What do I do well and/or enjoy in my present job?
- Where do I need to improve and/or develop my skills?
- Where and in what rôles do I see my future?
- What new knowledge, skills and insights will I need?
- What development methods have helped me in the past?
- What development opportunities are available to me now?
- What constraints or problems might I encounter?
- What support might I need/obtain from colleagues?
- What other resources will be available to me?

Fig. 11.4   *Suggested questions for personal development planning*

maintained, updated and annotated as necessary. For each development objective, you must state:

- **what** it is, expressed in a short phrase
- **how** you intend to achieve it – the development method
- **when** you will do this – the timescale for achievement
- **who** else will be involved in the process (if anyone).

You may find it useful to divide your objectives into *short-term development needs* and *longer-term career aims*, and to break down the latter into more manageable chunks in the form of sub-objectives, which can be incorporated into your short-term plan. Ideally you should update this document continuously, but you may find it easier to use a learning log on a day-to-day basis for this purpose, and then review your development plan at set points in the year.

Learning log

A learning log is a simple but powerful tool which helps you to ensure that twelve months' experience in a job is more than one month's experience repeated twelve times. (If you substitute 'years' for 'months' the argument is even more telling!) It reinforces the well-known learning cycle: having an experience; reviewing the experience; concluding from the experience; and planning the next steps. People who prefer an 'activist' learning style will be reluctant to write things down in this way, but experience shows that going through this process is the best way to make sure that you really do think about the experience, make sense of it, and do things differently in future. Only four or five headings are needed. Our suggestions are given in Figure 11.5. This format can also be used to record and evaluate more formal learning events, such as attendance at courses, in which case you may wish to indicate what your *personal aims* were in attending the event – note that this may not be the same as the event's advertised objectives!

ACTIVITY

Consider the development tools described and choose something which appeals to you. Find some unscheduled time in your diary – allow at least one to two hours. See what you can achieve in the time available.

Learning log

Date and event

[Identify a recent significant experience, and give it a meaningful name at the top of the log.]

What happened

[Provide a factual description of what happened, including what others did, but paying particular attention to your part in the events, and your feelings or thoughts *at the time.*]

Lesson learned

[Consider how what happened relates to what you know about people, groups or organizations. Does it lead you to change your view, or does your knowledge suggest any different approaches to what you did?]

Action planned

[Write down what you propose to do/how you will use this learning, eg something related to this event, or behaving differently in similar situations in the future, or developing yourself to handle such situations better.]

Fig. 11.5 *Suggested headings for learning logs*

References

1 Webb, S P, *Personal development in information work*, 2nd edn, Aslib, 1991, 1.
2 Line, M B, Re-engineering libraries for a lifelong learning society, *Logos*, 8 (1), 1997, 35–41.
3 Department for Education and Employment, *The learning age: a renaissance for a new Britain*, Cm 3790, HMSO, Introduction, para 16.
4 Aspey, A, Seeking motivation [Letter], *People Management* (10 December 1998), 23.
5 Special Libraries Association, *Competencies for special librarians of the 21st century*, Special Libraries Association, 1996 (available at http://www.sla.org/professional/competency.html).
6 Moore, N, Creators, communicators and consolidators: the new information professional, *Managing Information*, 3 (6), 1996, 24–5.
7 Library and Information Commission, *Building the new library network: a report to government*, Library and Information Commission,

1998, 235-7.
8   Kvebekk, M, Electronic discussion lists and professional development, *Personnel training and education*, **15** (2), 1998, 11-12.
9   Rees-Jones, L, Why not subscribe to the LA's new e-mail discussion list for solos? *Library Association Record*, **101** (4), 1999, 229.
10 Siess, J A, Flying solo: librarian, manage thyself, *American Libraries*, **30** (2), 1999, 32-4.
11 Guile, D and Fonda, N, *Performance management through capability*, Issues in People Management 25, Institute of Personnel and Development, 1998, vii.
12 Code of professional conduct. In *The Library Association Yearbook 1998-9*, Library Association Publishing, 1998, 210.
13 American Library Association, *Code of Ethics*, American Library Association, 1995.
14 Draft IIS guidelines for professional ethics for information professionals, *Inform*, **201**, 1998, 4-5.

Suggestions for further reading

Webb, S P, *Personal development in information work*, 2nd edn, Aslib, 1991.
   Defines personal development in the context of information work and describes methods of achieving this in different types of organization, with practical examples. Chapters cover the organization and the individual, interviews as a focus for personal development, management aspects, developing on your own, and the profession at large.
Elkin, J, Personal development: looking at further opportunities, *Assistant Librarian*, **90** (9), 1997, 139-44.
   Comments on the changing rôle of information professionals, arguing that newly qualified staff are 'embryonic professionals' for whom CPD and lifelong learning are essential. Lists competencies highlighted in recent survey of LIS employers and considers the potential contribution to CPD of Departments of Information and Library Studies.
Parry, J, Maintaining quality through continuing professional development, *Impact*, **1** (2), 1998, 25-9 *and* **1** (3), 1998, 34-7.
   Two-part article which defines CPD, explains the benefits to individuals and employers, and explores different options to consider in under-

taking CPD. Also looks at the management of CPD from both organizational and individual viewpoints, and offers advice on using appraisal schemes and the Library Association's CPD framework.

Professional competence

Beaulieu, M, Developing the information professional: whose responsibility? Educating and developing the information professional for success, *Impact*, **1** (7), 1998, 107-12.
   Discusses trends and developments in courses offered to aspiring professionals, noting the advent of multidisciplinary programmes (with computing, electronic publishing, etc) and describes some of the technical, social and organizational competencies expected of modern professionals, referring to the Special Libraries Association list of competencies.
Garrod, P, Skills for new information professionals (SKIP): an evaluation of the key findings, *Program*, **32** (3), 1998, 241-63.
   Based on in-depth research into the impact of IT on the skills and rôles of specialist and support staff in academic libraries. Highlights the need for communication and interpersonal skills, other personal qualities/behaviours, abilities in critical thinking and problem-solving and a supportive working environment, in addition to IT competence.

Development methods

Mumford, A, *Effective learning*, Training Extras Series, Institute of Personnel and Development, 1995.
   Concise guide (c40 pp) which explains how managers and professionals can develop their knowledge and skills by improving their ability to learn. Covers learning styles and skills, formal and informal learning opportunities, personal development plans, environmental influences, potential helpers, and 11 principles of effective learning.
Megginson, D and Whitaker, V, *Cultivating self-development*, Training Essentials Series, Institute of Personnel and Development, 1996.
   Guidebook for trainers and line managers (120 pp) which defines self-development, explains benefits and success factors, and describes various approaches and activities. Contains checklists to assess individual

and organizational readiness, identifies different types of learner, and provides annotated lists of key texts, workbooks and diagnostic tools.

Clutterbuck, D, *Learning alliances: tapping into talent*, Developing Practice Series, Institute of Personnel and Development, 1998.

Based on assumption that managers increasingly need to be facilitators of learning and can play many rôles. Explains four basic types of helper – coach, guardian, counsellor and networker – and 15 styles of mentoring behaviour. Presents mentoring as the integrating pivotal rôle, covering formal and informal programmes and relationships.

Skills development

Nofsinger, M M, Time management skills: a checklist, *College & Research Libraries News*, 57 (10), 1996, 648–50.

Aimed specifically at newly qualified information professionals, provides step-by-step guidelines amounting to 34 practical tips for clarifying service and personal objectives and goals, relating daily activities to overall priorities, identifying opportunities for delegation, planning daily schedules, managing paperwork, and finding time for projects.

Sampson, E, *30 minutes . . . to make the right impression*, Kogan Page, 1997.

Pocket guide (c60 pp) which explains how the way we look, move and sound affects our business and social relationships. Offers practical advice on dealing with various situations, including job interviews, meetings, presentations and social situations. Includes checklists and guidelines, and covers audience profiles, body language and vocal style.

Gleeson, K, *The high-tech personal efficiency program: organizing your electronic resources to maximize your time and efficiency*, John Wiley & Sons, 1998.

Detailed primer (c240 pp) on how to become better organized and more productive by developing effective working practices and improving your use of electronic tools. Sets out key work principles and then describes how to organize papers and files, how to manage plans and tasks, and how to deal with e-mail and web documents. Also covers work space, laptops and groupware, and provides glossary of c150 computer-related terms.

Morris, S and Smith, J, *Understanding mind maps in a week*, Hodder &

Stoughton, 1998.
Concise introduction (c100 pp) to mind mapping as a technique for recording, organizing and analysing information and ideas, and a way of improving understanding, planning, memory and creativity. Explains the concept, sets out basic rules, and discusses various uses, including decision-making, time management, note-taking and presentations.

Sussams, J E, *How to write effective reports*, 3rd edn, Gower, 1998.
Comprehensive guide (c140 pp) to planning, drafting and presenting reports, for managers and specialists. Separate chapters cover structure, layout, language, spelling and punctuation, and materials and equipment. Also provides advice on other means of communication, and includes exercises for self-analysis of style and effectiveness.

Career development

Burrington, G, *Equally good: women in British librarianship*, AAL Publishing, 1993.
Substantial survey (c300p) of ways to achieve success in life and work, containing 21 autobiographical profiles of women selected by their peers as professional rôle models, exemplifying career breaks, dual rôles, moving on, sectoral mobility and single-sector careers. Concludes with a review of common themes and issues, comments on 48 topics relevant to personal development, and gives information on good equal opportunities practice.

Noon, P, Managing to build a career, *Librarian Career Development*, 2 (3), 1994, 22-5.
Frank account of author's personal experience of undertaking a part-time MBA programme while working full-time in an academic library. Covers reasons for his decision, programme content, and both the drawbacks/challenges and benefits identified.

Hill, S J, Get that job: an introduction; letter-writing; form-filling and CV preparation, *Librarian Career Development*, 3 (1), 1995, 5-8; 3 (2), 1995, 22-5; *and* 3 (3), 1995, 24-7.
Three linked articles written by an experienced manager of a recruitment agency specializing in information-related posts. Outlines changes in the job market and skills requirements, and provides advice on career strategies and continuing professional development, followed by

detailed guidance on letters of application, forms and CVs.

Sellen, B-C (ed) *What else you can do with a library degree: career options for the 90s and beyond,* Neal-Schuman, 1997.

Substantial volume (335 pp) containing 62 personal accounts of librarians working beyond traditional settings. Organized in seven categories, ranging from related sectors (such as library supply and the book trade) through independent workers and business owners to more unusual examples (a risk-management researcher and an art dealer).

Dewar, D, Shock tactics for the job jungle, *Library Association Record,* **100** (12), 1998, 651.

Provides practical advice (based on personal experience) on surviving redundancy and finding another job. Advocates temporary contracts as a route back to permanent work (particularly for over-35s) and a valuable opportunity to broaden experience.

Appendices

PROFESSIONAL COMPETENCE MODEL
A checklist for personal development planning

GENERIC PERSONAL SKILLS
- Communication, oral and written
- Information, including use of IT
- Learning and research
- Numeracy, use of data
- Problem-solving
- Self-management (planning and managing time, developing oneself)
- Team working.

PROFESSIONAL/SPECIALIST INFORMATION SKILLS

- Collection development and management (eg selection, storage, preservation)
- Identification and evaluation of sources and services
- Information retrieval – searching, finding, filtering, etc
- Knowledge organization – cataloguing, classifying, indexing, metadata, thesauri
- Legal and regulatory aspects of information (eg copyright, data protection)
- Library housekeeping – acquisition, circulation, interlending, OPACs
- Presentation of information (eg abstracting, displaying, formatting, interpreting).

IT SKILLS

- Computer hardware and peripherals
- Database packages
- Electronic communication systems (eg e-mail, fax)
- Multimedia resources
- Network access (Internet/intranet, web browsers)
- Office automation tools (eg spreadsheets, word-processing)
- Presentation software (eg DTP, graphics).

BUSINESS AND MANAGEMENT SKILLS

- Accounting, budgeting and costing
- Change management
- Marketing, public relations and survey methods
- People/personnel management
- Project and programme management
- Quality assurance and performance measurement
- Strategic, tactical and operational planning.

ORGANIZATIONAL KNOWLEDGE AND SUBJECT UNDERSTANDING

- Culture and climate
- Customer groups and needs

- History and traditions
- Mission, vision and values
- Stakeholder interests
- Structure and systems
- Terminology of the field.

PERSONAL WORK BEHAVIOUR

- Achievement/results orientation
- Customer focus and concern
- Developing others
- Flexibility/adaptability
- Innovation and continuous improvement
- Leadership/initiative
- Strategic perspective.

CAREER DEVELOPMENT CHECKLIST
'The new ground rules for employability'

1   IDENTIFY YOUR TARGET MARKETS AND ASSESS NEEDS

- Do you know what kind of position you want next?
- Do you have long-range goals for your career?
- Do you have long-range goals for your personal life?
- Do you know what skills and new knowledge will be required to progress in your organization and/or your area of expertise?
- Have you considered how your current skills and experience could be applied to different career options?

2   IMPLEMENT A PERSONAL DEVELOPMENT STRATEGY

- Do you have the appropriate education and experience for the kind of job you want next?
- Do you take outside or organization-based courses or seminars that add to your managerial and technical expertise?
- Do you seek out individuals who have information and skills that you

need?
- Do you have a rôle model, mentor or champion from whom you can learn and who supports you in your professional goals?
- Do you regularly read newspapers, journals and books, both within your industry and profession and in management and business in general?

3 UNDERSTAND THE ORGANIZATIONAL ENVIRONMENT, POLICIES AND DIRECTIONS

- Do you actively seek information about what is happening, both in the areas in which you work and the wider organization?
- Do you know where work opportunities are increasing or declining?
- Do you know what organizations in your field of interest are looking for?
- Do you understand how influence works in your organization?
- Do you understand and use available support (formal and informal) to open up options?

4 DEVELOP YOUR PERSONAL (INTERNAL AND EXTERNAL) NETWORKS

- Have you developed contacts in other parts of your organization?
- Are you involved in cross-departmental activities or problem-solving groups?
- Do you keep in contact with people you have met at conferences and courses?
- Do you keep in touch with colleagues you have worked with in the past?
- Are you visibly involved in a professional organization and in contact with leaders in your particular field?

5 BUILD YOUR REPUTATION, BY PROVIDING HIGH QUALITY SERVICES

- Do you feel you have a good relationship with your boss and senior managers?
- Do you feel you have a good relationship with your peers and team?
- Do you speak and listen to customers (internal and external) regularly,

and check that you understand their needs?
- Do other people seek out your opinions on work-related subjects?
- Are you seen as a problem-solver and committed to action?

6 Evaluate your marketability

- Do you seek out feedback (external and internal) on your performance?
- Do you use feedback received to improve your performance?
- Do you know (from professional contacts) what value is put on your skills and expertise?
- Is your CV current and well-organized?
- Does your CV reflect your management accomplishments as well as your particular areas of expertise?

This checklist is modelled on the 'Career-fitness check' developed by GHN Limited (a coaching and counselling organization) and reproduced in the report by David Guile and Nickie Fonda cited above.[9]

12
Professional activities

This chapter covers:

- professional organizations
- benefits of professional involvement
- networking skills
- writing for publication
- delivering presentations
- committee work.

Introduction

Membership of a professional organization is one of the defining characteristics of a professional worker. The information profession is served by an impressive number of professional bodies, but many members fail to make the most of their professional associations. Such bodies fulfil a wide range of functions locally, nationally and internationally, in the UK, USA and many other countries around the world. This chapter considers the nature, challenges and benefits of professional involvement for both individuals and organizations. It also highlights the scope for developing your skills and your career through professional activities, and provides practical advice on getting started.

Professional options

The potential opportunities for the library and information worker wishing to get involved in professional activities are very extensive indeed. In the UK alone there are organizations that support employers (for example, Aslib and SCONUL), individuals (such as the Institute of Information Scientists and the Circle of State Librarians) or both (The Library Association). Professional organizations based in the USA include the American Library Association, American Society for Information Science and Special Libraries Association. Other countries have their own associations and there are also several international bodies, such as the International Federation of Library Associations and Institutions.

Each of these bodies offers its own distinctive mix of services, products and facilities. The Library Association (LA) home page, for example, provides links to:

- pages of information about the LA
- a press desk
- the LA Information Service
- professional issues pages
- medals and awards information
- organizations in liaison with the LA
- membership information
- careers and qualifications details
- job advertisements
- an events calendar
- the *Library Association Record*
- other LA publications
- training events and development programmes
- discussion documents
- links to relevant WWW sites.[1]

In addition to the national body most of these organizations have local branches and special interest groups (SIGs). A few of these are quite general in nature - for example, the LA Career Development Group (CDG) covers all sectors and subjects, although it caters particularly for newly qualified professionals; others are sector-specific but huge numerically (for example, the LA Public Libraries Group); while some are far more specialized and therefore have a much smaller membership base (like the LA Prison Libraries Group). Some highly specialist groups have become more mainstream (and expanded their membership) as the environment has changed; thus the LA Audiovisual Group, which changed its name and constitution to become the LA Multimedia Group, and then recently merged with the LA IT Group to become LAMIT - the LA Multimedia and Information Technology Group. Some local associations (for example, the branches of Aslib, the Institute and the LA) embrace all sectors in a geographical area; others (like the circles and divisions of LA groups) bring together sectoral and/or subject interests in a particular region or part of the country.

Some areas of the profession will always provide more options and opportunities for professional involvement than others. The healthcare information field, for example, offers an embarrassment of riches. The annual report of the LA Health Libraries Group (HLG) outlines:

- membership facts and figures
- committee activities
- events of the last twelve months
- working group activities
- subgroup activities
- work with related groups
- publication of monographs
- journal details.[2]

But this group is not the only option available to the information professional in the health field: Jane Farmer and Amanda Richardson's 1997 survey of this sector identified more than 24 other health-related groups of which HLG librarians were members.[3]

Your involvement with professional bodies can range from the largely *reactive* (keeping abreast of developments in the literature; attending conferences organized by fellow professionals) to the more *proactive* (writing journal articles yourself; entering into professional debates; presenting papers at events; becoming a committee member). In deciding which groups to join and how active a part to play, you need to take account of your professional and personal interests, your field of work, your geographical location, and the state and stage of your career. For many new professionals keen to take an active rôle in professional affairs, the LA Career Development Group or a local branch/circle offers a good way to embark on professional involvement in a highly supportive arena which is less daunting than beginning at the national level of these organizations.

REFLECTION

Consider the professional groups available. What options are there for professional involvement in your field?

Professional and personal benefits

Despite this wealth of options, many information professionals have little involvement in the wider profession. It is worth pausing to consider why this is the case. The reality of the situation is that no matter how supportive we might be of professional activity in *principle*, in *practice* it is not always so easy to get involved. Individuals and organizations often find they simply cannot afford the fees for expensive conferences. Moreover, we all have increasing pressures on our time, and time away from the workplace is frequently seen as too costly to contemplate (particularly if we are unclear about the benefits). In addition, people are sometimes deterred from participation because they are unsure about the skills required for the rôle which they are expected to fulfil.[4]

So why *should* we become actively involved in our profession? There are several benefits that deserve consideration, real benefits that can outweigh these undeniably forceful arguments. One obvious benefit is value for money. Every January the *Library Association Record* (as an example) contains at least one letter complaining about the cost of membership subscription fees. If people feel that all they get in return for their subscription is twelve copies of this journal, the fortnightly supplement *Library and Information Appointments* and 'free' membership of two Groups, the subscription may not seem to represent the best deal around! But a professional association *is* its membership: the more we use – or put into – our professional bodies, the more we shall see a real return on our investment. The following paragraphs outline other benefits for the active member.

- **Keeping in touch with professional developments.** One aspect new professionals often miss when they leave 'library school' is the opportunity for debating professional issues.[5] Wider professional involvement, whether through reading the professional press, attending conferences or evening meetings, or entering into e-mail list debates, allows the new professional to keep in touch with – and influence – current professional thinking.

- **Exposure to new ideas and alternative approaches.** It is all too easy to become totally focused on the practices of our own organization and to lose sight of alternative approaches to tackling particular management problems. With less movement in the job market and a decrease in new blood coming into many services, discussions with colleagues in other organizations is an effective way of finding fresh methods for solving universal problems.

- **Access to expert advice.** One of the key benefits of membership of professional bodies is the expert advice they can offer.[6] But this need not be restricted to using the officers of associations: the potential of using the 'invisible college', of consulting colleagues who are expert in their field, is often overlooked. By trawling the web or contacting the secretaries of specialist groups, you will be able to locate many well qualified and helpful colleagues. But remember, the invisible college is a two-way process and all professionals should expect to give as well as take!

- **Cost-effective training.** Most professional bodies run courses and seminars that are available to individual and corporate members at substantially reduced rates. Local events organized by branches and circles are generally particularly good value for money, as they tend to be very inexpensive and take up less time (often less than half a day). Low/no-cost evening meetings frequently fulfil a training or development function, even if they are not billed as such.

- **Accredited development.** Membership of the (UK) Library Association provides the opportunity to build on the theoretical foundations laid by your professional education and pursue your continuing professional development (CPD) within a hierarchy of qualifications, starting with Associateship (Chartership) and eventually progressing to Fellowship. CPD and professional involvement are inextricably linked. Working towards Chartership requires you both to demonstrate your understanding of – and ability to respond to – the changing wider environment, and to evaluate and record your development (for your Professional Development Report). It also provides a discipline that will prove invaluable for both professional and personal growth.[5] Formal recognition of your development and competence as represented by progression through different categories of membership is another valuable benefit of belonging to a professional body.

- **Vital network contacts.** An essential dimension of all of the above is networking and this is also a key benefit in itself, especially (as mentioned in the last chapter) for the solo professional, who may feel frustrated by the lack of peer contact. It is often argued that personal networking is essential for 'getting on in life' and there are some astonishing statistics quoted on the number of jobs that never get advertised.[7] Although much of this is questionable, one undeniable benefit for the job seeker is the chance to glean from contacts which organizations have a professional approach and which employers you would want (or not want) to work for. And of course, networking should be enjoyable, and fun!
- **Developing beyond and outside your current job.** Active involvement in a professional group can provide an opportunity for 'accelerated development' by giving you the chance to develop essential skills for the future, which you would not have the chance to do in your current post/organization – such as presentation, meetings and budgeting skills. Examples of skills development typically associated with professional activities are considered in the next section.

REFLECTION

Consider your current post and professional experience so far. Taking a strategic view of your professional development, what aspects of professional activity would bring the most benefits for you?

Developing your skills

As well as showing commitment, initiative and self-motivation, some of the more 'proactive' aspects of professional involvement can bring some very practical benefits. No matter how forward-looking and flexible our own organizations can be, there will always be scope for developing outside skills that you would not get the same chance to develop internally. The following sections explore some of the more common professional activities, their benefits and some practical considerations about involvement.

Networking

Networking has been identified by several commentators as one of the key management skills for the future, and one that you can learn – rather than something you do without thinking. Some of the potential benefits have already been mentioned in relation to personal development and career progression, but it is important not to overlook the direct benefits that a network of professional contacts can have in your day-to-day work. Information professionals are generally very willing to share their know-how with their peers, and the quickest way to answer an enquiry or solve a problem in the workplace is often to ask an experienced colleague based in your own service or at another organization.

Mark Griffiths of Nottingham Trent University (Department of Social Sciences) has provided the following tips for networkers:

1   **Network across the whole field.** Be aware of developments in your sector by talking to other professionals in your field and keeping up to date with possible areas of opportunity.
2   **Network within your organization.** Talk to people not just within your department but across the organization.
3   **Do not feel uncomfortable about networking.** It does not come naturally to a lot of people. If you feel uneasy about going into a room full of strangers, imagine how someone you admire, who is more self confident, would do it and try to emulate it.
4   **Networking is a reciprocal information resource.** Good networkers earn places in other people's lives. It's a bit like a bank account: you need to deposit before attempting to withdraw!
5   **Networking does not always have immediate pay-offs.** It is worth remembering that all contacts could potentially be useful – even if it might not seem a useful conversation at the time.
6   **Form mutual relationships.** This is often hard to begin with but persevere.
7   **Ask open questions and show interest.** Networking will be easier if open questions (eg who, what, when, where, how) are asked. Learn to be interested in what people say and identify their needs.
8   **Use your business card.** If you happen to speak to someone only momentarily, then use the back of your business card to write a message to maintain contact.

9 **Build up a relationship slowly.** Don't try and sell yourself the first time you meet someone.

10 **Use your network.** Once you have established networking contacts, make sure you put it to best use. Follow up and make sure you stay in touch – even if it is only a periodic e-mail.[8]

Writing for publication

Probably the most common first step for the new professional wishing to get actively involved in the wider professional world is to write a journal article. Local publications or national titles aimed at specific subject areas are a good starting point. *Impact*, the journal of the LA Career Development Group, is a popular choice for new professionals publishing for the first time.

Before you begin, it is important to think about why you are doing it. Enhancement of a *curriculum vitae* is undoubtedly a strong motivator, but this is not enough in itself.[9] Ultimately you must have something to say, something that colleagues in the profession will want to read and (ideally) find interesting or useful. The discipline of writing an article can be a good way of evaluating an experience or experiment, or checking your understanding of new concepts and techniques. Case studies can provide the basis for useful articles as they can show what you have learned and allow you to impart tips. Other practitioners can then avoid reinventing the wheel and be thankful to learn from your mistakes! If thinking about writing longer articles or books it is worth considering how existing reports, training materials, and the like might be adapted for publication.

There are some other considerations before embarking on the writing process. The best advice is common sense, but often overlooked:

- **Make it relevant and readable** – increasingly, academic research and publishing seems to be wilfully obscure, so try to avoid this pitfall!
- **Know your audience** – the terminology you would use for *Multimedia Information and Technology*, the *Library Association Record* and *The Guardian* would obviously be quite different.
- **Study the layout and presentation of your target journal** – note whether the articles are broken up into sections, and what formalities apply regarding references, abbreviations, abstracts, etc.

- **Keep it simple** – writers often try too hard to appear clever, and thus obscure their message. Good communicators communicate simply: above all, avoid 'poly-syllabic frenzy'.[10]
- **Consider your language and style** – determine whether you will say 'I', 'we' or 'it was discovered . . . ' Is the style of your chosen journal chatty or serious? Make sure you are consistent, and check that all your examples are gender-free.
- **Find an approach to writing that works for you** – think about it, and if necessary experiment to discover what suits you best. For example, do you plan in great detail before starting to write, or do you just allow the ideas to flow? Do you prefer to write in small chunks, or do you rattle off a whole article at one sitting? Do you compose on pieces of paper or go straight to the screen?
- **Read your work out loud** – this will help you to refine style and flow.
- **Get your masterpiece checked** – use a spell-checker and a human proofreader. If you can find colleagues with a good grasp of grammar and of your subject area, who will give you constructive, non-hurtful feedback, cherish them!

Perhaps most important of all – and most often overlooked – is the need to develop a relationship with your editor and his or her team. Writing articles is time-consuming and rejection is painful, so contact your prospective editor as early as possible, to see if he or she is interested in your ideas. State why you are qualified to write on the subject. The editor should either respond positively or point you in the direction of more suitable publications. Your editor can also give you details of formal requirements (such as word length, submission formats, etc) if they are not already stated in the journal. In addition, do not be afraid to talk with editorial staff. Remember that you are entering into a partnership, and it is in the interests of all parties for publications to succeed.

ACTIVITY

Consider your experience of problem-solving in the workplace. Could any of these experiences fruitfully be turned into an article? Write down what you see as the key benefits of writing for publication.

Delivering presentations

Another valuable opportunity for skills development is in giving presentations at professional meetings, conferences, seminars or workshops. This can be very daunting, especially if you do not feel that you are a natural born speaker – or comedian – but arguably this is the very reason you should embrace this form of professional activity.[11-12] If presentations are not actually required in your present post, you can be fairly certain that these skills will be needed in your next job.

Despite being a frightening prospect, presenting papers or giving talks in a professional setting has many benefits that often do not apply to presentations in the workplace. Your audience should be largely made up of keen individuals, who share your interests; this is rather different to delivering an induction/education session for students or other information service users! You will also have the chance to hone your skills in a non-hostile environment, where your biggest critic will be yourself. Always remember:

- An expert is someone who comes from somewhere else
- Your audience does not know what you do not know
- Your audience does not know what you have forgotten to include.

In addition, if presenting alongside other speakers, you will have the opportunity to watch their techniques and learn new skills, which you can take home to your organization. When presenting papers outside your own organization, it is important not to forget the skills you have developed 'at home', but you also need to be alert to the pitfalls of 'playing away'. If possible, organize the room to meet your needs in terms of tables, seating, etc, and make sure that you have worked out how unfamiliar equipment works. It also makes sense to liaise with other speakers beforehand, to ensure that you do not repeat what they say (or that they use all your best jokes). Finally, you can take comfort from the fact that the more presentations you give, the easier it gets; and you will find that a good presentation will give you an amazing buzz!

Committee membership

Writing articles and delivering presentations may – if you are successful – generate demand for more 'product', but publications and presentations are generally one-off commitments (which can be part of their attractiveness). The new professional concerned to make a more long-term impact should consider active committee membership.

The amount of work generated by committee activities can vary widely, depending on the committee joined and the rôle undertaken. Local branch/circle committees often provide a fertile place for growth for the new professional who can move from committee membership to officer status as he or she feels comfortable. Typical committee rôles include:

- **Chair** – generally concerned with coordinating and leading the group strategically, to ensure that it fulfils its objectives in an efficient manner; more specifically includes effective chairing of committee meetings.
- **Secretary** – typically involves organizing committee meetings (planning agendas, booking rooms, collating papers, arranging refreshments and writing minutes), coordinating group responses to wider initiatives (for example, 'green papers') and compiling reports, as well as formal communications with members, potential members and allied bodies. (These tasks are often shared with an assistant in larger committees.)
- **Treasurer** – responsible for the control and planning of group finances, in accordance with official accounting procedures, and liaising with auditors.
- **Events coordinator** – responsible for planning visits, presentations and conferences, from finding speakers to settling 'housekeeping' arrangements. (These tasks are sometimes shared by a sub-committee in larger groups.)
- **Publicity officer** – responsible for coordinating publicity and public relations for the group, which often includes managing an e-mail list and/or a website. (The latter may be handled by a separate web manager or sub-committee in larger groups.)
- **Journal editor** – can involve a wide range of tasks from commissioning and vetting copy to production and distribution of issues, depending on the size and frequency of the publication. For all but the smallest newsletters, these tasks are likely to be shared among various officers (such as an advertising manager, production manager and reviews editor) supported by an editorial board, and for larger journals this will be almost a full-time job.

Many of these rôles overlap and in a healthy group other committee members will support these officers – brave is the individual who plans a conference alone! Such responsibilities can obviously be very time consuming, and some negotiation will need to take place between the individual and his or her employer if committee activities take place during the working day. In this case, the benefits to the individual and organization must be explored. Finally, no-one should seek committee membership unless prepared to undertake a fair share of the work; people who join a committee solely to embellish a CV are soon found out.

REFLECTION

Consider the rôles outlined above. What benefits can you see for yourself and your organization in taking on such additional duties for a local/specialist group?

Organizational benefits

There is increasing pressure on everyone's time. As we have seen, professional involvement is not always easy to manage and can be extremely time consuming, so it is essential to be clear about why individuals – and organizations – should support this. On top of the practical benefits outlined above, one further argument can be put forward. From his research across a number of large organizations, Harvey Coleman has argued that the way we (and our services) are judged (and promoted) is made up of a combination of three elements:

- the work we do – 10%
- our image within the organization – 30%
- our visibility (the extent to which people know about our work) – 60%.[13]

Although we cannot succeed with image alone and no substance, just doing the job is not enough. It is important for us to raise our profile and the obvious way to do this is through developing our networking skills, our writing and publication skills, our presentation skills, our meeting and political/committee skills. All these can be honed by active involvement in the wider professional world.

REFLECTION

Consider Coleman's arguments. How do they relate to you? Consider other professionals you know. How does this model relate to them?

How should personal professional involvement be handled at an organizational level? As managers we need to evaluate professional involvement and balance it with the day-to-day concerns of service provision. It is crucial for us to take a strategic view and (where possible) promote professional activities to our staff. Staff can develop skills (meeting skills, presentation skills, writing skills) of direct relevance to the workplace. At times of limited job opportunities this can usefully provide new challenges and improve staff morale. Ultimately this will reflect well on your organization and should attract a higher calibre of candidate when posts become available. So, when someone comes up to you at a conference (as can happen!) and says 'you're a dynamic bunch at your institution, I'm always reading about what you are up to,' you will definitely feel that the investment is worthwhile!

References

1   Available at http://www.la-hq.org.uk/directory/menu.html.
2   Contact the LA for details of availability.
3   Farmer, J and Richardson, A, *Attitudes to librarianship and information science education and academic-practitioner liaison: report of a survey conducted for the Library Association Health Libraries Group*, The Robert Gordon University, Faculty of Management, School of Information and Media, 1997, 9.
4   ibid, 42-3. Farmer and Richardson found that 82% of practitioners agreed or strongly agreed that it is valuable for practitioners to be involved in LIS course development, but 56% said they would not be willing to do so because of financial restraints, lack of time, or lack of teaching skills.
5   Becoming a professional, *Library Association Record*, 100 (5), 1998, 254-5.
6   Broughton, S, No fat cats at HQ, *ELG News*, (Summer 1998), 14-15.
7   Jago, A, Stepping up the career ladder: step one: what to look for and where to find it, *Assistant Librarian*, 89 (4), 1996, 60-2.

8 Griffiths, M, Networking: a skill to be learnt? *Network (The Nottingham Trent University Alumni Association)*, (Autumn 1998), 16.

9 Heery, M, Why do academic librarians write articles?, *SCONUL Newsletter*, **1**, 1994, 14–17.

10 Skelton, J, Writing skills, *Practice Nurse*, **13** (4), 1997, 212–16.

11 Heery, M, Funny peculiar, *SCONUL Newsletter*, **11**, 1997, 35–6.

12 Kempster, G, How I have got where I am going: putting into practice what you have learned, *Assistant Librarian*, **90** (10), 1997, 146–9

13 Quoted in Willis, L and Daisley, J, *Springboard: women's development workbook*, Hawthorn Press, 1990, 33.

Addresses

American Library Association
50 East Huron Street
Chicago, IL 61611, USA
Tel: (toll-free number) (1)-800-545-2433
Fax: (1) (312) 440-9374
http://www.ala.org/

American Society for Information Science
8720 Georgia Avenue, Suite 501
Silver Spring, MD 20901-3602, USA
Tel: (1) (301) 495-0900
Fax: (1) (301) 495-0810
http://www.asis.org/

Aslib, The Association for Information Management
Staple Hall
Stone House Court
London EC3A 7PB, UK
Tel: 020 7903 0000
Fax: 020 7903 0011
http://www.aslib.co.uk/

The Institute of Information Scientists
44-45 Museum Street
London WC1A 1LY, UK
Tel: 020 7831 8003
Fax: 020 7430 1270
http://www.iis.org.uk

International Federation of Library Associations and Institutions
POB 95312
2509 CH The Hague, Netherlands
Tel: (31)-(70)-314-0884
Fax: (31)-(70)-383-4827
http://www.ifla.org/

The Library Association
7 Ridgmount Street
London WC1E 7AE, UK
Tel: 020 7255 0500
Fax: 020 7436 7218
http://www.la-hq.org.uk/

Special Libraries Association
1700 Eighteenth Street, NW
Washington, DC 20009-2514, USA
Tel: (1) (202) 234-4700
Fax: (1) (202) 265-9817
http://www.sla.org/

Standing Conference of National and University Libraries (SCONUL)
102 Euston Street
London NW1 2HA, UK
Tel: 020 7387 0317
Fax: 020 7383 3197
http://www.sconul.ac.uk/

Suggestions for further reading

Seely, J, *The Oxford guide to writing and speaking*, Oxford University Press, 1998.

Clearly set out with summary guidelines and 'you try' exercises at the end of each section. Covers most elements of written and oral communication, including fax and e-mail communication, job applications, organizing meetings and giving presentations (with particular attention to targeting specific audiences) and concludes with the writing process.

Pantry, S, Moving forward along networks, *Library and Information Appointments*, 2 (3), 1999, [1–2].

Defines networks, identifies 11 different types in the library and information community, and outlines how they have evolved and are used, including training networks, special interest groups, the 'invisible college', action groups and e-mail networks.

Coult, G, Get a life! Become active in a special interest group, *Managing Information*, 6 (3), 1999, 20-1.

Considers the benefits of belonging to a special interest group: explores typical group activities (notably organizing events) and identifies networking as a key benefit. Includes checklists on what makes a good committee member and the benefits of active participation.

Writing for publication

Heery, M, Why do academic librarians write articles? *SCONUL Newsletter*, 1, 1994, 14–17.

Argues that the primary purpose of writing must be to help practising librarians and questions whether the scholarly publication is the most suitable medium. Notes predominance of 'sexy' subjects (like IT) rather than other central but less exciting developments, and reflects on potential of electronic communication as a future forum for professional debate.

Day, A, *How to get research published in journals*, Gower, 1996.

Introductory guide (c140 pp) aimed at researchers, students and faculty. Advocates a step-by-step approach to ensure proper consideration of objectives and audience (editors, referees and readers) before moving on to drafting and style; includes advice on reviewing the literature, targeting journals, writing abstracts and presentation of manuscripts.

St Clair, G, Steps toward writing a sure thing, *Library Administration and Management*, **11** (1), 1997, 11–14.

Argues that writing an article should not be carried out in isolation and asserts that successful authors reach out to others for assistance in creating their work, for example in selecting the right journal, placing the work in the context of existing literature/research, seeking help with statistical design and execution, and using peers to review their work.

Jackson, M E, Becoming a published author: eight simple steps for librarians, *Library Administration and Management*, **11** (1), 1997, 15–18.

Provides straightforward instructions and succinct tips on how to get published, covering why you should strive to be published, the search for a suitable topic, choice of medium, deciding on a collaboration strategy, identifying potential publication sources, finding time to write, working with your publisher, 'getting rich and famous', and copyright.

Schuman, P G and Harmon, C, From book idea to contract, *Library Administration & Management*, **11** (1), 1997, 19–25.

Written by the President and a director of an established professional press (Neal-Schuman Publishers) as a guide for inexperienced authors. Explains – with checklists – how publishers evaluate proposals and price publications, and offers advice on choosing and approaching a publisher and vetting a contract, with comments on typical clauses.

Carley, H, How to get published, *Library Association Record*, **100** (3), 1998, 131.

Explains the aims of Library Association Publishing as a professional association's press, itemizes what the publisher needs to see in order to evaluate a publication proposal, and offers suggestions for producing a publication without writing a large text by yourself.

Giesecke, J, Preparing research for publication, *Library Administration & Management*, **12** (3), 1998, 134–7.

Argues the need to write about our research and to make it interesting so that others can learn from it. Explores the component elements of both theoretical and practical articles, identifies and reviews common errors, considers the difficulties of translating from one publication medium to another (such as thesis to article) and offers some tips for success.

Di Vecchio, J, Transforming an oral presentation for publication, *Library Administration & Management*, **12** (3), 1998, 138–41.

Identifies the essential differences in the 'dynamics' of oral and written presentations, contrasting the non-linear approach, two-way dialogue, and use of nuances and non-verbal communication in the former, with the clarity of purpose, language and layout required in the latter. Offers tips for successful transformations (including ruthless editing, re-reading and testing on others) and concludes with a bibliography of general and LIS-specific texts.

Presenting papers

Mandel, S, *Effective presentation skills*, Kogan Page, 1987.
Practical guidebook, which begins with a self-analysis questionnaire, and then offers the reader an array of tips on dealing with anxiety, planning presentations, structuring talks, using visual aids (with 'avoid this' examples), and preparation and delivery techniques.

Stevens, M, *Improving your presentation skills: a complete action kit*, Kogan Page, 1987.
Open learning workbook providing step-by-step guidance to developing core presentation skills; covers tailoring information to your audience, use of language, delivery and impact.

Rawlins, K, *Presentation and communication skills: a handbook for practitioners*, Macmillan Magazines Ltd, 1993.
User-friendly introduction, well laid out with many activities. Provides extensive coverage of planning presentations (more than half the book) as well as delivery and evaluation.

Denny, R, *Speak for yourself: tested techniques for improving your communication and presentation skills*, Kogan Page, 1994.
Popular book aimed primarily at people involved with presentation and sales work; uses an anecdotal approach, and includes useful sections on mastering nerves and good/bad habits.

Comfort, J, *Effective presentations*, Oxford University Press, 1995.
Multimedia package based on a 35-minute video, accompanied by a student's book, audio cassette and teacher's book, suitable for group use or self-study. Covers writing and structuring presentations, starting and finishing, using visual aids, handling questions, and evaluating presentations. Illustrated throughout with examples of 'good' and 'bad' practice.

Index

Page numbers in italics refer to suggestions for further reading.